Organized Crime and Networks

This collection explores organized crime and terror networks and the points at which they intersect. It analyses the close relationships between these criminalities, the prevalence and ambiguity of this nexus, the technological elements facilitating it, and the financial aspects embedded in this criminal partnership.

Organized Crime and Terrorist Networks is the outcome of empirical research, seminars, workshops and interviews carried out by a multinational consortium of researchers within 'TAKEDOWN', a Horizon 2020 project funded by the European Commission. The consortium's objective was to examine the perspectives, requirements and misgivings of front-line practitioners operating in the areas of organized crime and terrorism. The chapters collected in this volume are the outcome of such analytical efforts. The topics addressed include the role of Information and Communication Technology in contemporary criminal organizations, terrorism financing, online transnational criminality, identity crime, the crime-terror nexus and tackling the nexus at supranational level.

This book offers a compelling contribution to scholarship on organized crime and terrorism, and considers possible directions for future research. It will be of much interest to students and researchers engaged in studies of criminology, criminal justice, crime control and prevention, organized crime, terrorism, political violence, and cybercrime.

Vincenzo Ruggiero is Professor of Sociology at Middlesex University in London. He has conducted research for many national and international agencies, including the European Commission and the United Nations. Since 2010 he has published the following single-authored books: *Penal Abolitionism* (2010), *The Crimes of the Economy* (2013), *Power and Crime* (2015), *Dirty Money* (2017) and *Visions of Political Violence* (2019). In 2016 he was given the Lifetime Achievement Award by the American Society of Criminology for his contribution to Critical Criminology.

Routledge Studies in Crime and Society

Cyber-risk and Youth
Digital Citizenship, Privacy and Surveillance
Michael Adorjan and Rosemary Ricciardelli

Gun Studies
Interdisciplinary Approaches to Politics, Policy, and Practice
Edited by Jennifer Carlson, Harel Shapira and Kristin A. Goss

The Myth of the 'Crime Decline'
Exploring Change and Continuity in Crime and Harm
Justin Kotzé

Execution by Family
A Theory of Honor Violence
Mark Cooney

Changing Narratives of Youth Crime
From Social Causes to Threats to the Social
Bernd Dollinger

Human Enhancement Drugs
Edited by Katinka van de Ven, Kyle J.D. Mulrooney and Jim McVeigh

Organized Crime and Terrorist Networks
Edited by Vincenzo Ruggiero

Private Security and Domestic Violence
The Risks and Benefits of Private Security Companies Working With Victims of Domestic Violence
Diarmaid Harkin

For more information about this series, please visit: www.routledge.com/Routledge-Studies-in-Crime-and-Society/book-series/RSCS

Organized Crime and Terrorist Networks

Edited by Vincenzo Ruggiero

Routledge
Taylor & Francis Group
LONDON AND NEW YORK

First published 2020 by Routledge

2 Park Square, Milton Park, Abingdon, Oxon, OX14 4RN
605 Third Avenue, New York, NY 10017

Routledge is an imprint of the Taylor & Francis Group, an informa business

First issued in paperback 2020

Copyright © 2020 selection and editorial matter, Vincenzo Ruggiero; individual chapters, the contributors

The right of Vincenzo Ruggiero to be identified as the author of the editorial matter, and of the authors for their individual chapters, has been asserted in accordance with sections 77 and 78 of the Copyright, Designs and Patents Act 1988.

All rights reserved. No part of this book may be reprinted or reproduced or utilised in any form or by any electronic, mechanical, or other means, now known or hereafter invented, including photocopying and recording, or in any information storage or retrieval system, without permission in writing from the publishers.

Notice:
Product or corporate names may be trademarks or registered trademarks, and are used only for identification and explanation without intent to infringe.

British Library Cataloguing-in-Publication Data
A catalogue record for this book is available from the British Library

Library of Congress Cataloging-in-Publication Data
Names: Ruggiero, Vincenzo, editor.
Title: Organized crime and terrorist networks / edited by Vincenzo Ruggiero.
Description: Milton Park, Abingdon, Oxon ; New York, NY : Routledge, 2020. |
Series: Routledge studies in crime and society | Includes bibliographical references and index.
Identifiers: LCCN 2019018246 (print) | LCCN 2019021855 (ebook) | ISBN 9780429435102 (eBook) | ISBN 9781138351745 (hardback : alk. paper)
Subjects: LCSH: Terrorism–Finance. | Organized crime–Finance.
Classification: LCC HV6441 (ebook) | LCC HV6441 .O742 2020 (print) | DDC 364.106–dc23
LC record available at https://lccn.loc.gov/2019018246

ISBN: 978-1-138-35174-5 (hbk)
ISBN: 978-0-367-78441-6 (pbk)

Typeset in Bembo
by Wearset Ltd, Boldon, Tyne and Wear

Contents

List of figures	vii
List of tables	viii
Notes on contributors	ix

1 Introduction 1
  VINCENZO RUGGIERO

2 Organized crime and terrorist networks 8
  VINCENZO RUGGIERO WITH THE
  TAKEDOWN CONSORTIUM

3 Hybrids: on the crime-terror nexus 26
  VINCENZO RUGGIERO

4 The online crime-terror nexus: using booter services
  (stressers) to weaponize data? 42
  ROBERTO MUSOTTO AND DAVID S. WALL

5 The role of information and communication
  technology (ICT) in modern criminal organizations 60
  ANDREA TUNDIS AND MAX MÜHLHÄUSER

6 The rise of low-tech attacks in Europe 78
  ANDREW MONAGHAN

7 Global system dynamics in the relationships between
  organized crime and terrorist groups 100
  INMACULADA MARRERO ROCHA

8 **Understanding the crime-terrorism nexus through a dynamic modelling approach** 117
FLORIAN HUBER, BERNHARD JÄGER, IDO EREV, DORON COHEN, SERGIO BIANCHI AND MATTEO E. BONFANTI

9 **Terrorism financing and the crime-terror relationships as challenges for security in Europe** 141
JAVIER RUIPÉREZ CANALES

10 **Tackling the nexus at the supranational level** 156
MATTEO E. BONFANTI AND LUKAS MEYER-DAETSCH

11 **Identity crime in the UK** 181
AIDA FAZELY

Index 202

Figures

4.1	The crime-terror nexus connections	44
4.2	Subscribing users and date of payments	53
4.3	Size of DDoS attacks over years	54
8.1	Cube Model	120
8.2	Cases with different levels of risk	121
8.3	Allocation of the case	125
8.4	Allocation of the case	128
8.5	Allocation of the case	130
8.6	Pathway of Case 1	131
8.7a	Example 1: IS active in different domains at the same time	133
8.7b	Example 2: Case x changing domains from OC to TN	134
8.8	Hypothesized case location changes by different PPPR measures	136
11.1	UK Payments identity-related fraud figures in millions of pounds	196

Tables

2.1	Cross-tabulations of effect of actions for crime reduction across professional types	13
2.2	Cross-tabulations of effect of actions to reduce organized criminality	13
2.3	Cross-tabulations of effect of actions across professional types	19
4.1	Plan subscriptions	50
4.2	Plan subscriptions	52
4.3	Most active users in the ticket forum	54
8.1	Requirements for the model development	119
8.2	Allocation based on the case analysis	125
8.3	Allocation based on the case analysis	127
8.4	Allocation based on the case analysis	129
11.1	Number of identity-related fraud cases per year	197

Contributors

Sergio Bianchi is General Director of the International Organisation Agenfor. He collaborates with the Italian Ministry of Justice as researcher on radicalization and de-radicalization policies. Orientalist and Middle East expert, Dr Bianchi specializes in the field of Muslim minorities and has carried out in-depth research into security issues and geopolitics, supporting the idea that Islam may be a resource to counter the terrorist threats. Among his recent books *Low Intensity Conflicts in a Liquid World* (2016), *Is Islamism a Threat?* (2015), *Jihadist Radicalisation in European Prisons* (2010), *The Italian Right Wing Parties in the Age of Leadership* (2008). His articles and video productions news have been featured in national and international newspapers and TV channels. He is fluent in Italian, Arabic, German and English. Dr Bianchi is a RAN C.o.E. member.

Matteo E. Bonfanti is Senior Researcher at the ETH Center for Security Studies in Zurich. He holds a PhD from the Scuola Superiore Sant'Anna of Pisa. Dr Bonfanti's research activities focus on the governance implications generated by targeted initiatives adopted by the EU and its Member States to foster their internal security. These include the development and adoption of new technical, technological and organizational solutions to enhance policing and intelligence cooperation, cyber security, as well as crisis and emergency management. He has been actively involved as a researcher in several EC and EDA funded projects in the field of security since 2010.

Doron Cohen is currently a PhD candidate at the Technion in Israel. His main research interests lie in clarifying basic behavioural puzzles, such as why people invest too much or too little effort in achieving their goals, and why and how people change their behaviour in response to uninformative feedback from their previous choices. Doron Cohen holds a BA in Psychology and Management from Tel-Aviv University and an MSc in Cognitive Psychology from the Technion.

Ido Erev holds a PhD in quantitative psychology and is professor of Behavioural Science and Economics at the Israel Institute of Technology. He is also President Elect of the European Association for Decision Making. His research focuses on the effect of experience on choice behaviour. Among the contributions of this research is the discovery of a robust experience-description gap: people exhibit oversensitivity to rare events when they decide on the basis of descriptions of incentive structures, but experience reverses their bias and leads to underweighting rare events.

Aida Fazely has a diverse background in the field of criminology, ranging from time spent in the commercial sector in security, business crime and fraud to the academic analysis and understanding of these topics. Identity-related crimes are her main interests, an area where she undertook her PhD research and worked with major banks and retailers in the UK, contributing to the evaluation and impact of identity theft and fraud. Partnerships and multi-agency crime prevention approaches are her second area of interest.

Florian Huber is a senior researcher at SYNYO GmbH in Vienna. He has been coordinator of EU-H2020-Projects such as TAKEDOWN and SciChallenge as well as national projects such as Counter Stories. Furthermore, he represents SYNYO in other European projects including MINDb4ACT, MIICT, CHAMPIONs and ARMOuR. He holds a PhD in Sociology from the University of Vienna and has experience in empirical research on urban issues, migration, violent extremism and social inequality. Before joining SYNYO, he worked as a post-doc-researcher at the University of Vienna and had several university teaching positions.

Bernhard Jäger is Research Manager and Department Lead at SYNYO. He holds a master degree in sociology and a bachelor in communication studies. As project researcher at the Department of Criminal Law and Criminology at the University of Vienna, he gathered extensive knowledge on criminal behaviour, policing, criminal justice and crime prevention. At SYNYO Bernhard has conceived and managed many funded projects (e.g. FP7, H2020) in which he also extended his knowledge of Cyber Security, Organized Crime and Terrorist Networks and Radicalization. Since 2017 he is responsible for the overall coordination of research projects at SYNYO.

Inmaculada Marrero Rocha is a Political Scientist, Senior Lecturer of International Relations at the University of Granada and Executive Secretary of the Euro-Arab Foundation for Higher Studies. She completed her Graduate studies at the Institut de Hautes Études Internationales of University of Geneva, and was Fulbright Scholar at American Studies Institute at the University of Delaware (USA). She achieved professional experience in foreign institutions such as the European Institute of Public Administration in Maastricht (Netherlands) and the Geneva Center for Security Studies in Geneva (Switzerland). She has been Visiting professor at Smith College of Massachusetts (USA), the Loyola School of Law (Los Angeles, USA) and Università degli Studi di Cagliari (Italy).

Lukas Meyer-Daetsch holds an MA in International Relations/Political Science from the Graduate Institute of International and Development Studies (IHEID) in Geneva, Switzerland. He was a visiting academic at the Fletcher School of Law and Diplomacy, Tufts University, Medford, USA. His areas of research include violent extremism, terrorism and crime, law enforcement and intelligence cooperation. He is currently working on the protection of civilians in armed conflicts, focusing on the dynamics between counter-terrorism measures and humanitarian action.

Andrew Monaghan is a Criminologist. His areas of expertise are self-generated images in online pornography and online risks, and more recently European terrorist attacks. He worked as a Post-Doctoral Researcher on the Horizon 2020 Project. He is currently working as lecturer at Middlesex University.

Max Mühlhäuser is a full professor at Technische Universität Darmstadt and head of Telecooperation Lab. He holds key positions in several large collaborative research centres and is leading the Doctoral School on Privacy and Trust for Mobile Users. He and his lab members conduct research on The Future Internet, Human Computer Interaction and Cybersecurity, Privacy and Trust. Max founded and managed industrial research centres, and worked as either professor or visiting professor at universities in Germany, the US, Canada, Australia, France, and Austria. He is a member of acatech, the German Academy of the Technical Sciences.

Roberto Musotto is a Research Fellow at the School of Law, University of Leeds and a practising lawyer. He holds a PhD in Economics. He has relevant expertise in serious crimes and their economic implications, focusing on their commercial, corporate and cyber aspects. His research employs theory and methods from network science and law and economics.

Javier Ruipérez Canales is Projects and Research Manager at the Euro-Arab Foundation for Higher Studies, where he has been working in different positions for the last ten years. He was awarded the title of Engineer in Naval Architecture by the Polytechnic University of Madrid. He holds two Postgraduates degrees, respectively in Sustainability and Corporate Responsibility and Cooperation and Development Public Policies Management. He is a PhD candidate in the Social Sciences Department of the University of Granada. With an extensive experience in European research projects in the fields of security, education and social intervention, he is member of the European International Studies Association and the Official College of Naval Engineers. Formerly, he was the Delegate in Andalusia of the organization Economists Without Borders.

Andrea Tundis is a Senior Researcher and his areas of expertise are infrastructure protection, internet organized crime and human safety. In 2014 he got a PhD degree in Systems and Computer Science from the DIMES department at University of Calabria (Italy). He is currently working at the Department of Computer Science at Technische Universität Darmstadt (TUDA) in Germany and member of the Telecooperation Division (TK).

David S. Wall is Professor of Criminology in the Centre for Criminal Justice studies, School of Law, University of Leeds, UK where he researches and teaches cybercrime, identity crime, organized crime, policing and intellectual property crime. He has published a wide range of books aand articles on these subjects and he also has a sustained track record of interdisciplinary funded research in these areas from a variety of Research Councils and Government Agencies.

1 Introduction

Vincenzo Ruggiero

When in 1613 Cervantes wrote a delectable short story about a criminal organization operating in Seville, he was unaware that only a few centuries later would the debate on organized crime finally spark off and, currently still rampant, take numerous competing directions. His *Rinconete and Cortadillo* are independent thieves who, in Seville, realize that their independence is at risk. In the town, Mr Monipodio requires the payment of a duty from all those operating in illegal activities and markets (Cervantes, 1952). Monipodio is fervidly religious and well connected with important people, including law enforcers, while his 'soldiers' deliver punishment against 'unregistered' lone criminals or on behalf of customers who intend to eliminate enemies or competitors. Rinconete and Cortadillo are astounded by the careless manner in which justice is administered in Seville, and fearful that the members of that 'infamous academy' would make their work more difficult and dangerous, they leave and seek elsewhere a more apposite environment for their professional development (Ruggiero, 2003).

Cervantes was also unaware that several of the characteristics he highlighted would provide as many angles for analyses of organized crime to come. Cultural aspects, for instance, have been addressed, among others, by Hess (1973), Hobsbawm (1971) and Sciascia (2002), entrepreneurship by Arlacchi (1983), Santino and La Fiura (1990) and Scalia (2016), flexibility and professionalism by Hobbs (1995, 2013), Albanese (2014) and Paoli (2014). Organized crime as power syndicate features in the work of Block (1991), Antonopoulos and Papanicolaou (2018), von Lampe (2016), Dino and Pepino (2008), Abadinsky (1990), Einstein and Amir (1999). More general analyses are found in Holmes (2016), Sergi (2017) and most recently by Hall (2018). Finally, organized crime as illegal governance has been dealt with by Gambetta (1992), Varese (2010), Campana and Varese (2018).

Readers are kindly asked not to put this book down straight away, because this brief introduction will not display yet another endless review of the literature that is normally reiterated in every work devoted to organized crime. Nor will this book attempt to formulate yet a new 'redefinition' of the subject matter, as such an attempt would be churlish in the face of a phenomenon that constantly evolves and changes according to time, context and the politico-economic philosophy prevailing in it. The notions of organized crime discussed in this volume are those that lend themselves to a comparative examination with the findings of an empirical research carried out between 2017 and 2018 (more about the research later).

The area of terrorism is similarly crowded, and a proper review of the literature would consider, first of all the Bible, then the Jacobins, Fichte, Burke (Ruggiero, 2019). Terrorist attacks feature, in the form of state assassinations, in the guidelines released by the CIA for the benefit of its operational members in 1953 (Stevenson, 2019). While interest in state terrorism appears to be declining, those focusing on the current times may want to examine the work of Sageman (2017), Schmid (2011), Gerges (2015), Badiou (2016), Bibes (2001) and many others. Those fascinated by the relationship between religion and terror could scan Armstrong (2014) or Juergensmeyer, Kitts and Jerryson (2013). Terrorism interpreted as the reaction to the invasion and the secularization of the sacred (Ginzburg, 2015) can be found in Balibar (2015, 2018) or in Eagleton (2005; 2018), while for purely secular perspective one needs to look at all those political theories that link radical social change with the use of collective violence, those, in other words, which see belligerence as a salvific midwife that helps the delivery of a new millenarian order.

But again, the literature on terrorism, in this book, will only be referred to when the views collected in our research are compared with other perspectives and findings.

Takedown

The objective of the TAKEDOWN Project was to examine the perspectives, requirements and misgivings of front-line practitioners operating in the areas of organized crime and terrorism. Funded by the European Commission, TAKEDOWN focused its research on the activities, the causes of, and responses to, these two types of criminality, recording the views of social workers, teachers, law enforcers and other experts. The TAKEDOWN Consortium was formed of teams based in Austria, Belgium, Bulgaria, the Czech Republic, Germany, Italy, Poland, Romania, Slovakia, Spain, Switzerland and the UK (for the methodologies adopted in the research process see Chapter 2). Initially, some members of the consortium were somewhat reluctant to undertake a joint examination of organized crime and terrorism, the two being regarded as distinct phenomena. In fact, to analyse them together was seen by some as an example of the questionable practice to include under the same heading everything one may dislike. Later, it was unanimously accepted that 'hybrids', namely organizations that possess the traits of both organized crime and terrorism, were worth investigating with a view, on the one hand, to ascertaining to what extent such overlap between the two manifests itself and, on the other, to contesting their very existence.

On completion of the empirical research, members of the consortium addressed some specific aspects that had not received sufficient attention in the process, expanding their analysis into areas only alluded to by our informants and/or touched upon by other studies. The chapters collected in this volume are the outcome of such analytical efforts.

Chapter 2 presents and discusses the findings of the Takedown research into the perceptions of front-line practitioners around organized crime and terrorist networks. The material collected in the research is then compared with other findings and previous analyses produced on the same topics. Chapter 3 deals with hybrids, noting that the constitution of networks involving conventional criminals and terrorists is often problematic, thus making a joint analysis of crime and terror theoretically challenging. Chapter 4 offers ideal-typical models of organized crime and terrorism against developments in the socio-political and technological spheres. Online crime is the focus of Chapter 5, which examines the role of information and communication technology in the activities of modern criminal organizations. With Chapter 6, the book then moves on to consider low-tech forms of terrorism, implying that advanced technology is not a constant feature of contemporary attacks. Chapter 7 returns to the crime-terror nexus, while Chapter 8 proposes an understanding of such nexus through a dynamic modeling approach. How organized crime and terrorism share financing strategies is the object of the analysis offered in Chapter 9, which is followed by an examination, in Chapter 10, of the strategies to tackle both at the supranational level. Finally, Chapter 11 shows how technology shapes new criminal actors (identity fraudsters) who defy traditional typologies of offending behaviour.

Pleasure, evil and technology

It may be unnecessary to provide readers with guidelines as to how the following chapters could be interpreted, because the chapters speak for themselves, informed as they are by their own logic and redacted with their own vocabulary. What may be useful, however, is to offer some supplementary observations intended to foreground a number of general concepts which are hidden, or at times implied, in the individual contributions.

For ancient philosophy, prudence enables people to become virtuous (Aristotle, 1995), while the nascent 'science' of economics turned it into a modality to become successful (Wootton, 2018). Western thought managed to locate utility, profit and power, which the Greeks and Romans regarded as debased values, among the priorities of human action. The logic of endless pursuit of pleasure and wealth accompanied this slow mutation, with virtue becoming a pure tool for their achievement. Most criminological concepts took shape on the background of this shift: for example, the endless pursuit of wealth was associated with anomie, competition with relative deprivation, utility with differential association, and power with routine activity theory. Pleasure, one could argue, is a distinctive trait characterizing the crimes of the powerful, particularly if we consider that it is projected into the future, in the sense that what is illegally obtained guarantees a succession of future pleasure (Ruggiero, 2015). Maximizing wealth and profits, which is a dogma in economics, is also an injunction in crime, where instrumental reasoning of an economic nature constantly migrates to inspire predatory conduct.

It is in this light that the alarm around transnational organized crime should be read. The Council of Europe (2014), for example, attempted to identify the social and economic damage caused by this type of criminality, highlighting the way in which it benefits from certain legal loopholes, it uses sophisticated methods to conceal activities and the proceeds of crime, it take advantage of globalization and of information and communication technologies (ICTs). In brief, transnational organized crime is accused of following an economic logic and the instrumental reasoning of entrepreneurs. A practical extension of dominant philosophies, the obscenity of transnational organized crime finds its ideal incubation in official narratives and justifications. Hence, perhaps, the ambiguity of institutional concerns about this type of criminality, which can be attributed to any economic actor, in the illicit as well as in the licit sphere. The Council of Europe worries about the negative impact on national economies, the money lost through tax evasion, the semi-legality of certain occupational sectors, all of which 'undermine the credibility and competitiveness of a state's financial and commercial actors' (ibid.: 9). But are these concerns addressed to specific criminal organizations or to the current routine of legitimate markets?

The confusion is compounded when priorities are set in the realm of institutional responses. It is asserted, in this respect, that the main problem does not appear to be a lack of legal instruments, but rather their implementation in practice. Detection, investigation and prosecution are said to be hampered by the very nature of the crimes being committed, leaving us uncertain whether the subject matter is the economy itself or some criminal group operating in it. Mystification also arises when cooperation with the private sector is advocated, begging the question whether the public sector is, in fact, among the perpetrators. To its credit, the Council of Europe clarifies in a few lines that the type of criminality it is concerned about enjoys the support of a 'wide range of professionals, for example lawyers, accountants, financial advisers, corrupt officials, judges, politicians and chemists. Without the support of these professionals, transnational organized crime would not succeed' (ibid.: 18). The question remains, however, whether this clarification falls in the 'bad apple' logic or whether it contains a more radical critique of market mechanisms.

There is another important variable that springs up with increasing frequency, and this is technology. For instance, the debate on cybercrime prompts questions such as: has this type of crime changed the features of conventional crime? To what extent is it organized? Is it mainly perpetrated by career criminals or by white-collar individuals and groups? The substantial rise of cybercrime may or may not be simultaneous with the decline of other conventional criminal activity (Levi et al., 2017). However, the development of technology encourages further questions, perhaps of a more interesting nature.

Access to technology creates a wide range of opportunities for extremely diverse individuals and groups. The skills perfected through its use have no relationship with specific subcultures, criminal learning processes, social disadvantage, labelling or symbolic interactions. They are not acquired within distinct enclaves where techniques of neutralization are elaborated. Rather, they are a new manifestation of a participatory spirit that appears to nullify differences and inclinations, bringing to the fore what phenomenologists would describe as the life worlds of everyone and all. Think of the sociopolitical debates taking place through social media. On the one hand, such debates contain a progressive element, in that they see the participation of knowledgeable and articulate people alongside uninformed or inarticulate people. On the other hand, what often emerges from this democratic participation amounts to stereotypes, prejudices and inimical banality. Some vicious attacks launched online against designated victims do not remind us of the banality of evil but of the evil of banality.

Technological skills can be used for criminal purposes by diverse actors because the crimes they enable require no physical contact with victims: like drone operators, cyber-criminals face a screen and ignore the damage they cause to their victims together with their very identity. Lack of empathy is the characteristic of cybercrime, as technology transcends any notion of morality or, perhaps, it incorporates it, turning its social and economic utility into a moral value in its own right. This is why among cyber-criminals we find professional predators, terrorists or amateurs, irreverent youth and derisive pranksters who experience the thrill of violating moral laws and display their distaste for normative restraint. The exponential growth of technology and its productive application outstrip the capacity of humankind to use them responsibly. Our moral imagination has simply failed to keep pace with our technological capability (Todorov, 1999; Dews, 2013).

Technology means efficiency, and the latter often supersedes honesty, as it offers opportunity for adaptation and innovation, of a legitimate or deviant type. The overwhelming emphasis on efficiency triggers new perceptions so that causal relations are obscured and narrative linearity is lost. One's conduct ceases to be precisely linked to the effects it causes, while the ensuing disorientation prevents from grasping the importance of events. 'The consequence is a pushing and shoving of images, events and information, which makes any lingering contemplation impossible. Thus, one zaps through the world' (Han, 2017: 41). In this sense, efficiency requires 'never dwelling anywhere', as the use of technology requires haste, the type of speed necessary in a race (Virilio and Lotringer, 2002). Efficiency aided by haste, as already argued, leaves moral imagination behind, increasing the fragmentation of our experience and the depersonalization of our relations.

In Kantian terms, technology reduces the potency of will in the sense of 'practical reason' (reason that makes us act in conformity with a universal principle) and expands will as our spontaneous power of choice (which is guided by egoistic instrumental reasoning). Self-reflection is discouraged and incorporated in technology: torpor and inertia prevail, while one is held back from rational exertion. It is not hyperbolic to describe cybercrime as evil, particularly if we follow the Hegelian argument that evil arises when subjects turns inward, isolate themselves, exalt their power of choice, 'failing to acknowledge the shared human world in which [their] very existence is grounded: being evil means singularizing myself in a way that cuts me off from the universal' (Dews, 2013: 90).

In conclusion, pleasure, evil and technology may not be the explicit themes addressed in this book, but they are variables that traverse the different chapters, like a latent, at times imperceptible filigree. Further themes will necessarily have to emerge in the future in order to make sense of increasingly unpredictable forms of criminality.

References

Abadinsky, H. (1990), *Organized Crime*, Chicago: Nelson-Hall.
Albanese, J.S. (2014), *Organized Crime: From the Mob to Transnational Organized Crime*, London and New York: Routledge.
Antonopoulos, G.A. and Papanicolaou, G. (2018), *Organized Crime. A Very Short Introduction*, Oxford: Oxford University Press.
Aristotle (1995), *Politics*, Oxford: Oxford University Press.
Arlacchi, P. (1983), *La mafia imprenditrice*, Bologna: Il Mulino.
Armstrong, K. (2014), *Fields of Blood*, London: Vintage.
Badiou, A. (2016), *Our Wound Is Not So Recent*, Cambridge: Polity.
Balibar, E. (2015), *Violence and Civility*, New York: Columbia University Press.
Balibar, E. (2018), *Secularism and Cosmopolitanism*, New York: Columbia University Press.
Bibes, P. (2001), 'Transnational Organized Crime and Terrorism in Colombia', *Journal of Contemporary Criminal Justice*, 17: 243–258.
Block, A. (1991), *Organizing Crime*, Dordrecht: Kluwer.
Cervantes, M. (1952), *Three Exemplary Novels*, London: Cassell.
Campana, P. and Varese, F. (2018), 'Organized Crime in the United Kingdom: Illegal Governance of Markets and Communities', *British Journal of Criminology*, 58: 1381–1400.
Council of Europe (2014), *White Paper on Transnational Organised Crime*, Strasbourg: Council of Europe.
Dews, P. (2013), *The Idea of Evil*, Oxford: Wiley-Blackwell.
Dino, A. and Pepino, L. (eds) (2008), *Il metodo mafioso*, Milan: Franco Angeli.
Eagleton, T. (2005), *Holy Terror*, Oxford: Oxford University Press.
Eagleton, T. (2018), *Radical Sacrifice*, New Haven and London: Yale University Press.
Einstein, S. and Amir, M. (1999), *Organized Crime: Uncertainties and Dilemmas*, Chicago: Office of International Criminal Justice.
Gambetta, D. (1992), *La mafia siciliana*, Turin: Einaudi.

Gerges, F.A. (2015), *ISIS. A History*, Princeton: Princeton University Press.
Ginzburg, C. (2015), *Paura, reverenza, terrore*, Milan: Adelphi.
Hall, T. (2018), *The Economic Geographies of Organized Crime*, New York and London: The Guilford Press.
Han, B.-C. (2017), *The Scent of Time*, Cambridge: Polity.
Hess, H. (1973), *Mafia*, Bari: Laterza.
Hobbs, D. (1995), *Bad Economies*, Oxford: Oxford University Press.
Hobbs, D. (2013), *Lush Life: Constructing Organized Crime in the UK*, Oxford: Oxford University Press.
Hobsbawm, E.J. (1971), *Primitive Rebels*, Manchester: Manchester University Press.
Holmes, L. (2016), *Advanced Introduction to Organized Crime*, Cheltenham: Elgar.
Juergensmeyer, M., Kitts, M. and Jerryson, M. (eds) (2013), *The Oxford Handbook of Religion and Violence*, Oxford: Oxford University Press.
Levi, M., Doig, A., Gunder, R., Wall, D. and Williams, M. (2017), 'Cyberfraud and the Implications for Effective Risk-Based Responses: Themes from UK Research', *Crime, Law and Social Change*, 67: 77–96.
Paoli, L. (ed.) (2014), *The Oxford Handbook of Organized Crime*, Oxford: Oxford University Press.
Ruggiero, V. (2003), *Crime in Literature*, London and New York: Verso.
Ruggiero, V. (2015), *Power and Crime*, London and New York: Routledge.
Ruggiero, V. (2019), *Visions of Political Violence*, London and New York: Routledge.
Sageman, M. (2017), *Understanding Terror Networks*, Philadelphia: University of Pennsylvania Press.
Santino, U. and La Fiura, G. (1990), *L'impresa mafiosa*, Milan: Franco Angeli.
Scalia, V. (2016), *Crime, Networks and Power*, London: Palgrave Macmillan.
Schmid, A.P. (ed.) (2011), *The Routledge Handbook of Terrorism Research*, London and New York: Routledge.
Sciascia, L. (2002), *Il giorno della civetta*, Milan: Adelphi.
Sergi, A. (2017), *From Mafia to Organized Crime*, London: Palgrave Macmillan.
Stevenson, T. (2019), 'Finer Points of Murder: A Recent History of Political Assassination', *Times Literary Supplement*, 11 January: 8–9.
Todorov, T. (1999), *Facing the Extreme: Moral Life in Concentration Camps*, London: Weidenfeld and Nicolson.
Varese, F. (ed.) (2010), *Organized Crime: Critical Concepts in Criminology*, London: Routledge.
Virilio, P. and Lotringer, S. (2002), *Crepuscular Dawn*, New York: Semiotext(e).
Von Lampe, K. (2016), *Organized Crime*, London: Sage.
Wootton, D. (2018), *Power, Pleasure and Profit*, Cambridge: Harvard University Press.

2 Organized crime and terrorist networks

Vincenzo Ruggiero with the TAKEDOWN Consortium

Introduction

Practitioners dealing with organized crime and terrorist networks develop views around the activities and causes leading individuals to join such networks. They also evaluate the effectiveness of responses to these phenomena and, in a reflective fashion, the adequacy of the professional setting in which they operate. Causation aspects have been addressed by many criminological schools of thought, including positivism, functionalism, labelling, strain, conflict and control theory. These theories attempt to identify the drivers of both phenomena while hypothesizing the pathways of offenders into organized criminality and terror activities. The practitioners who acted as informants in this research drew on their own direct experience in dealing with both, highlighting the constraints, difficulties and misunderstandings hampering their routine work, but they also expressed views that find an echo in the criminological literature. As responses to organized crime and terrorism are inevitably linked to their perceived causes, informants in this research project also expressed views on the efficacy of existing legislation and the structural make-up of the organizations in which they worked. This chapter examines such views in light of analyses and previous research conducted into organized crime and terrorism.

Methodology

Using a mixed methodology that includes a quantitative empirical framework with qualitative inputs from interviews, focus groups and workshops, this research canvassed the views of key commentators in the field. The respondents were selected from law enforcement agencies, policy makers, the academic community, practitioners and other stakeholders in the area of prevention of organized crime and terrorism. A quantitative survey was conducted to engage front-line practitioners and professionals. Focus groups were then carried out with experts and law enforcement agents. Finally, workshops were conducted with solution providers in the field of security.

In more detail, interviews were held with informants based in the following countries: Austria, Belgium, Bulgaria, Czech Republic, Germany, Italy,

Poland, Romania, Slovakia, Spain, Switzerland, and the UK. Six interviews were carried out with relevant experts engaged at the EU level, and three with researchers established in the surveyed countries but whose expertise was not country focused. These were experts on terrorism and organized crime in Europe in general. Among the interviewees, researchers constituted the highest number of responders (53 interviews, 47.3 per cent), followed by practitioners (24 interviews, 21.4 per cent), and policy makers (13 interviews, 11.6 per cent). These latter served at the national level (members of national parliaments), while some of them operated at the local or international level. Responders labelled as practitioners often decided to hide their affiliation and name. Those who did state their affiliation had a variety of tasks: the sample included police officers, people working for NGOs, in prisons, in agencies fighting terrorism or organized crime, and social workers involved in prevention. Some responders were categorized with mixed-connotation labels (22 interviews, 19.6 per cent): these respondents were experts in multiple fields of activities, thereby allowing interviewers to gain insights into multifaceted perspectives.

An online survey gathered data on the practices and views of front-line professionals. The survey took place between 24 May and 16 September 2017 and targeted a niche pool of respondents rather than the general population, which explains the sample size of 519. Regarding the demographics, more than 65 per cent of the respondents were male and a majority was between 30 to 40 years old. The survey covered a total of 23 countries, 15 different professions that fall into the category of first-line-practitioners and 12 different areas of work within these professions. The findings were generated via the use of SPSS software.

Eleven focus groups were organized in eight countries across the European Union. The focus groups engaged 107 law enforcement agents and front-line practitioner organizations working on organized crime or terrorist networks. Finally, workshops were organized with solution providers, professionals and experts in the field of security. The workshops took place in Darmstadt, Reggio Calabria, Barcelona and Brussels, involving some 40 professionals. Each workshop aimed to highlight current challenges, available solutions as well as possible societal and ethical issues.

Findings

Organized crime activities

There was a sense that knowledge of the organized crime and terrorist phenomena is insufficient. This lack of knowledge was highlighted in the survey as well as in the qualitative research based on workshops, focus groups and interviews. Among the experts interviewed the point was made that more cooperation between researchers and practitioners, along with less emotional attitudes on the part of public bodies, would contribute to a better understanding of both phenomena. Those interviewed also stressed the importance of collaborating with external experts, particularly in the relatively 'unknown' area of cybercrime. Interviews, moreover, brought to the fore the need for an international platform for the exchange of information. The majority of respondents (60 per cent), however, mentioned drug production/distribution and cybercrime, along with the smuggling of people, as the main activities of organized crime. In their view, these require more effective prevention or response policies and strategies. Only in a minority of national contexts was it felt that the activities of organized crime include forays into the licit world thanks to the partnership with, and the support or tolerance of, official political representatives and/or legitimate entrepreneurs.

Two main points need to be highlighted here. First, the research process led to no distinction being made between professional and organized crime. The former is characterized by a horizontal structure in which agents operate as peers, planning schemes together, executing them, and sharing proceeds. By contrast, the latter implies a distinction between planning and execution, a wage relationship between a patron and an agent, and a degree of invisibility: agents may ignore the motivations and the very identity of those recruiting them (Arlacchi, 1994; Armao, 2000; Ruggiero, 2000; Dino, 2008). The activities mentioned by our informants, to be sure, may be carried out by both professional and organized criminals, but the emphasis was only placed on the latter. Second, the activities conducted by organized crime in the official arena, which concerned only few of the experts interviewed, were neglected by the majority of informants contacted through the quantitative as well as the qualitative research.

Previous research proved that organized criminal groups who gain access to the legitimate economy and the political apparatus complete the evolution hypothesized by Peterson (1991), whereby this type of crime traverses a number of successive stages: a predatory, a parasitic, and finally a symbiotic stage. While some groups may fail to undergo a similar evolution, thus stagnating in conventional criminal markets, others may instead succeed, therefore straddling legality and illegality.

By focusing on conventional criminal activities, many of our respondents overlooked the instances in which organized crime invests into the official economy, engages in the delivery of services and in the formation of partnerships with legitimate actors. Criminal networks, which facilitate such nonconventional activities, were also neglected (Dino and Ruggiero, 2012; Ruggiero, 2017). This aspect constitutes the focus of more recent research studies, which show how such criminal networks are perceived. The ruling elites in business and politics are seen as inhabitants of a distant sphere, which attracts with equal force licit as well as illicit actors. Disillusioned citizens, in other words, perceive the existence of menacing entities formed of a variety of powerful coteries whose actions and strategies are relatively obscure. These entities are not depicted as conventional or traditional forms of organized crime, but rather as mixed consortia linking legality and illegality. Financial institutions are seen as key components of such consortia, whose activities include hiding bribes, enabling tax evasion by politicians and entrepreneurs and performing money laundering on behalf of criminal organizations (Whyte and Wiegratz, 2016; Ruggiero, 2017; Libera, 2018; Shaxson, 2018).

In brief, informants focused their attention mainly on conventional criminal activities, namely organized groups that remain confined to illicit markets.

Organized crime drivers

'Being raised in a criminal environment' scored very high among our respondents (66 per cent), whereas 'Discriminatory police tactics against certain groups and individuals' scored very low (7 per cent). Families were regarded as part of such criminal environment. Some participants in the focus groups claimed that legal restrictions on police work was a problem for those involved in the investigation of human smuggling, a problem also encountered in the identification of criminals due to data protection laws. The analysis of our quantitative data also shows that joining organized crime networks was perceived as being associated less with mental difficulties and instability than with lack of opportunities (45 per cent). It is interesting to locate the responses received in our survey within the traditional and contemporary debate around the causes of organized crime.

From the perspective of the Positivist School of criminology, the variable 'tradition' plays a crucial role (Lombroso, 1971). 'Criminal environments' and 'families' return in subsequent interpretations in the form of 'backwardness' or 'archaism'. These are analyses that address organized crime from a 'cultural' perspective (among the most celebrated are Hess (1973) and Hobsbawm (1971)). Belonging to the same cluster are contributions focused on the perpetuation of organized forms of criminality, which is said to derive from the lack of popular stigma attached to those involved. Subcultural theorists, for instance, would argue that members of criminal organizations are not regarded as individuals belonging to a distant and censurable social universe, nor are they associated with immorality or elicit contempt (Cohen, 1955; Cloward and Ohlin, 1960). Our respondents, by emphasizing the 'learning process' implied in being 'raised in a criminal environment', located their views in the tradition of subcultural theories.

Echoing strain theory, the relative majority of participants in the online survey singled out 'lack of opportunities' as a causation variable. Merton's (1968) deviant adaptation of the 'innovative' type comes to mind, namely a solution adopted by those who pursue the official goals of money and success through alternative illicit means. The quantitative parts of the research, on the other hand, failed to provide the nuanced descriptions found in the 'social disorganization' tradition, that is to say descriptions of organized crime as micro-societies characterized by a surrogate social order (Downes and Rock, 1988; Thrasher, 1927; Shaw, 1930; Whyte, 1943; Landesco, 1969). While police discrimination against certain individuals and groups was deemed irrelevant by our respondents, some classical literature, instead, focuses on the participation of the police themselves in organized criminality (Landesco, 1969). Finally, the variable 'low self-control' (Gottfredson and Hirschi, 1990) did emerge in interviews and workshops, but notions of organized crime as service provider in contexts characterized by lack of trust were not (McIntosh, 1975; Gambetta, 1992; Varese, 2010, 2017).

Measures against organized crime

Respondents mainly opted for the creation of special police/law enforcement units (49 per cent) and discarded the idea that new drug legislation would have an effect on the fight against organized crime (22 per cent). Little attention was devoted to the potential of labour market reform and improved welfare provision (20 per cent). The analysis of our quantitative data reveals that the policing and criminal justice group of our informants did not necessarily see harder tactics as effective prevention tools. Participants in focus groups stressed the importance of integrating young people and empowering them, namely making them able to express their opinions and reach independent decisions. More involvement of civil society was advocated, along with more material resources and training for law enforcers and investigators. Interviews with experts revealed unsatisfactory feelings around the problem of agency cooperation and transnational coordination of responses. They also emphasized how institutional responses are often driven by emergency situations and determined by the search for political consensus. Some interviewees stressed the importance, in the fight against organized crime, of establishing proper protection for whistle-blowers. The analysis of quantitative data shows a prevalence of non-criminal justice professionals favouring human and social approaches to reduce the incidence of organized crime (44 per cent). The analysis also reveals that aims and objectives in combating this type of crime are shared across occupational roles. Some law enforcers involved in focus groups lamented the inadequacy of cybercrime units and the need to liaise with the private sector, particularly commercial banks. Respondents involved in workshops stressed the need for strong coordination, communication and alignment of national and international laws that regulate the field of cyber security. Interviewees pointed out the need for more strategic, comprehensive, prevention measures, but also for techniques able to evaluate the effectiveness of such measures.

For further analysis, data was manipulated to collapse those participants working in criminal justice related fields (criminal justice (CJ) professionals) and those working in other domains such as education and youth work (non-CJ professionals). Comparing criminal justice professionals to non-criminal justice professionals, we see a difference in where they believe reductions in criminality could occur (Table 2.1).

Two findings are worth attention. First, respondents within both groups did not substantially differ in their appreciation of job creation, increased

Table 2.1 Cross-tabulations of effect of actions for crime reduction across professional types

Variables	CJ professionals %(n)	Non-CJ professionals %(n)	Significance
Social welfare	28 (63)	40 (36)	4.08★
Job creation	48 (61)	53 (87)	0.81, NS
Increased policing	28 (33)	31 (47)	0.33, NS
Sentence enhancement	34 (41)	38 (60)	0.60, NS
Increased therapy	24 (30)	35 (55)	4.00★

Note
★ Denotes significant association at the $p < 0.05$ level. The analysis illustrates those participates who responded to the question as either having a moderate or strong effect.

policing and sentence enhancement as preventive tools. The main differences between the two cohorts were recorded in relation to social welfare and therapeutic measures. Surprisingly, the policing and criminal justice group did not see harder tactics in a positive light. Table 2.2 below explores an additional set of actions perceived as potentially effective to reduce organized criminality.

The most notable differences in the opinions of criminal justice and non-criminal justice professionals pertain to rehabilitation, investment in schools and drug legalization. The majority of all participants, therefore, expressed relatively similar views regardless of their social role, suggesting that increased cooperation between professionals could be fruitful.

But let us provide a general backdrop against which the responses received might be better understood.

Backdrop

Informants advocated a mixture of measures connoted by a social as well as a technical character. Educational programmes aimed at spreading civic awareness were prioritized, as were projects promoting social inclusion. In line with anti-drug policies already operational across Europe, the majority of respondents called for tackling demand through informative public health campaigns and supply through international agency cooperation. Scepticism

Table 2.2 Cross-tabulations of effect of actions to reduce organized criminality

Variables	CJ professionals %(n)	Non-CJ professionals %(n)	Significance
Increased rehabilitation	33 (41)	38 (62)	0.77, NS
Special units	51 (63)	49 (80)	0.17, NS
Investments schools	37 (46)	43 (67)	0.88, NS
Legalize prostitution	18 (19)	18 (24)	0.02, NS
Legalize drugs	20 (31)	27 (36)	0.24, NS
Community policing	40 (50)	42 (67)	0.05, NS

about the introduction of new legislation led to the neglect of the potential effect of decriminalizing the use of some drugs. As already mentioned, positive views were expressed about labour market reform and improved welfare provision. In this respect, research conducted by institutional agencies (Europol, 2011) and independent investigators alike (Hobbs, 2013; Dino, 2016) depicts organized crime as 'employer' attracting individuals who find no suitable occupation in the official labour market. With legitimate occupations being increasingly characterized by precarious conditions and poor wages, organized crime may well appear as a more appealing labour recruiter. Social prevention, therefore, should attempt to make legitimate work competitive, in ethical and material terms, with illegitimate occupations.

Prioritizing, as most informants did, the use of special tools and enforcement units appears to be consistent with the common strategies already used by European governments, which consist of 'dismantling criminal organizations by dismantling their leadership structures in order to fragment them into minor and more manageable groups' (Ferreira, 2016: 43). Measures have included a mixture of undercover operations, raids, privacy-piercing approaches, and, increasingly, collaboration with intelligence services and international policing agencies. Some observers would judge such strategies ineffective, particularly in developed countries, while in developing countries they risk, it is feared, to 'intensify pre-existing conflicts, turf wars, and generate smaller, less predictable and more violent groups fighting fiercely for smaller turfs' (ibid.: 43). In brief, the old dilemma whether monopolistic organized crime causes more harm than disorganized crime remains unsolved (Andreano and Siegfried, 1980). For this reason, some academic researchers would suggest that efforts to eradicate organized crime should rely less on conventional crime-control activities than on the alteration of the incentive structures in place in the economic and the political sphere (Milhaupt and West, 2000). Hence the broad structural suggestions emanating from the European Parliament (2016): increasing public finding for schemes in underdeveloped regions, implementing economic growth strategies, enforcing and strengthening the regulations governing national and international financial institutions, prosecuting money-laundering enablers, developing international schemes of asset recovery, and harmonizing standards for confiscation.

It has to be noted, that while informants in this research also stressed the importance of patrimonial measures, they failed to appreciate the role that the allocation of funds to problematic regions could play. In fact, they called for more funds, resources and training to be allocated to law enforcers rather than to society at large.

As mentioned above, informants were perplexed about the way in which the effectiveness of strategies and measures can be assessed. Their perplexity may derive from the fact that strategies and measures mainly target closed enclaves of socially and culturally homogenous individuals, in other words they confine their intervention to conventional criminal activities, or the underworld, while overlooking the connections this establishes with the overworld. As already noted, only in reference to specific national contexts (for instance, Bulgaria), was the unwillingness of government to sever the links between organized crime and the official world pointed out.

It is difficult to explain the unsatisfactory feelings expressed by informants around the problem of agency cooperation and transnational coordination of responses. The Maastricht Treaty includes articles concerning police cooperation and addresses the growth of organized crime as a product of the process of integration. First regarded as an issue to be tackled under the Third Pillar (the intergovernmental pillar), the fight against organized crime gave rise to police and judicial cooperation and new systems and procedures to improve the sharing of information. In 1990 member states stipulated the Convention on Laundering, Search, Seizure and Confiscation of the Proceeds of Crime, which was turned by the Council into a directive in 1991. Under the directive, states were forced to implement legislation against money laundering, 'but also to ensure that their financial institutions would register and report unusual and suspect transactions to the competent authorities' (Fijnaut, 2015: 574).

Cooperation among member states stepped up in the aftermath of the assassination of Palermo investigative judges Falcone and Borsellino in 1992, and resulted in the establishment of Europol in 1995. European concerns around organized crime were also intensified by the collapse of the Soviet Union and the threat of new forms of criminal activity emanating from its former satellite states in Eastern Europe (Dunn, 1996). An 'Action Plan to Combat Organized Crime' was produced in 1997 under the banner of the Treaty of Amsterdam, instructing member states to integrate prevention, investigation and prosecution and harmonize their legislations. In a cumulative process, policies and strategies were devised under the successive presidencies of the European Council, and in 1999 Eurojust was created, namely a multinational European team of national prosecutors and police officers. A European Police College was founded while a Financial Intelligence Unit tasked with information sharing about money laundering was set up (Fijnaut, 2015). In brief, the unsatisfactory feelings conveyed by informants may testify to the difficulties member states encounter when they attempt to translate general principles and guidelines (or even instructions) into routine practical action. Or, as informants argued, may derive from their perception that institutional responses are often driven by emergency situations and determined by the search for political consensus.

As for the technical measures advocated, increasing the quality of equipment and training of police forces scored high (about 40 per cent). Support was given to the European Parliament suggestions to strengthen the regulations governing the activities of financial institutions and the prosecution of money-laundering enablers (see Directive 2014/42/EU of the European Parliament and of the Council of 3). But along with the importance of patrimonial measures, the crucial role of special units for the fight of organized crime seemed to be prioritized.

Terrorist activities

In general terms, also in the area of terrorism more cooperation between researchers and practitioners was deemed necessary for a better understanding of the phenomenon. The highest number and proportion of respondents stressed that propaganda and recruitment require more effective prevention. In the focus groups, however, it was argued that common definitions of violent extremism, radicalization and terrorism are needed, and that the emotional public reaction to such phenomena hampers their understanding. The analysis of our data shows a generalized concern among respondents about terrorism financing and cyber terrorism (10 per cent), with some interviewees lamenting that expertise in this area is underused by official agencies. One important finding was that the invasion of countries was not deemed to stop terrorism, but rather encourage it. It is interesting to compare this concern with research findings on this specific issue and other aspects of terrorism.

Working closely with Islamic fundamentalists, Sageman (2017) gained an intimate understanding of how propaganda and recruitment take place. He observed the development of networks which transform socially isolated individuals into warriors, and noted that affiliation is normally a bottom-up process, with young people volunteering to join the organization. Friendship and kinship bonds emerged as key factors in shaping the networks. In brief, propaganda and recruitment, the concerns of our informants, occur through micro-social dynamics which are little known to law enforcement and, therefore, can hardly be influenced by outsiders.

The necessity to clarify definitions is perceived in the existing literature as it was by the majority of our respondents. However, the emotional public reaction to terrorism, regarded by respondents as detrimental, seems to be perfectly understandable when targeting preferences are examined. Research conducted on this aspect reveals that soft targets are 'dominant and increasing, while particularly well-protected targets are almost totally avoided' (Hemmingby, 2017: 25). In other words, the general public is more exposed than high-ranking individuals or highly symbolic buildings or premises such as parliaments, governmental institutions or business headquarters.

The point was made by the relative majority of informants (12 per cent) that the invasion of a country may be followed by organized violent resistance, and that invasions may destabilize regimes and trigger sectarian attacks. The example of Libya was referred to (Ismael and Ismael, 2013), while research suggests that over 30 per cent of the founders of ISIS were former members of the Ba'athist secret services of Iraq, who enact a form of revenge, responding to the invasion of their country with indiscriminate attacks (Gerges, 2015; Lynch, 2015).

Terrorist drivers

In the opinion of the majority of respondents (60 per cent), individuals join terrorist networks because they are raised in a culture that promotes extreme ideological views. Psychological-personality disorders, in their view, have a moderate influence (42 per cent). In the focus groups some participants underlined the social exclusion of young people joining terrorist networks and their search for stability when joining them. Emphasis was also placed on vulnerability and lack of guidance and security on the part of families. A strong association between economic exclusion, isolation and alienation was found in our data analysis (53 per cent), which also showed the respondents' stress on the influence of leadership figures (52 per cent).

Cultures promoting extreme ideological views have been studied by scholars who have attempted to find in sacred texts the cause of contemporary terrorism. (Kennedy, 2016; Small, 2016; Adonis, 2016). Challenging causations derived from foundational texts, other scholars have underlined how the Quran is replete with suggestions around dialogue, peace and the development of harmonious interfaith relationships (Horkuc, 2009; Wills, 2016). Finally, the argument has been made that not Islam, but religion in general has always played a role in war and terrorist violence, even in advanced secular countries (Buc, 2015; Sacks, 2015; Hassner, 2016).

Research into psychological factors has linked terrorism with collective animosity against injustice and power. The final step on a narrowing staircase (Moghaddam, 2005), the choice of terror is said to appeal to individuals who believe they have no voice in society and who express a 'significance quest' (Victoroff and Kruglanski, 2009). One of the causes identified in the literature is the feeling of 'weakness, irrelevance, marginalization and subordination experienced by Muslim people', combined with the memory of the glorious past of a great transnational civilization (Toscano, 2016: 123). The 'reactionary utopia' of the Caliphate is explained in these terms, namely as the result of frustration determined by the gap between expectations and achievement. The frustration thesis seems to apply to both prevailing models of terrorism: 'the fanatic who is outside any appeal to rationality, and the calculating actor who lacks any capacity for human empathy' (McDonald, 2013: 11).

Research has also examined terrorism as a corollary of social exclusion: extremists are said to come from the poorest and rundown parts of cities, where youth are raised in large housing estates and where trouble flares up periodically. Accounts illustrate the fractured lives of young second-generation migrants, their alienation, exclusion, family size, poverty and disrupted upbringings. Some traverse the pathways from home to care and from crime to prison, struggle within the education system, and display all the 'predictors of criminal behaviour' (Walklate and Mythen, 2016: 337). However, 'It is erroneous to presume that material deprivation works in a simple and/or straightforward manner in relation to the propensity to commit violence'

(Walklate and Mythen, 2016: 338). To claim that inequality and social injustice are the main causes of terrorism neglects the fact that there is no terrorism in the 50 countries listed by the United Nations as the poorest, least developed, most unjust and unequal. As Sen (2015: 165) has argued,

> The simple thesis linking poverty with violence is empirically much too crude, both because the linkage of poverty and crime is far from universally observed, and because there are other social factors ... Calcutta is not only one of the poorest cities in India – and indeed in the world – it so happens that it also has a very low crime rate.
>
> (Ibid.: 165)

In sum, our respondents overstressed social and structural factors as causes of terrorism, although they also highlighted the 'search for stability' that encourages young people to join terrorist networks. Their views on cultures promoting violence find controversial treatment in research, while findings in the psychological domain may suggest that more attention to this area of investigation should be devoted.

Measures to decrease terrorism

The majority of respondents thought that cross-border cooperation between police and intelligence agencies to facilitate monitoring, arrest and disruption would have the strongest effect (52 per cent), and that military action abroad to target terrorist leaders and infrastructure has no effect. Pre-emptive intelligence was called for, mainly in interviews and workshops. Opinions collected in focus groups addressed the issue of legal documentation for young migrants who otherwise 'get lost in the system'. New comers, it was argued, should receive appropriate support and guidance. Social workers, it was noted, needed to be properly trained in order to 'connect' with young people at risk. Often, their lack of religiosity was regarded as an obstacle preventing such connection. Other actors to be involved in the preventive process, it was remarked, include community leaders, religious leaders, victims and families. One problem raised during the course of interviews with experts was that preventive and other measures are commonly the result of mere public pressure. Preventive work, according to some interviewees, should also take place in prison institutions. Finally, it was felt that policy-making processes should be evidence-based and that a wider involvement of Muslim communities is necessary.

As in the previous section on organized crime, an analysis was undertaken to explore whether there were any significant differences in the views of criminal justice and non-criminal justice professionals in the arena of prevention.

Two major differences stand out. First, non-criminal justice professionals scored much higher in relations to 'social welfare' and slightly higher in

Table 2.3 Cross-tabulations of effect of actions across professional types

Variables	CJ professionals %(n)	Non-CJ professionals %(n)	Significance
Equipment	42 (25)	48 (41)	0.61, NS
Social welfare	21 (12)	43 (32)	6.48★
Job creation	33 (19)	36 (29)	0.06, NS
Increased policing	33 (20)	35 (27)	0.50, NS
Special police	53 (32)	49 (41)	0.21, NS
Increased therapy	34 (19)	33 (26)	0.02, NS

Note
★ Denotes significant association at the $p < 0.01$ level. The analysis illustrates those participants who responded to the question as either having a moderate or strong effect.

relation to 'job creation'. Second, they also revealed a higher propensity for improved technical tools such as 'equipment'. Let us interrogate research and other sources on these points.

Official agencies seem to share the view that cross-border coordination has a strong effect. In this respect, an Agenda on Security for the period 2015–2020 was set out by the European Commission, detailing the concrete tools to be used in joint anti-terrorist work (European Commission, 2015). Technical anti-terrorist preventive measures adopted within the EU include exchange of DNA data, which is also carried out in the fight against other forms of cross-border crime (Santos and Machado, 2016), along with the introduction of new counter-terrorism legislation in most member states. Glorification and incitement are now widely criminalized.

As for military intervention, most available literature oscillates between suggestions to deal with terrorism through the rule of law and deprecation for unnecessary military action. While EU citizens overwhelming believe that institutional action against terrorism and radicalization is insufficient (European Parliament, 2016), states reacting with pure military force are said to imitate the illusions and delusions of those groups or individuals they are trying to combat (English, 2016). The dangers of what is termed a 'forever war' are highlighted: 'Say the word "war" and the rule of law often implodes' (Rakoff, 2016: 80). This is the view, among others, of distinguished law experts, who find themselves in disagreement when the judiciary avoids to scrutinize anything 'embarrassing' from far-reaching surveillance to torture or the use of drones (Todorov, 2014; Fiss, 2016). Equal controversy surrounds the use of 'disposition matrix' or 'kill lists' that spell out who has to be hit by a long-distance unmanned missile (Hayden, 2016).

In the UK, a study has examined the emotional impact of counter-terrorist strategies on Muslim communities, while several authors have focused on how such strategies increase fear and encourage suspicion and racism (Mythen and Walklate, 2006; Ahmed, 2015; Abbas and Awan, 2015). Finally, counter-terrorist wars have also been judged as serious obstacles to the delivery of humanitarian aid (Gill, 2016). It should be added that, when there is a disconnect between the depiction of terrorist threat as presented by official agencies and the perception of large sectors of the public, responses to terror attacks fail to gain the support they would need (Smith et al., 2016). The disconnect is likely to widen, at least in the UK, after the publication of the Chilcot Report, showing the disastrous outcome of the institutional deceit leading to the invasion of Iraq (Chilcot, 2016; Wheatcroft, 2016).

Informants did not specify the type of pre-emptive intelligence measures they would stand for, nor did they seem to be aware of the considerable controversies surrounding them. For instance, some schemes have been located among the 'pre-crime' strategies adopted in many Western countries. These strategies are said to centre state action on sheer suspicion, whereby individuals and groups are targeted without a specific charge being formulated. Anticipating risk, in this sense, tends to integrate national security into criminal justice, to the detriment of civil and political rights (McCulloch and Pickering, 2009). Anti-terrorism, from this perspective, is said to become a threat to democracy (Wolfendale, 2007; Zedner, 2000). It is hard to determine whether this is one of the cases in which, according to respondents, measures where implemented as a response to public pressure. Scant attention is devoted to the importance, as underlined in interviews, of the religiosity of social workers. On the other hand, some research findings are available on prevention in prison and in the financial arena, where terrorist organizations find affiliates and resources respectively (Hamm, 2007; 2013).

Examples of community involvement as proposed by informants are relatively common across Europe. For example, prevention is pursued through targeting families, both those affected by the radicalization of one or more of their members and those who feel the need to protect their offspring from the radicalization process. In the UK, FAST (Families Against Stress & Trauma) is one such initiative, engaged in making people aware of the risks of the Internet and the violent messages it can convey. Although more controversial, the 'Prevent' programme, launched in the UK in 2003 as one of the four elements of CONTEST, the government's counter-terrorism strategy, is inspired by similar aims, mobilizing in particular teachers and lecturers in the detection of embryonic signs of radicalization.

'Agenfor Media' is also engaged in preventing radical escalation, and produces videos and printed documents. These explain how to deal with vulnerable groups and individuals of Muslim faith from an Islamic perspective. The area of radicalization in prison is covered, while an informative social media channel is provided informing on wars and insurgents in several regions (www.agenformedia.com/dossier/preventing-radical-escalations).

Community-led (or social media) initiatives also take the form of testimonies and life stories of individuals affected by radicalization aiming to reduce the appeal of terrorist organizations.

The 'Viennese Network Deradicalization and Prevention' is active in the Austrian capital and operates in the field of education. The network elaborates and assesses policies and strategies, addresses social inequality and vulnerable groups, focusing, among other things, on gender and sexism (information gathered through focus groups). In Spain, 'Women without Borders' address mothers in the attempt to raise their awareness of extremist ideologies, aiming at the creation of a future without fear and violence (information gathered through focus groups).

Finally, some research proves that certain forms of community policing can promote Muslims' willingness to cooperate with investigators in terrorist prevention. While intrusive counter-terrorism policies and practices alienate the communities being addressed, perceptions of police legitimacy and fair policing appear to have a strong bearing on Muslims' behaviour. Cooperation with the police, in such cases, takes place despite 'the salience of identity within the current political discourse about terrorism and Islam' (Madon, Murphy and Cherney, 2017: 1144).

Our respondents proposed measures that share some components with these initiatives. For instance, when advocating the legal documentation and identification of young migrants (lest they 'get lost in the system'), support was given to control systems based on community forms of policing. These would encourage the willingness of ordinary people and groups to cooperate in the preventive process, favouring at the same time the provision of support and guidance to youth. Our informants indicated that a crucial role in these initiatives should be played by social workers, community and religious leaders, victims and families, namely all figures, professional or not, involved in the projects described above.

Analyses of the unintended consequences of policy interventions and strategic tactics suggest that 'sometimes these interventions have created backlash effects that led to greater numbers of crimes' (Chermak, Freilich and Caspi, 2010: 139). As an alternative, participation of extremists (or those they purportedly represent) in policy-making is advocated (Dugan and Young, 2010: 164).

In sum, the majority of our respondents concurred that military action abroad has no effect, although details regarding the backlash of such action were not captured in the research process. Similarly, cross-border cooperation between police and intelligence agencies was advocated, but the danger of adopting a pre-crime strategy and targeting individuals and groups on mere suspicion was not reckoned with. In other words, no potential unintended consequences of increased 'monitoring, arrest and disruption' were anticipated.

Conclusion

Informants involved in this research study made no distinction between professional and organized crime and mainly limited their attention to the activities carried out by the former in criminal markets. In brief, with few exceptions, they neglected the operations conducted by criminal organizations in the official economy and in the legitimate world in general. When discussing the causes of organized crime, they tended to pinpoint learning processes and embrace variables belonging to the tradition of subcultural, control and strain theory. The main dissonance between their views and those found in the criminological literature were manifest in the role they attributed to law enforcers and in the lack of appreciation of the surrogate social order, governance or trust provided by organized crime. In response to organized crime, they advocated social measures whose effectiveness is acknowledged in the criminological literature. They called for technical preventive measures which are also encouraged or implemented at the European level.

On terrorism, this research found a mismatch but also some coincidence between the views of informants and those expressed in previous theoretical and empirical work. The mismatch was particularly evident with respect to propaganda and recruitment, while the coincidence pertained to the effect of invasions and wars on the spread of terrorist activity. The role of cultures which encourage extreme forms of violence, as compared with previous analyses and findings, was overstressed, as was the causative role of the material condition experienced by those joining terrorist networks. Interestingly, there was a high degree of consonance around responses to terrorism, as the types of measures suggested are discussed and valued in the literature and, in part, are already implemented across Europe. This would prove that the process some informants hoped for, which should bring researchers and practitioners closer together is, if only partly, already underway.

Acknowledgements

Funding has been received from the European Union's Horizon 2020 Research and Innovation Programme under Grant Agreement N. 700688.

References

Abbas, T. and Awan, I. (2015), 'Limits of UK Counterterrorism Policy and its Implications for Islamophobia and Far Right Extremism', *International Journal for Crime, Justice and Social Democracy*, 4: 16–29.

Adonis (2016), *Violence and Islam*, Cambridge: Polity.

Ahmed, S. (2015), 'The Emotionalization of the War on Terror: Counterterrorism, Fear, Risk, Insecurity and Helplessness', *Criminology and Criminal Justice*, 15: 545–560.

Andreano, R. and Siegfried, J. (eds) (1980), *The Economics of Crime*, New York: John Wiley.

Arlacchi, P. (1994), *Addio Cosa Nostra. La vita di Tommaso Buscetta*, Milan: Rizzoli.

Armao, F. (2000), *Il sistema mafia. Dall'economia-mondo al dominio locale*, Turin: Bollati Boringhieri.

Buc, P. (2015), *Holy Wars, Martyrdom and Terror*, Philadelphia: University of Pennsylvania Press.

Chermak, S.M., Freilich, J.D. and Caspi, D. (2010), 'Policymakers and Law Enforcement Must Consider the Unintended Consequences of Their Proposed Responses to Extremist and Terrorist Groups', in Frost, N.A., Freilich, J.D. and Clear, T.R. (eds), *Contemporary Issues in Criminal Justice Policy*, Belmont: Wadsworth.

Chilcot, J. (2016), *The Report of the Iraq Inquiry*, London: HMSO.
Cloward, R. And Ohlin, L. (1960), *Delinquency and Opportunity*, New York: The Free Press.
Cohen, A. (1955), *Delinquent Boys: The Culture of the Gang*, New York: The Free Press.
Dino, A. (2008), *La mafia devota*, Rome/Bari: Laterza.
Dino, A. (2016), *A colloquio con Gaspare Spatuzza*, Bologna: Il Mulino.
Dino, A. and Ruggiero, V. (2012), 'Il metodo mafioso', special issue of *Studi sulla Questione Criminale*, VII (1): 1–130.
Downes, D. and Rock, P. (1988), *Understanding Deviance. A Guide to the Sociology of Crime and Rule Breaking*, Oxford: Clarendon Press.
Dugan, L. and Young, J. (2010), 'Allow Extremist Participation in the Policy-Making Process', in Frost, N.A., Freilich, J.D. and Clear, T.R. (eds), *Contemporary Issues in Criminal Justice Policy*, Belmont: Wadsworth.
Dunn, G. (1996), 'Major Mafia Gangs in Russia', *Transnational Organized Crime*, 2 (2–3): 63–87.
English, R. (ed.) (2016), *Illusions of Terrorism and Counter-Terrorism*, Oxford: Oxford University Press.
European Commission (2015), *Commission Takes Steps to Strengthen EU Cooperation in the Fight against Terrorism, Organised Crime and Cybercrime*, Press Release, Strasbourg 28 April, http://europa.eu/rapid/press-release_IP-15-4865_en.htm (accessed 20 January 2018).
European Parliament (2016), *Expectations for EU Action. Fight against Terrorism and Radicalisation*, Strasbourg: Public Opinion Monitoring Unit.
Europol (2011), *EU Organised Crime Threat Assessment*, The Hague: Europol Public Information.
Ferreira, O.R. (2016), 'Violent Mexico: Participatory and Multipolar Violence Associated with Organized Crime', *International Journal of Conflict and Violence*, 10(1): 40–60.
Fijnaut, C. (2015), 'European Union Organized Crime Policies', in Paoli, L. (ed.), *The Oxford Handbook of Organized Crime*, Oxford: Oxford University Press.
Fiss, O. (2016), *A War Like No Other: The Constitution in a Time of Terror*, New York: New Press.
Gambetta, D. (1992), *La mafia siciliana. Un'industria della protezione privata*, Turin: Einaudi.
Gerges, F.A. (2015), *ISIS. A History*, Princeton: Princeton University Press.
Gill, P. (2016), *Today We Drop Bombs, Tomorrow We Build Bridges*, London: Zed Books.
Gottfredson, M. and Hirschi, T. (1990), *A General Theory of Crime*, Stanford: Stanford University Press.
Hamm, M.S. (2007), *Terrorism as Crime*, New York: New York University Press.
Hamm, M.S. (2013), *The Spectacular Few. Prisoner Radicalization and the Evolving Terrorist Threat*, New York: New York University Press.
Hassner, R.E. (2016), *Religion on the Battlefield*, Ithaca: Cornell University Press.
Hayden, M. (2016), *Playing to the Edge: American Intelligence in the Age of Terror*, Harmondsworth: Penguin.
Hemmingby, C. (2017), 'Exploring the Continuum of Lethality: Militant Islamists' Targeting Preference in Europe', *Perspectives on Terrorism*, 11: 25–41.
Hess, H. (1973), *Mafia*, Bari: Laterza.

Hobbs, D. (2013), *Lush Life: Constructing Organized Crime in the UK*, Oxford: Oxford University Press.

Hobsbawm, E.J. (1971), *Primitive Rebels*, Manchester: Manchester University Press.

Horkuc, H. (2009), *Said Nursi: Makers of Islamic Civilization*, Oxford: Oxford University Press.

Ismael, J.S. and Ismael, S.T. (2013), 'The Arab Spring and the Uncivil State', *Arab Studies Quarterly*, 35: 229–240.

Kennedy, H. (2016), *The Caliphate*, Harmondsworth: Pelican.

Landesco, J. (1969), *Organized Crime in Chicago*, Chicago: University of Chicago Press.

Libera (2018), *Sulla percezione e la presenza di mafie e corruzione*, www.libera.it/schede-630-rapporto_liberaidee (accessed 22 October 2018).

Lombroso, C. (1971), *L'uomo delinquente*, Turin: Bocca.

Lynch, M. (2015), *The New Arab Wars: Uprising and Anarchy in the Middle East*, New York: Public Affairs.

Madon, N.S., Murphy, K. and Cherney, A. (2017), 'Promoting Community Collaboration in Counterterrorism: Do Social Identities and Perceptions of Legitimacy Mediate Reactions to Procedural Justice Policing?', *British Journal of Criminology*, 57: 1144–1164.

McCulloch, J. and Pickering, S. (2009), 'Pre-Crime and Counter-Terrorism', *British Journal of Criminology*, 49: 628–645.

McDonald, K. (2013), *Our Violent World. Terrorism in Society*, London: Palgrave Macmillan.

McIntosh, M. (1975), *The Organisation of Crime*, London: Macmillan.

Milhaupt, C.J. and West, M.D. (2000), 'The Dark Side of Private Ordering: An Institutional and Empirical Analysis of Organized Crime', *The University of Chicago Law Review*, 15: 41–98.

Merton, R. (1968), *Social Theory and Social Structure*, New York: The Free Press.

Moghaddam, F.M. (2005), 'The Staircase to Terrorism. A Psychological Exploration', *American Psychologist*, 60: 161–169.

Mythen, G. and Walklate, S. (2006), 'Criminology and Terrorism: Which Thesis? Risk Society or Governmentality?', *British Journal of Criminology*, 46: 379–398.

Peterson, M. (1991), 'The Changes of a Decade', *Criminal Organizations*, 6 (3–4): 20–22.

Rakoff, J.S. (2016), 'Terror and Everybody's Rights', *New York Review of Books*, 29 September: 80–82.

Ruggiero, V. (2000), *Crime and Markets*, Oxford: Oxford University Press.

Ruggiero, V. (2017), *Dirty Money. On Financial Delinquency*, Oxford: Oxford University Press.

Sacks, J. (2015), *Not in God's Name. Confronting Religious Violence*, London: Hodder and Stoughton.

Sageman, M. (2017), *Understanding Terror Networks*, Philadelphia: University of Pennsylvania Press.

Santos, F. and Machado, H. (2016), 'Fighting Cross-Border Crime and Terrorism in the EU', paper presented at the European Society of Criminology Conference, Munster University, 21–14 September.

Sen, A. (2015), *The Country of First Boys and Other Essays*, Oxford: Oxford University Press.

Shaw, C. (1930), *The Jack-Roller: A Delinquent Boy's Own Story*, Chicago: University of Chicago Press.

Shaxson, N. (2018), *The Finance Curse: How Global Finance is Making Us All Poorer*, New York: Bodley Head.
Small, T. (2016), 'Wars of Religion', *Times Literary Supplement*, 23 September, Middle East Special Feature: 1–12.
Smith, B.K., Figueroa-Caballero, A., Chan, S., Kovacs, R., Middo, E., Nelson, L., Palacios, R., Yelimeli, S., Stohl, M. (2016), 'Framing Daesh: Failures and Consequences', *Perspectives on Terrorism*, 10: 42–52.
Thrasher, F. (1927), *The Gang: A Study of 1,313 Gangs in Chicago*, Chicago: University of Chicago Press.
Todorov, T. (2014), *The Inner Enemies of Democracy*, Cambridge: Polity.
Toscano, R. (2016), 'Il tempo della paura', *Micro Mega*, 2: 119–128.
Varese, F. (ed.) (2010), *Organized Crime: Critical Concepts in Criminology*, London: Routledge.
Varese, F. (2017), *Mafia Life*, London: Profile.
Victoroff, J. and Kruglanski, A.W. (eds) (2009), *Psychology of Terrorism: Classic and Contemporary Insights*, London: Psychology Press.
Walklate, S. and Mythen, G. (2016), 'Fractured Lives, Splintered Knowledge: Making Criminological Sense of the January, 2015 Terrorist Attack in Paris', *Critical Criminology*, 24: 333–346.
Wheatcroft, G. (2016), 'Tony Blair's Eternal Shame: The Report', *New York Review of Books*, 13 October: 42–44.
Whyte, F.W. (1943), *Street Corner Society*, Chicago: University of Chicago Press.
Whyte, D. and Wiegratz, J. (eds) (2016), *Neoliberalism and the Moral Economy of Fraud*, London and New York: Routledge.
Wills, G. (2016), 'My Koran Problem', *New York Review of Books*, 26 September: 16–19.
Witte, R. (1996), *Racist Violence and the State*, London: Longman.
Wolfendale, J. (2007), 'Terrorism, Security and the Threat of Counter-Terrorism', *Studies in Conflict and Terrorism*, 30: 75–92.
Zedner, L. (2000), 'The Pursuit of Security', in Hope, T. and Sparks, R. (eds), *Crime, Risk and Insecurity*, London and New York: Routledge.

3 Hybrids

On the crime-terror nexus

Vincenzo Ruggiero

Introduction

The crime-terror nexus transpires in embryonic forms in some contributions of classical criminology. Such contributions do not describe clear overlaps between terrorism and organized crime, but simply allude to the proximity of some forms of political violence with conventional criminality. Sedition, for Beccaria, combines political as well as criminal elements, and being socially devastating, constitutes the only offence against which capital punishment is justified. Similar opinion is expressed by Bentham in respect of the crimes against the state. The latter, moreover, criticizes the Declaration of Human Rights approved by the French government after the Revolution because it is the fruit of an insurrection, therefore of terrorist violence and crime. Positivist analysis hints at a crime-terror nexus, when it detects in some forms of political violence the outcome of individual personalities that would be induced to violent criminality even without being inspired by a political idea. Functionalism, in its turn, links homicide with strong forms of binding with sets of moral values which may characterize political as well as criminal subcultures. Chicago sociologists, as we shall see, provide the most glaring example of how politics and organized crime groups can shape symbiotic alliances, while conflict theorists tend to argue that all forms of violent hostility originate from struggles between groups over material as well as political power. Symbolic interactionism, finally, is more interested in how institutional and anti-institutional violence affect each other.

These contributions will be examined in some detail in the following pages, with the purpose of ascertaining to what extent they constitute premonitions of contemporary events. Such events have led observers to posit the existence of an overlap between terrorism and crime, particularly organized crime, as many terrorist organizations complement their military capability with functioning infrastructures and profitable activity in economic ventures as well as in crime. The validity of the notion of hybrids, namely of an undeniable crime-terror nexus, is advocated by some and contested by others, and the pages below will provide the main arguments and the most relevant empirical material offered by the two parties. What will emerge is an analytical landscape indicating that the overlap between terrorism and organized crime is, at the very least, controversial and, at times, merely prompted by the strong disapproval or revulsion that both elicit. Similarities and differences between the two forms of criminality will be highlighted, as will the ambiguity of the very notion of 'crime-terror nexus'. In the last section of this chapter such ambiguity will come to the fore with particular emphasis, when the relationships linking organized crime and terrorism respectively with the establishment will be focused upon. It may be helpful, however, to set off with a concise outline of definitions of organized crime and terrorism found in criminology.

Criminological definitions

The best-known definitions of organized crime found in the criminological tradition can be classified very succinctly as follows. Some hinge on strictly quantitative aspects: the number of individuals involved in a criminal group is said to determine the organizational degree of that group (Ferracuti, 1988; Johnson, 1962). Organized crime is also said to differ from conventional crime for the larger scale of its illegal activity (Moore, 1987). Other definitions focus mainly on a temporal variable, that is on the time-span during which illegal activities are conducted. The death or incarceration of a member of an organized crime group, therefore, does not stop the activities in which the group is involved.

Criminologists who focus attention on its structural characteristics observe that organized crime operates by means of flexible and diversified groups. Such a structure is faced with peculiar necessities due to its condition of illegality. First, the necessity, while remaining a 'secret' organization, to exert publicly its coercive and dissuasive strength. An equilibrium is therefore required between publicity and secrecy that only a complex structure is able to acquire. Second, the necessity to neutralize law enforcement through *omertà*, corruption and retaliation. Finally, the need to reconcile its internal order, through specific forms of conflict control, with its external legitimacy, through the provision of occupational and social opportunities (Cohen, 1977).

Frequently, definitions of organized crime revolve around the concept of 'professionalism': its members, it is suggested, acquire skills and career advancement by virtue of their full-time involvement in illegality. The concept of professionalism, however, clashes with that of normalization, through which some observers describe the increasing flexibility of criminal markets, the constructed nature of the notion of organized crime, and the involvement of diverse actors in a domain where professional criminals once prevailed (Hobbs, 2013). Other authors prefer to concentrate on the collective clientele of organized crime. The latter is therefore identified with a structure involved in the public provision of goods and services which are officially deemed illegal. Organized crime groups, in this view, simply fill the inadequacy of institutional agencies, which are unable to provide those goods and services, or perhaps officially deny that demand exists for them. The contribution of McIntosh (1975) is to be located in this perspective. She notes that organized crime is informed by a particular relationship between offenders and victims. For example, even the victims of extortion rackets often fail to report the offenders, less because they are terrified than 'because they see the extortionist as having more power in their parish than the agents of the state' (ibid.: 50). It may be added that the victims may also recognize their 'protector' as an authority more able than its official counterpart to distribute resources and opportunities. Among the goods provided, trust and protection are singled out as paramount. These, which should be supplied by the state, may under certain circumstances become the preserve of private entrepreneurs, namely organized crime. Therefore, this type of crime is purported to be an industry for the supply of private protection and the distribution of trust to economic actors who would otherwise be unable to interact safely (Gambetta, 1992). In the case of the mafia, for example, its strength as an industry for the supply of protection and trust is deemed a consequence of traditional popular distrust of the official agencies, and of foreign domination before them. This line of analysis is partly endorsed by Varese (2010), who proposes to consider the organized crime phenomenon as part of the broader category of governance. His suggestion is that a crucial distinction should be drawn between producers of goods and services, and suppliers of forms of regulation, protection and governance. The form of governance alluded to here is one that usurps the functions of the state in societies where sovereign rule is inadequate, a form of governance from below which extends power beyond the state and into the realms of civil society (Edwards and Levi, 2008; Ruggiero, 2012; Sergi, 2017).

Moving on to violent conflict, this has been an object of study in criminology since the very inception of the discipline. Before the word 'terrorism' gained common use, early criminologists dealt with both institutional and anti-institutional violence. Classical criminology, particularly the work of Cesare Beccaria (1965) and Jeremy Bentham (1967), regarded political violence as a breach of the social contract binding citizens and authority together. The focus of Beccaria, for instance, was on 'state savagery' and, at the same time, on 'crimes of sedition'. He linked institutional violence (torture, capital punishment, assassinations and other forms of state violence) with violent outbursts directed against the state. From a contemporary perspective, we can summarize his thought as follows: excessive state violence provokes violent responses by non-state agents.

Positivist criminologists studied regicides, romantic murderers and violent anarchists and looked at the social and psychological causes of political violence. While in general they thought that violent action against the system retained an 'evolutive' character, in the sense that it accelerated social change, when faced with specific forms of terrorist acts they judged those acts as emanating from monomaniac individuals who would be violent even if not inspired by political beliefs. Their distinction between rebellion and revolution was, in this respect, crucial. The former, in their view, was conduct caused by insanity, moral madness, narcissistic martyrdom or suicidal drive. The latter was an evolutionary process which, without necessarily resorting to violence, aimed at social change and improved social justice. It is noteworthy that this school of thought formulated a notion of 'suicide missions' well before these became common currency in the present times, as they described anarchists who assassinated aristocrats in the middle of the streets as individuals whose principal aim was an 'honourable death' or 'indirect suicide' (Lombroso, 1894).

Within the functionalist tradition, Durkheim's seminal study of suicide and homicide offers tools and arguments that can be extended to the analysis of political violence and terrorism. Durkheim associates the rise of homicide with the growth of those collective sentiments whose interest obsessively resides in the group, the family, or the state. The feelings that lie at the base of the cult of such entities may be in themselves conducive to murder. When the family, the group, the state, or for that matter a political idea or a religious belief, appear to be the supreme good, their importance transcends the sympathy and compassion due to the individual or people in general. Like some forms of suicide, terrorism and political violence in general may be the result of excessive integration in a creed, an identity, or of a strong form of binding to a set of moral values (Durkheim, 1996).

Looking at the contributions of the Chicago School of sociology in the first decades of the twentieth century, we find a penetrating analysis that echoes aspects of the contemporary debate. The study of migrants' communities and excluded groups brought to light the connections between organized crime and political violence. Criminal organizations, while conducting their illicit business, acted as the violent arm of political parties, using terroristic forms of intimidation, particularly during electoral campaigns (Landesco, 1969). Rival candidates were attacked or kidnapped, in a climate that turned political competition into violent interpersonal conflict. Subsequent criminological analysis focuses, rather, on collective conflicts, describing societies as composed of competing groups and contrasting value systems. Political violence, from a conflict theory perspective, is interpreted as the outcome of struggles for the attainment of material and ideological power.

Finally, symbolic interactionism can be useful for the causative explanation of terrorism. This school of thought examines the relational dynamics that produce harmony or conflict, in other words, how interacting individuals and groups determine their mutual conduct. In this view, state and non-state entities engage in acts of terror when both feel that they have no space left for peaceful interaction.

From enterprise to network

It is worth supplementing the overview presented so far with some additional observations.

Some organized crime groups do not limit their activities to conventional offending. Successful organized crime, for example, manages to establish partnerships with the official world, particularly with business enclaves and political representatives. When unable to do so, criminal groups remain pariah organizations operating in the underworld, and are destined to exhaust their resources and energies within the restricted realm of illicit markets. Organizations leaping onto the 'overworld', by contrast, are required to adopt a business style, a conduct, a strategy and a 'vocabulary of meaning' helping them to blend in the environment receiving them. They may still 'commute' between legality and illegality, but their new status will force them to identify allies, sponsors, mentors and protectors. In brief, they will be required to develop the negotiation skills characterizing an economic consortium or a political party.

It is at this point that organizations develop the features of networks, and this process may be followed by conventional criminal groups as well as by terrorist groups. The difference, however, is that organized crime networks imply the alliance between highly heterogeneous groups and individuals, each with a distinctive cultural and ethnic background, who may establish common goals on an occasional or long-term basis. Actors operating in conventional criminal networks are socially 'fuzzy', in the sense that their exploits and careers overlap with those of others who are apparently radically different from them. Such networks shape grey areas where licit, semi-licit and overtly illicit economies overlap (Ruggiero, 2017). Terrorist networks, by contrast, require a substantial degree of homogeneity among participants, who may 'offer' what they can, from donations to logistical support. Of course, participants may also offer 'action' and their own life, when they engage in missions inspired by the terrorist group with which they ideologically identify. However, while conventional criminal networks imply a form of *collective behaviour*, terrorist networks show signs of *collective identity*. The latter, inevitably, brings to the fore a concept of social movement, of contentious politics, an idea of social change inscribed in a specific teleology or imagined finalism. Later, when more directly addressing hybrids, this aspect will receive some of the attention it deserves.

It seems that only after the events of 9/11 has criminology resumed any specific interest in political violence, at least in its variant commonly termed terrorism (random violence against civilians) (Freilich and LaFree, 2015). For example, there are scholars who advocate the application of criminological theories of 'common' violence to the analysis of political violence, arguing that both types of violence are directed to the achievement of goals. Both aim at extracting something from someone; moreover, at least by perpetrators, both are presented as the outcome of provocation by the victims (Ruggiero,

2006). From a different perspective, the suggestion has been made that the principles of situational crime prevention should also be applied to terrorism. According to this view, after identifying and removing the opportunities that violent groups exploit to mount their attacks, situational measures implemented through partnerships among a wide range of public and private agencies will assist with this task. In other contributions the point is put forward that conventional crime is characterized by tensions and dynamics that also underpin many forms of terrorism. Issues of shame, esteem, loss, and repressed anger, alongside the pursuit of pride and self or collective respect, which provide important tools to criminological analysis, may also help establish a taxonomy of terrorism.

Looking at the formation of terrorist networks, the point has been made that the invasion of a country may be followed by organized violent resistance, and that invasions may destabilize regimes and trigger sectarian attacks (see Chapter 2). It is estimated, incidentally, that over 30 per cent of the founders of ISIS are former members of the secret services of Iraq, who enact a form of revenge, responding to the invasion of their country with indiscriminate attacks (Gerges, 2015; Lynch, 2015). This imitative dynamic echoes aspects of symbolic interactionism mentioned above. In a similar vein, scholars have focused on criminalization, labelling processes and phobias which enhance rather than decelerate the radicalization of those who find themselves on the receiving end (Mythen and Walklate, 2006; Ahmed, 2015; Abbas and Awan, 2015; Khan, 2016).

An enduring distinction, however, connotes the criminological field. Organized crime appears to be motivated by the accumulation of wealth:

> Though the evasion or neutering of state control and the corruption of officials may assist in the criminal enterprise, the generation of profit and the control of illicit markets is the primary focus of organized crime rather than any grasping of power for political ends.
>
> (Campbell, 2014: 230)

Terrorism, on the other hand, remains characterized as violence motivated by political, ideological, or philosophical considerations, aimed at civilians to 'generate fear and cause damage, and to coerce a government to act in a particular manner' (ibid.).

The following two sections gather, respectively, views positing a strong crime-terror nexus and views highlighting some tentative components of such nexus.

Hybrids and overarching etiologies

A notion of hybrid, combining conventional with political criminality, emerges in some etiologies focused on excluded and marginalized groups.

For example, the processes leading to involvement in organized crime groups or/and in terrorist networks, from some analytical perspectives, appear to be very similar. Such processes are said to stem from severe forms of inequality or from the resentment and humiliation suffered by the young components of minority groups. While older settlers chose where to live and partly maintained the culture of their country of origin, the young distanced themselves from that culture without acquiring a new one: 'the danger that ruins life in the poor districts is not Islam or multiculturalism… it is deculturation' (Todorov, 2014: 168). 'Deculturation' is one of the characteristics of failed democracies, which are based on a winner-take-all logic whereby the losers are left with no place to occupy. Becoming involved in crime or in political extremism, in this situation, amounts to 'pure and simple regression that offers a mixture of sacrificial and criminal heroism' (Badiou, 2016: 56). Failed democracies, while wreaking destruction, encourage revenge, which is formalized through the mythology of tradition or the cult of the swaggering outlaw.

Overarching etiologies based on relative deprivation, however, neglect the substantial differences between terrorism and organized crime. Organized crime groups may use violence as a supplementary tool of negotiating their presence on markets, or with the system. Violent political groups, on the contrary, use violence as a signal of their unwillingness to negotiate with a system they would rather demolish. Their action transcends the immediate result they achieve, and prefigures, realistically or not, a different set of achievements which will be valued in a future, rather than in the current society.

Another overarching theory revolves around the techniques of neutralization identified in criminology research, and may well describe the ideological process whereby organized crime groups as well as violent political groups come to terms with the effects of their acts. The denial of the victim is operated through the perception of the victim as wrongdoer, the condemnation of the condemners through their association with immorality, and finally the appeal to higher loyalties through the appropriation of the ideals and practices of one's subculture, one's political or religious creed. Techniques of neutralization, however, seem to belong to an ex post repertoire of motivations mobilized by offenders in order to fill the moral void they presumably experience. They are, in sum, a defensive device that may temper moral disorientation. In this sense, terrorism and conventional or organized crime display very similar characteristics, although such similarity may be insufficient to give rise to hybrids of the two.

Violent political groups, however, may pursue material gain as a means to reproduce and enhance their military apparatus and to acquire growing symbolic status, namely a capacity to step up their propaganda and hence their visibility. Along with offences aimed at the material reproduction of their organization, contemporary terrorists, who appear to ignore the ethical boundaries often respected by their counterparts of the 1970s and 1980s, are said to engage in crimes that their predecessors would find revolting: espionage, drug smuggling, gun running, money laundering, cell phone and credit card theft, immigration violations, extortion and prostitution (Hamm, 2007). Moreover, some contemporary perpetrators of terrorist acts are drawn from the offender population, although they do not consider themselves common criminals. Instead, they often see themselves as freedom fighters whose unlawful acts are motivated by a just cause and not by personal gain (Hoffman, 2006).

With the purpose of reproducing themselves, terrorist groups may acquire expertise in conventional criminality and through this pursue a form of 'empire-building' that transcends their original political goal. Violent political groups who cease their operations, moreover, may find at their disposal not only unlawful expertise and skills, but also arms and infrastructures and, after the dismissal of their organization, may use what they possess to start a career in criminal markets. Looking at 'terrorism as crime' from a particular angle, organized forms of criminality have been described as 'lifeblood of terrorist groups', and include all forms of acquisitive offences that mafia-type organizations would perpetrate (Hamm, 2007).

The growing dimension of transnational crime activities is regarded as a contributing factor to the blurring of the two phenomena, expressed through the development of alliances, the sharing of methods, and ultimately the merging of groups (Makarenko, 2004). Some authors see the evidence in the European Union of linkages between crime and terror as immense, 'although the scholarly literature has shied away from these associations' (Makarenko and Mesquita, 2014: 259). Specific elements characterizing the crime-terror nexus are detected when criminals and terrorists engage in similar activity, or 'relate symbiotically, as when they exchange drugs for weapons' (Grabosky and Stohl, 2010). The two appear to have developed networked organizational forms and technological skills that enhance their capacity and resilience. The interface between organized crime groups and terrorism, as suggested by Grabosky and Stohl, reflects the need of the latter to support themselves and their operations, but also the politicization of ordinary criminals who eventually join terrorist groups. The reverse process is also possible, with individuals turning from fighters into criminals after the continuing exchange between the two parties of information, knowledge and assets for mutual benefit. Involvement in cigarette smuggling and counterfeiting by terrorist groups has been revealed (Shelley and Melzer, 2011; Carrapico, Irrera and Tupman, 2014), while hybrids have been detected in the Islamic Maghreb, where crime groups and terrorists respond to specific material and political demands from local populations (Rosato, 2016). Terrorist groups are also attributed the power to control large enterprises, such as the gas fields in Eastern Algeria, close to the Libyan border. The case prompts the conclusion that the 'interaction of crime, corruption, and terrorism is having a tremendous impact on both security and the global economy' (Shelley, 2014: 1). Among the victims of such hybrids, or entangled criminal entities, the following are listed:

'economic growth, employment, security, development, and the sustainability of the planet' (ibid.: 4–5).

Analysts do emphasize that criminals are motivated by a broad spectrum of reasons, like personal enrichment, passion or revenge, while terrorists are led by what they believe is a higher cause (Foster, 2012). And yet, the separation of the two groups is sometimes deemed difficult. Of course, the presence of former criminals in terrorist groups is not unprecedented. But the phenomenon is now described as more pronounced and more visible. Research conducted by the ICSR (International Centre for the Study of Radicalisation and Political Violence) suggests that in many European countries, the majority of jihadist foreign fighters are former offenders. The findings of this study, however, do not confirm the merging of criminals and terrorists as organizations, but of their social networks and environments.

> Criminal and terrorist groups have come to recruit from the same pool of people, creating (often unintended) synergies and overlaps that have consequences for how individuals radicalize and operate. This is what we call the *new* crime-terror nexus.
>
> (ICSR, 2016: 3)

Whether new or old, the nexus is particularly emphasized by law enforcement agencies, which include within their remit the support of member states in preventing and combating all forms of serious international crime through the exchange of criminal intelligence. Perhaps the concern and focus on 'serious international crime', inevitably, leads agencies to adopt a joint approach to the two. The British National Crime Agency (NCA) follows the same route, providing a general definition that embraces a considerable range of groups and activities, some of which could be labelled organized crime groups while some others are labelled terrorist organizations. It is from the perspective of legal prosecution and law enforcement that the borders between terrorism and conventional and/or organized crime continue to be regarded as particularly blurred.

Other empirical studies do show that terrorist organizations may, when convenient, procure the services of criminal groups to further their political goals (Gallagher, 2016; Picarelli, 2006; Roth and Sever, 2006). In the recent past, among the hybrid organizations simultaneously pursuing material and political gain Colombian narco-terrorism appeared to be outstanding: 'The number of assassinations and bombings generated by the cartels was very substantial… [so that] a categorical exclusion of the criminal motivation from a definition of terrorism does not seem to be warranted' (Schmid, 2011: 66). Yet another case study of narco-terrorism in Colombia by Bibes (2001) indicates that, over the past 30 years, leftist guerrilla groups and right-wing paramilitaries have largely depended on drug cartels to help finance their political objectives. Bibes also describes instances where cartel leaders have in turn hired terrorist groups to carry out violent acts to achieve their own goals.

Similarly, Neumann and Salinas de Frías (2017) state that there have been crossovers and common interests between criminal and terrorist organizations for several decades: as early as the 1980s, namely during the rise of Pablo Escobar. A study of Mali's Al-Qaeda in the Islamic Maghreb (AQIM) proves that this terrorist organization, while principally aiming at disposing of the Mali government and establishing a Caliphate, does act in conjunction with narco-traffickers (Boeke, 2016). The Taliban have at times depended on Afghanistan's heroin production, while suggestions are also made that formerly politically motivated groups can develop conventional economically motivated organized crime syndicates (Hausken and Gupta, 2016). This development, however, is said to take place when terrorist organizations cease to be funded by benefactors and donors. Thus, following an end of hostilities with the state, members of the Colombian FARC and the provisional IRA, it is assumed, have turned into purely profit-seeking organizations, relying on their terrorist skills to accumulate wealth (Byrne, 2009).

Ultimately, the crime-terror nexus is found in the shared skills that terrorists and criminals may have developed in outmanoeuvring law enforcement and the techniques acquired in committing property offences.

> Jihadists not only condone the use of "ordinary" criminality to raise funds, they have argued that doing so is the ideologically correct way of waging jihad. Combined with large numbers of former criminals in their ranks, this will make financing attacks through crime not only possible and legitimate but, increasingly, their first choice.
> (ICSR, 2016: 4)

It is time to bring more controversial aspects of the debate to the fore.

The ambiguity of joint analyses

While the word 'terrorism' is not even mentioned in the detailed index of a recent important handbook on organized crime (Paoli, 2014), the phrase 'organized crime' recurs in many contemporary contributions on political violence and terrorism. This may be because both forms of crime are analysed against the variables offered by the sociology of organizations, which offers useful conceptualizations for the understanding of collective behaviour in delimited structures. Terrorism and organized crime, in this respect, may be similar because both deploy an organizational layout. An objection, in this respect, could be that any group of people acting in concert can be viewed as a social organization, therefore, it is not only organized crime and terrorism that lend themselves to a joint analysis, but also any couple of aggregations of individuals who perform collective action. As a way of overcoming this ambiguity, the following explanation referring to organized crime groups as opposed to terrorism has been offered: 'Their primary motivation is usually financial gain' (Holmes, 2016). However, if the focus is on illegal structures rather than illegal activities, the concern is how organizations relate to states.

Attempts to influence state officials are commonly made by organized criminals, who mainly pursue impunity for their offences and, when engaged in the official economy, seek contracts to carry out some form of state-funded public work (Abadinsky, 2013). The goal is, in such cases, of an economic rather than a political nature. 'Commonly, the lack of political goals is seen as a defining characteristic of organized crime that distinguishes it from ideologically and religiously motivated terrorist and insurgent groups' (von Lampe, 2016: 263).

The controversy around motivation accompanies the debate on hybrids, with some authors underlining the divine or political command obeyed by terrorists as opposed to greed commanding organized crime groups. In an attempt to identify differences and similarities, the suggestion has been made that the association of terrorism with organized crime mitigates the hideous and noxious operations of the former and that, comparatively, the latter is granted a higher moral status. Among the similarities, characteristics such as secrecy, ruthlessness, intimidation and the use of front organizations are mentioned. Among the differences, motivations, the nature of the relationship with governments and the media and the type of victimization are enumerated (Schmid, 1996, 2011).

Focusing on environments and milieus, rather than on the merging of organizations, it may appear that terrorism and organized crime recruit from similar pools of people, creating (often unintended) synergies and overlaps. However, the recruitment of street offenders will hardly make terrorist groups resemble organized crime: perhaps car thieves will become lone attackers, not men of honour of powerful mafias.

There is, in sum, disagreement around the nexus between organized crime and terrorism, its nature and scope, with some commentators arguing that such nexus amounts to nothing more than temporary marriages of convenience. While generalizable statements are unhelpful, distinctions are identified that might clarify the issue. The proliferation of hybrids, it is felt, may be likely in certain contexts more than in others, for instance in areas experiencing armed conflicts. On the other hand, lack of trust between the two types of membership may hamper collaboration, which entails added risk to groups inured to avoiding risk. For this reason, new types of organizations, distinct from both organized crime groups and terrorist groups, may be springing which service both criminals and terrorists with illicit services. These new groups may well be sponsored by legitimate states. In other words, the explanatory power of the crime-terror nexus is questioned, as it is considered to be based on insufficient evidence (Carrapico, Irrera and Tupman, 2014). Rather than focusing on the linkages between organized crime and terrorist groups, which are regarded as sporadic and short-lived, some propose to reorient attention on the links between criminal organizations and the state. 'A research agenda that prioritizes the local dynamics of interactions between criminal networks, militant ideologies, society and the state is likely to produce more nuanced analyses than an over-reliance on these binary approaches' (Lewis, 2014: 337). A further distinction pertains to sovereign-bound groups as opposed to sovereign-free groups, the former 'defined by their goal of establishing a new and separate state' (Picarelli, 2006: 13), and the latter 'concerned with profits and authority in illicit markets rather than sovereignty and authority over neighbourhoods and regions' (ibid.: 15).

There remains a feeling that the debate on hybrids belies an attempt to group under the same rubric all conducts most human beings would find repellent, hence the widespread attempts to carry out joint analyses of such conducts. See for example how all organized criminality is often attributed to terrorism, including human smuggling and trafficking. Terrorist groups are said to establish, with this transnational criminal activity, bonds of dependence with those they help relocate, who end up radicalizing (Neumann and Salinas de Frías, 2017). In fact, those smuggled or trafficked may end up hating more their traffickers than their employers, as proven by research that excludes participation of terror groups and other centralized organizations in such activities (Zhang, 2008; Sanchez, 2015; Campana and Varese, 2016; Campana, 2018).

In this respect Europol (2015), responding to hyperbolic depictions of the hybrid phenomenon, stresses that, at least in the EU, the nexus between organized crime and terrorism remains limited:

> In light of the available evidence, convergence between organized crime and terrorism in the EU seems a limited phenomenon. Terrorist and organized crime groups have learned to adapt to changing circumstances such as governmental interventions or changed environments. This makes their structure, activities and methods opportunistic in nature [...]. Based on the cases available in the Europol databases, it can be concluded that convergence often consists of isolated incidents.
>
> (Ibid.: 9)

Whether hybrids are rare or frequent, it is the heuristic value of joint analyses of organized crime and terrorism that could be questioned. Terrorism, like other forms of political violence, combines defensive and offensive strategies, a combination without which action could hardly be triggered. Such strategies may include ways of overcoming a presumed moral disorientation, but must provide, at the same time, strong, unequivocal guidance for individuals and groups to act. This combination of strategies coalesce in the form of collective identity, which transcends pure role or group identity, in that it refers to shared self-definitions and common efforts towards the production of social change. Collective identity offers orientation in a moral space and gives rise to a sense of self-esteem and self-efficacy; it also prompts what is worth doing and what is not in organizational terms, leading individuals to appreciate their capacity to change the surrounding environment. The cause pursued may not be 'higher', but it is certainly 'different'.

Political violence, therefore, is one of the outcomes of organized identity, and entails high degrees of subjectivity, so that some features of social life are no longer seen as part of misfortune, but of injustice. Along with techniques of neutralization, political violence needs to elaborate an interpretive 'frame alignment' with the activists it intends to mobilize. The potential recruits possess a coherent body of knowledge about past experiences that can be utilized for the interpretation of the present. This constitutes a schema or 'frame' with which terrorist groups must align in order to attract sympathizers and adherents (Snow et al., 1986; Ruggiero, 2010). Moreover, violent political groups draw on their specific repertoires of action accumulated through long periods of conflict. Such repertoires consist of a legacy, made of cultural and political resources: they contain sets of action and identity derived from shared understandings and meanings, they are cultural creations that take shape in social and political conflict.

Every expression of political violence seeks to represent a contentious political issue, and to speak not only to the authorities but to social movements from which it claims to emanate. It is this purported (and at times real) link with social discontent and 'anger' that makes terrorism a distinct violent manifestation. It is also its righteousness, be that religious or secular, that makes it different from other expressions of criminality. Terrorists fight for what they think will be a future system, their justification is 'transcendental' and 'historical', in the sense that only history, in their view, will judge on the morality of their action. Terrorist violence is, in the view of those using it, a foundational force, that is expected to create a new system and designate a new authority. It is norm-oriented, in that it is meant to create new norms in the name of generalized beliefs.

This has significant implications for prevention and institutional responses. Successful organized crime groups are normally emboldened by alliances with complicit or complacent establishment actors, while violent political groups normally rely on the supposed ideological advocacy of anti-establishment groups. When such groups distance themselves from those who, through the exercise of terror, claim to represent them, the perpetrators of terror start losing their imagined justification and find themselves fighting a private war, one that only exists in their head. Terrorist groups of the past have declined when social movements have radically severed the symbolic and material links on which such groups believed they could rely. Anti-establishment non-violent forces expressing contentious political views were (and still are) more effective in fighting terrorism than action emanating from the establishment. By contrast, the weakening of organized crime may occur when efforts are made to sever the links between crime groups and the actors of the establishment who are associated with them, whether due to subjective choice or by virtue of objective shared interests. Organized crime, in other words, may decline when the elite (politicians and business people) will distance themselves from it. In brief, prevention of terrorism has a possibility of success when it originates from the relatively 'lower' strata of society, while prevention of organized crime may temper the phenomenon when the higher strata of the institutions are targeted. The difference is notable, and joint analyses of the two may hamper and meddle with the identification of potentially effective policies.

Conclusion

We have to 'collar' the crime, not the criminal, suggested a crucial analytical strategy referred to white-collar crime, meaning that some offences may be committed by individuals of high rank and reputation, conventional criminals bereft of any reputation at all, and consortia formed by both. In this chapter the suggestion has been made that, when dealing with terrorism and crime, we have to 'collar' the criminal instead. We have seen how criminological thought, while defining organized crime and political violence as two separate entities, offers some examples of hybrids incorporating the two. It does so, particularly, through etiologies that attribute to both types of criminality similar causations. The crime-terror nexus has emerged at times as strong and undeniable and at other times as tentative and ambiguous, depending on the work examined. The ambiguity of such nexus has been ascribed to the nature of political violence, its relationship with contentious politics, and its views of the law and the state. Lack of consensus still persists in this area, with the unfortunate consequence that prevention and enforcement strategies may prove contradictory and fallacious.

References

Abadinsky, H. (2013), *Organized Crime*, New York: Praeger.
Abbas, T. and Awan, I. (2015), 'Limits of UK Counterterrorism Policy and Its Implications for Islamophobia and Far Right Extremism', *International Journal for Crime, Justice and Social Democracy*, 4: 16–29.
Ahmed, S. (2015), 'The Emotionalization of the War on Terror: Counterterrorism, Fear, Risk, Insecurity and Helplessness', *Criminology and Criminal Justice*, 15: 545–560.
Badiou, A. (2016), *Our Wound is Not so Recent*, Cambridge: Polity.
Beccaria, C. (1965 [1765]), *Dei delitti e delle pene*, Turin: Utet.
Bentham, J. (1967 [1776]), *A Fragment of Government. With an Introduction to the Principles of Morals and Legislation*, Oxford: Basil Blackwell.
Bibes, P. (2001), 'Transnational Organized Crime and Terrorism in Colombia', *Journal of Contemporary Criminal Justice*, 17: 243–258.
Boeke, S. (2016), 'Al Qaeda in the Islamic Maghreb: Terrorism, Insurgency, or Organized Crime?', *Small Wars and Insurgencies*, 27: 914–936.
Byrne, E. (2009), 'Nexus of Terror', *Intersec*, 19: 10–12.
Campana, P. (2018), 'Out of Africa: The Organization of Migrant Smuggling across the Mediterranean', *European Journal of Criminology*, 15: 481–502.
Campana, P. and Varese, F. (2016), 'Exploitation in Human Trafficking and Smuggling', *European Journal of Criminal Policy and Research*, 22: 89–105.
Campbell, L. (2014), 'Organized Crime and National Security: A Dubious Connection?', *New Criminal Law Review*, 17: 220–251.

Carrapico, H., Irrera, D., Tupman, B. (2014), 'Transnational Organized Crime and Terrorism: Different Peas, Same Pod?', *Global Crime*, 15: 213–218.
Cohen, A. (1977), 'The Concept of Criminal Organization', *British Journal of Criminology*, 17: 97–111.
Durkheim, E. (1996), *Professional Ethics and Civic Morals*, London: Routledge.
Edwards, A. and Levi, M. (2008), 'Researching the Organization of Serious Crime', *Criminology and Criminal Justice*, 8: 363–388.
Europol (2015), www.europol.europa.eu/content/page/europol%E2%80%99s-priorities -145 (accessed 12 October 2016).
Ferracuti, F. (ed.) (1988), *Forme di organizzazioni criminali e terrorismo*, Milan: Giuffré.
Foster, J.F. (2012), 'Criminals and Terrorists: An Introduction to the Special Issue', *Terrorism and Political Violence*, 24: 171–179.
Freilich, J.D. and LaFree, G. (2015), 'Criminological Theory and Terrorism', *Terrorism and Political Violence*, 27: 1–8.
Gallagher, M. (2016), 'Criminalized Islamic State Veterans. A Future Major Threat in Organized Crime Development?', *Perspectives on Terrorism*, 10: 51–57.
Gambetta, D. (1992), *La mafia siciliana. Un'industria della protezione privata*, Turin: Einaudi.
Gerges, F.A. (2015), *ISIS. A History*, Princeton: Princeton University Press.
Grabosky, P. and Stohl, M. (2010), *Crime and Terrorism*, London: Sage.
Hamm, M.S. (2007), *Terrorism as Crime*, New York: New York University Press.
Hausken, K. and Gupta, D.K. (2016), 'Determining the Ideological Orientation of Terrorist Organizations', *International Journal of Public Policy*, 12: 71–97.
Hobbs, D. (2013), *Lush Life: Constructing Organized Crime in the UK*, Oxford: Oxford University Press.
Hoffman, B. (2006), *Inside Terrorism*, New York: Columbia University Press.
Holmes, L. (2016), *Advanced Introduction to Organised Crime*, Cheltenham: Edward Elgar.
ICSR (2016), *Criminal Pasts, Terrorist Futures*, London: ICSR.
Johnson, E. (1962), 'Organized Crime: Challenge to the American Legal System', *Criminal Law, Criminology and Police Science*, 53: 1–29.
Khan, S. (2016), *The Battle for British Islam. Reclaiming Muslim Identity from Extremism*, London: Saqi.
Landesco, J. (1969), *Organized Crime in Chicago*, Chicago: University of Chicago Press.
Lewis, D. (2014), 'Crime, Terror and the State in Central Asia', *Global Crime*, 15, 337–356.
Lombroso, C. (1894), *Gli Anarchici*, Turin: Bocca.
Lombroso, C. and Laschi, R. (1890), *Il delitto politico e le rivoluzioni*, Turin: Bocca.
Lynch, M. (2015), *The New Arab Wars: Uprising and Anarchy in the Middle East*, New York: Public Affairs.
Makarenko, T. (2004), 'The Crime-terror Continuum', *Global Crime*, 6: 129–145.
Makarenko, T. and Mesquita, M. (2014), 'Categorising the Crime-terror Nexus in the European Union', *Global Crime*, 15: 259–274.
McIntosh, M. (1975), *The Organisation of Crime*, London: Macmillan.
Moore, M. (1987), 'Organized Crime as Business Enterprise', in Edelhertz, H. (ed.), *Major Issues in Organized Crime Control*, Washington: Government Printing Office.
Mythen, G. and Walklate, S. (2006), 'Criminology and Terrorism: Which Thesis? Risk Society or Governmentality?', *British Journal of Criminology*, 46: 379–398.

Neumann, P. and Salinas De Frías, A. (2017), *Report on the Links between Terrorism and Transnational Organised Crime*, Strasbourg: Council of Europe.

Paoli, L. (ed.) (2014), *The Oxford Handbook of Organized Crime*, Oxford: Oxford University Press.

Picarelli, J.T. (2006), 'The Turbulent Nexus of Transnational Crime', *Global Crime*, 7: 1–14.

Rosato, V. (2016), '"Hybrid Orders" between Terrorism and Organized Crime', *African Security*, 9: 110–135.

Roth, M.P. and Sever, M. (2006), 'The Kurdish Workers Party (PKK) as Criminal Syndicate', *Studies in Conflict and Terrorism*, 30: 901–920.

Ruggiero, V. (2006), *Understanding Political Violence*, Maidenhead: Open University Press.

Ruggiero, V. (2010), 'Armed Struggle in Italy', *British Journal of Criminology*, 50: 708–724.

Ruggiero, V. (2012), 'Organizing Crime', in Gounev, P. and Ruggiero, V. (eds) *Corruption and Organized Crime in Europe*, London and New York: Routledge.

Ruggiero, V. (2017), *Dirty Money. On Financial Delinquency*, Oxford: Oxford University Press.

Sanchez, G. (2015), *Human Smuggling and Border Crossing*, London and New York: Routledge.

Schmid, A.P. (1996), 'The Links Between Transnational Organized Crime and Terrorist Crimes', *Transnational Organized Crime*, 2, 40–82.

Schmid, A.P. (ed.) (2011), *The Routledge Handbook of Terrorism Research*, London and New York: Routledge.

Sergi, A. (2017), *From Mafia to Organized Crime*, London: Palgrave Macmillan.

Shelley, L.I. (2014), *Dirty Entanglements. Corruption, Crime, and Terrorism*, Cambridge: Cambridge University Press.

Shelley, L.I. and Melzer, S.A. (2011), 'The Nexus of Organized Crime and Terrorism: Two Case Studies in Cigarette Smuggling', *Journal of Comparative and Applied Criminal Justice*, 32: 43–63.

Snow, A.D., Burke Jr, E., Worden, S.K. and Benford, R.D. (1986), 'Frame Alignment', *American Sociological Review*, 51: 464–481.

Todorov, T. (2014), *The Inner Enemies of Democracy*, Cambridge: Polity.

Varese, F. (ed.) (2010), *Organized Crime: Critical Concepts in Criminology*, London: Routledge.

von Lampe, K. (2016), *Organized Crime*, Thousand Oaks: Sage.

Zhang, S. (2008), *Chinese Human Smuggling Organizations*, Stanford: Stanford University Press.

4 The online crime-terror nexus

Using booter services (stressers) to weaponize data?[1]

Roberto Musotto and David S. Wall

Introduction

For some years now, the cybersecurity community has speculated about the formation of dark networks with criminal and terroristic intents. Those criminal groups facilitate crime and fear online (Wu and Knoke, 2017) while also organizing and protecting the criminals involved through their powerful connections. The actions of these groups are qualitatively different to groups of online criminals who simply commit crimes, a subtle, but important difference. While the speculation of their existence has been great, the evidence and indeed logic for such groups is less forthcoming and this chapter seeks to address this knowledge imbalance. While we are finding that most current online criminal organizations are very ephemeral in nature and are not sustainable in the longer term (see Musotto and Wall, 2017), we anticipate that recent adaptive changes in the cyber-threat landscape are creating high impact cybercrimes such as Data Breaches, Ransomware, DDoS (Distributed Denial of Services) and crimes of extortion and political revenge. Cybercrimes which increasingly weaponize data, but also are high yield and create a logic for the creation of a more sustainable (mafia or IS) type model of crime groups (see our definition of sustainable crime groups in Chapter 4 of this collection). Such groups specifically seek to protect criminals and terrorists under its umbrella, invest their crime proceeds in the legitimate economy or in spectacular fearful attacks to increase their wealth, power and influence and ultimately their resilience and sustainability. As stated earlier, we believe that there is currently little evidence of such phenomena online but argue that their emergence is only a matter of time. This chapter explores some known models of cybercrime that could be used by terror groups to attack infrastructure. It explores a specific case study, to illustrate the differences and challenges: booter services (or stressers as they are commonly known) which can be used to deliver DDoS attacks for multiple purposes but also infrastructure attacks. The chapter then identifies the main legal challenges that online crime-terror groups pose before exploring some socio-legal solutions. The first part of this chapter reviews the existing literature and analyses the legal and technical aspects of stressers as they will be referred to. The second part focuses on the StressSquadZ service and forum as case study. The third part discusses the findings and concludes.

The crime-terror nexus

The crime-terror nexus is considered to be an emerging global threat (Shein, 2018). But, despite varying definitions in the literature (Makarenko, 2001, 2003, 2004; Shelley and Picarelli 2002, 2005; Naylor, 2002) there is a general lack of agreement about what the nexus really is (see Chapter 3). Shelley and Picarelli (2002 and 2005), for example, refer to the crime-terror nexus as a series of pathways that lead towards the cooperation of the two groups. Naylor (2002), on the other hand, describes it as a malicious technique employed by governments to repress multiple political and economic rights (p. 10), while for Makarenko (2002) it is a term covering multiple kinds of operational contacts between illicit organizations. The crime-terror nexus, therefore, relates primarily to the common traits that organized crime and terror groups might share. So, notwithstanding the disagreements over definitions, the nexus either refers to some features of terror organizations adapted by organized crime for their own use, or to terrorist organizations deploying activities typical of organized crime. This 'convergence' is described as 'the endorsement' of activities that are specific to one criminal or terrorist group (Makarenko, 2012). Alternatively, the nexus is regarded as a *hybrid* which co-exists within the same groups, what Dishman (2001: 58) refers to as groups that are 'political by day' and 'criminal by night'. Moreover, the nexus can refer to forms of collaboration between groups with different aims (Makarenko, 2012). Pure hybrids may be rare, as suggested by Europol (2015: 9), which limits their presence 'to isolated incidents'. Such 'rare' cases, however, display a key characteristic, namely collaboration through alliances and other kinds of agreements between groups. Figure 4.1 visualizes these connections, where money or business opportunities appear to be the gel binding crime and terror groups. Connections seem to be looser once the structure of these groups is analysed.

It is possible to define the structures of organized crime and terror networks by looking at a series of models that can be applied to both. Looking at organized crime, Albanese (2011), for example, suggests differentiating between the Hierarchical Model, the Ethnic-Cultural Model and the Entrepreneurial Model. *The Hierarchical Model* is found in traditional 'Mafia' organized crime structures and the more traditional terrorist groups, such as the IRA. The groups are organized according to a top-down leadership with one person (or controlling group) on top of pyramidal structure and many soldiers at the lower levels, with a number of levels of authority in between the levels. *The Ethnic/Cultural Model* shares a common heritage that engages in both low-level and high-level crime to the benefit of the entire group. Ethnic, Cultural or Religion ties bind the group together and individuals mostly control their own activities to achieve a common goal which may be criminal or terror oriented. *The Enterprise Model* differs from the hierarchical and ethnic/cultural models, mainly because the organized crime groups and terrorist networks operate more like legitimate business enterprises but focus upon illicit instead of legitimate markets (Cornell, 2006). These groups are rarely organized in a centrally structured way, rather, they operate along the same principles that govern legal markets, although they maintain and extend their share in illicit markets, thus responding to a variety of needs and demand on the part of their consumers. The aims of the groups falling within the organized crime enterprise model are mainly profit driven, and yet, profit can be used to fund terror campaigns. According to part of the literature (Hutchinson and O'Malley, 2007; Makarenko, 2004), cooperation between different groups is possible, but criminal organizations will never be able to identify themselves fully with terror groups, because of the different purposes that drive them. This three-way differentiation is useful for delineating specific group orientations, even if in practice a combination of each of the models is possible. See, for example, Figure 4.1 which reworks Makarenko's table (2012) of known crime-terror alliances to show how a crime-terror nexus can be connected. It illustrates how connected cartels combine hierarchical, ethnic/cultural and enterprise models of organized crime and terror groups.

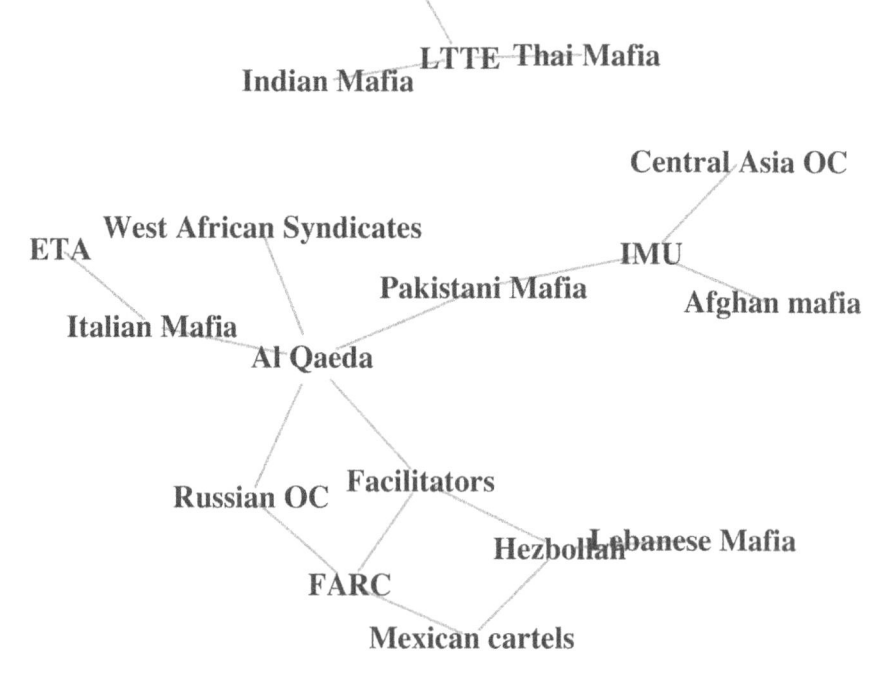

Figure 4.1 The crime-terror nexus connections.

Source: Reworked Makarenko's (2012) table of known Crime-Terror alliances.

What is still missing from this discussion is consideration of how online and offline organized crime and terror networks achieve their goals, particularly the various ways in which they express power to achieve them. Lukes (1974, 2005) conceptualizes power at three different levels of discussion which can be usefully applied to this discussion.

The first dimension of power is coercive, based on threat as a means for the achievement of goals. This is expressed through the use or threat to use private, military-like force. But, in practice, actual violence can frustrate the ultimate goal of the organization by, for example, bringing unwanted attention at particularly sensitive points in an operation. Organized crime groups and many terror groups usually want to frighten the public into compliance, so they will express power in subtler ways because, despite public and media expectations, direct violence attracts adverse police attention and disrupts illegal operations of all types. In this context, cyber-attacks are potentially a more powerful political tool. Once the attack is carried out, and the attackers get high media coverage, a climate of insecurity spreads among institutions and the general public and pushes for political and policy responses. Online, the WannaCry ransomware cyber-attack to NHS in 2017 (Corera, 2017; Boiten and Wall, 2017) is a good example of this type of expression of power. Whether the impact was intended or not, it instantly created fear and disruption. According to the UK Department of Health and Social Care (DHSC), the WannaCry attack created over £92 million in damages and it pushed DHSC to spend £60 million in 2017–2018 in cyber-resilience infrastructure, with an additional £150 million investment planned for the following three years (Field, 2018). The Not-Petya ransomware attack that followed later in the year is reputed to be possibly 'the most devastating cyberattack in history' (see Greenberg, 2018). Ransomware encrypts computer data until a ransom is paid for a code to release the data. Usually it strikes at random, though it is becoming more targeted, making it very profitable for criminals (Wall, 2018). Ransomware fits into the crime-terror nexus debate because companies pay the ransom (extortion) money without actually knowing to whom they are paying.

Lukes' second dimension of power is expressed through corruption and manipulation. Through corruption, members of criminal organizations may be protected from investigation or prosecution, while through manipulation they can interfere with electoral systems, for example by reducing or increasing the options of voters (Nichols, 2018).

Lukes' third dimension of power consists in the subtler manipulation of ideas, aimed at changing the structure of thought, empowering certain ideologies and making them acceptable. This manipulation results in the blurring of the boundaries between legitimate and illegitimate conduct. In the case of terror networks, political or religious ideologies can shape views as to which ends are desirable and which are not. For an example of how online operations can attempt to change views and values, see the role of social media in the 'fake news' phenomenon (BBC, 2018). Similar operations, when conducted by terror organizations, may lead to overestimating their actual power and, ultimately, may even determine the types of institutional responses adopted.

The crime-terror nexus online: principles and evidences

Once the discussion on the (offline) crime-terror nexus is transposed to on an online context, it is possible to focus on the use of cyber-assisted, cyber-enabled and cyber-dependent information technologies (Wall, 2013). Such technologies operate at multiple levels, in communicative as well as organizational term (Shelley and Picarelli, 2002). They are used to spread terror and to contact foreign/transnational organizations, but also to launch attacks against systems that will have real-time effects. Ransomware has been mentioned (see WannaCry) as a form of attack, but Distributed Denial of Service (DDoS) tools have been increasingly used to attack systems with great effect and explored in this chapter in greater detail. Before showing examples of crime-terror attacks where a nexus can be found, a definition and rationale of DDoS follows here.

DDoS attacks paralyse computer networks by flooding them with data coming from various sources and blocking their access systems, thus disrupting their operations. Data mobilization (or weaponization) slows or makes online services unavailable, or even makes the system vulnerable to further attack, theft of data, or ransom. The impact of such attacks is economic, consisting of loss of time and resources, but also loss of reputation. DDoS can also create fear when they disable infrastructure. Even resilience measures which try to decrease potential disruption by installing larger servers to support heavier traffic or creating honeypot traps (which slow down and identify malwares entering a system network) are being challenged by a growth in the number of such attacks (Krupp, Backes and Rossow, 2016). Morales (2018) illustrated this growth and found that, in 2007, the peak DDoS attack sizes were 24 gigabytes. A decade later, in the first quarter of 2018, the peak attack sizes had grown to 1.7 terabytes, almost 1,000-fold increase (Morales, 2018). As the DDoS expands, new facilitating actors (brokers) are emerging who supply tools, in exchange for a few dollars, pounds or bitcoins, for everyone to become a cyber-criminal. Stressers are DDoS-for-hire services (a variant of crimeware-as-a-service) which are deployed by cyber actors, pranksters, and hacktivists to prevent the access of specific web sites.

As suggested above, DDoS attacks are an exercise of Lukes' first dimension of power. They are one of the most rapidly proliferating cybercrimes as they achieve a range of outcomes for offenders, although offender motivations and victims vary considerably. This raises the interesting question as to whether DDoS attacks epitomise new forms of the online crime-terror nexus or whether they mark the development of totally new criminal groups. At the hard end of the DDoS attack spectrum, for example, some attacks are clearly designed to inflict maximum damage upon victim organizations, as in the case of cyberwarfare, and attackers are motivated by the economic or political opportunities arising from that damage or disruption. Ponemon, for example, found that the maximum cost of an outage caused by DDoS more than doubled from $1 million in 2010 to more than $2.4 million in 2016 (Kassner, 2016). But, at the softer end of the same spectrum, in contrast, other DDoS attacks are designed to irritate or to test system security, with offenders clearly more interested in trying to impress friends (or businesses) with their expertise than to cause serious damage. These typologies will be explored in greater detail in future publications, but in this chapter, we look to a main enabler of DDoS attacks, the stresser service. Stressers are semi-legal IT services, which, for a fee, enable their clients to mobilize DDoS attacks to conduct legitimate penetration tests of computer systems (with consent) to improve their security, but in so doing, can facilitate more malicious attacks. This raises several important questions, for example, are they legally justifiable or are they just a hidden form of crime-ware-as-a-service that might cause extremely fearful consequences? Moreover, to what extent does their organizational form illustrate that they are new online crime-terror groups? The answers to these questions will provide new insights and inform existing debates on the topic.

Some examples of online crime-terror organizations are already available. One of the very first politically motivated cyberattacks targeted Estonia in 2007 (Traynor, 2007). With the interruption of internet communication and websites down, the spread of fake news undermining the Russian ethnic minority sparked frightful riots. In December 2016, a DDoS tool, called the 'Caliphate Cannon', was released in a deep web forum linked with ISIS and institutional websites linked to the governments of Egypt, Iraq, Jordan and Yemen were targeted (Wolf, 2017). Despite the evocative name, there was nothing terrifying about the 'Cannon', because it was quite weak due to the network structure supporting it.[2] Similar to the Estonia case, the 2017 DDoS attack on the Ukrainian postal service's (Ukrposhta) website (BBC, 2017), shortly after a ransomware attack on the main strategic websites by Russian criminals, provided examples of how these techniques can be helpful to achieve political goals. It is still hard, however, to identify who was actually responsible for these attacks: whether they were coordinated acts by criminal and terrorist groups, or, whether they were attempts to pursue both criminal and terrorist aims, which makes the existence of the crime-terror nexus hard to prove in these cases. While such events are often framed within the dystopic tropes of terror, actual evidence of the creation of terror is not apparent, so analysts must be careful when labelling events as terror events. Not least, because it can also influence outcomes.

The make-up and operation of a booter service that can be used to launch DDoS attacks

In the remainder of this chapter we analyse stressers because they negotiate a peculiar position in a very grey area, as both legitimate and illegitimate online service tools. Using network analysis to analyse a data set taken from a now defunct stresser, we observe how they share some characteristics with offline criminal and terror organizations, but, equally, also some well-known legitimate online service providers. This will be shown by drawing from recent cases and investigations such as the Lizard Squad, Mirai malware, but mainly from the specific case study of a stresser provider called StressSquadZ (a pseudonym). Using the data gathered from the forum and the activity of its members in a period of six months, from its opening to its closure, we focused upon the service provided, the users and their transactions. We found that most DDoS attacks had very low impact in terms of damage, and they also generated relatively small revenues, but this was set against almost nonexistent risks in terms of being caught and a small transaction window. Some, of course had more serious consequences.

What are stressers?

Stressers are online services whose primary rationale is to test the service and traffic capacity of a network or website. Like many web-based services, they can be legally bought or exchanged for other goods and it is possible to find many companies offering a range of tools and services to suit their different clients' needs. The stresser and the stress testing it can be used for is considered legal by the providers so long as the site owner agrees with it and tests can be run legitimately and legally on its network. It appears, however, that the misuse of such tools is also tolerated and rarely prevented. In fact, in some cases the lack of prevention is tantamount to encouragement of abuse of service. In defence of stressers, it is important that companies and governmental websites keep their websites up under conditions of heavier traffic and this is where a stresser can assist in developing resilience so long as its use is consented by the site owner. The main usage is, however, usually more malicious, for example, in the case of John Kelsey Gammell, an electronic technician from New Mexico, who admitted to buying subscriptions for DDoS-for-hire services to launch attacks against businesses that had either fired or declined to hire him again. He also tried to recruit people with similar interests on social media to launch his own DDoS-for-hire service business (Claburn, 2018). Business organizations and Government agencies are usually the main targets of DDoS attacks, but the likes of gaming websites, for example, are also regularly affected as well by those seeking revenge for losses or financial gain by trying to interrupt the operating algorithms.

Many individuals, with an interest in IT, trial these attacks from a very young age, and most are young adults under the age of 20 (Hall, 2016; NCA,

2017). They pay for stressers to maliciously deploy software to launch DDoS attacks and they are often, seemingly, unaware of the broader consequences of their actions (Claburn, 2018). See, for example, the case of Adam Mudd who created a malware called Titanium Stresser when he was only 15 years old and sold it online, He also used it to launch attacks upon websites, gamers and colleges. He allegedly profited from the malware by almost $400,000, and the Titanium Stresser was one that the Lizard Squad developed further for its own ends (Corfield, 2017).

Once a stresser group forms, it is relatively easy for users to carry out successful attacks against bigger targets. This was the case of Lizard Squad, which attacked Sony PlayStation, Xbox Live, Tor Network and Blizzards Warcraft (Amir, 2018). The organization of this group was extremely ephemeral in terms of its composition and activities, making it more difficult for law enforcement agencies not only to track down individuals, but also to correctly prosecute them for their illicit actions. In fact, once such a group disappears following completion of a criminal activity, some of its surviving members will simply reform with others to create a new group, using their knowledge, and frustrating policing efforts. After multiple arrests of alleged members from online gangs, it appears that some continue to operate under a different name. For example, some of Lizard Squad appear to have reformed as BigBotPein, which released the Mirai malware and its variants in 2016 (Amir, 2018). This is the same botnet used in August 2017 to attack and blackmail Lloyds Banking Group and Barclay's banks, infecting 1.25 million Deutsche Telekom routers (Schwartz, 2017).

Most users of stressers seek to achieve criminal goals, so the providers and the clients are effectively online organized crime groups. Especially as DDoS attacks are usually performed without the website owner's knowledge; even if the use of the site (facility) is justified on the grounds that it can be used for legitimate stress testing (FBI, 2017). Stressers create a cost to society (as mentioned earlier) by preventing access to businesses and disrupting their operations, with the effect of damaging their reputation in the market place and reducing business and profit. They also create major challenges for law enforcement.

In most jurisdictions, laws exist to provide police and criminal justice systems with the powers to arrest, prosecute and imprison DDoS attackers, plus seize their computers and other electronic devices used as well as the proceeds of their crimes, which are also included within the investigative powers for cases of suspected terrorism or organized crime. The US Computer Fraud and Abuse Act (18 US Code 1030), for example and the UK Computer Misuse Act (1990 *c*.18) are legislative measures in two of many jurisdictions. But, the laws focus upon the DDoS attackers rather than those who actually facilitate the attacks – the brokers who operate the stressers. While DDoS attacks are hard to intercept quickly by law enforcers, it may, however, be possible to increase law enforcement powers to disrupt stressers when they are being used for criminal purposes and link/ conspiracy between the stresser and attacker can be shown. Alternatively, introducing regulations making providers sure that they know their customers (know your customer), or making sure that only approved payment systems are being used. Plus, also increasing the crime prevention mission by advising companies and governments to protect themselves by increasing their network bandwidth, multiplying their website providers, filtering out traffic, performing stress-tests, looking for spikes in traffic or avoiding using cryptocurrencies or PayPal when paying for a stresser. These measures could increase the security of targets but also potentially reduce the amount of damages and compensation paid by the company when the attack has not been prevented (Porter, 2017). Also underlying these measures is a need to understand the nature of the stresser as crimeware-as-a-service and to this end we analyse a case study.

The StressSquadZ case study

We acquired anonymized forum data and website details from a stresser that had been taken down by policing agencies and shared with us thanks to DutchSec intelligence. The StressSquadZ website we analysed appeared to have been registered in multiple locations around the world under the same owner name. We focused upon how the stresser group was organized and used a social network analysis approach to explore the various types of service provided and the users and their transactions. StressSquadZ offered their clients various levels of service at different prices that ranged from $0.01 (which could be a tester for the payment system) to $249.99. A total of 359 payments were recorded and were clustered according to the amount an individual paid. Each transaction was attached to a specific delivery plan, of which there were a total of 16. They started with trials and ended with premium services. The payments and subscription plans were found to be clustered around users and directed towards their chosen payment and subscription. Therefore, the users who picked the trial $1.99 plan (plan 1 in Table 4.1) were the majority – they paid 183 times. After the trial plans, the next

Table 4.1 Plan subscriptions

Plan	Subscribers
1	183
16	87
2	44
3	20
4	8
23	6
6	4
5	3
13	2
20	1
10	1

popular category were the monthly subscriptions, although some users moved through different plans, say, from first choosing a trial plan to taking out a subscription plan. Seventy-three users upgraded their subscription, from trial plans to monthly subscriptions or to yearly or lifetime affiliations.

The cheap trial plans did not allow users to perform full-power attacks and were limited in time. That is the reason why we see in the graph users that are tied to more plans. When they were checked with the timing of the payments, however, it is possible to notice an evolutionary pattern from the trial service to lifetime subscriptions, suggesting a pathway into higher cost and more impactful plans. We also found that specific users displayed different consumer behaviour patterns: one user, for example, bought five trial plans, possibly because they were enough for his or her needs rather than pay more for a more powerful service. In pure marketing terms, this technique attracts more people at a price set under or close to the actual cost of running the tool. At the same time, the trial plan encourages subscribers to switch and pay for a more expensive service. The majority of subscribers first bought a trial plan before buying a higher cost plan. Only 53 of the trial users did not upgrade to different plans. Please note that we are assuming that those who bought a trial plan either did not know how to use a stresser and tested it with the least economic effort possible or they knew already how to use stressers but did not know the service in question. Yet, some of them clearly knew already how to use the service and managed to get a satisfactory result before upgrading to a more powerful subscription.

Some clients, on the other hand, never upgraded because the service did not suit their needs, or they did not possess the skills to run an attack (e.g. script-kiddies or wannabes). Furthermore, there were also users who knew very well how to run stressers and needed a service that was strong enough to take down larger websites. These users paid the highest costs for the higher-grade services, and in some cases, received a bespoke service. This finding was obtained by comparing the quantitative data with the qualitative results extracted from the forum data. More experienced users sought to buy a tailored service with features that beginner users did not. Another observation was that not all the users in the discussion forum made purchases or subscribed to plans and there was a relatively low level of engagement. Only 285 users (out of 1451) were subscribers to trials or other plans. This finding is also noted in the wider crime forum literature (see, for example, Karami, Park and McCoy, 2016). We interpret this finding as the interest being generated about the service. Users join the club because they have heard about it in other forums or from other users and they are curious about its capabilities. They confirm these by reading forum threads, which in this case study were structured in a help-desk format (see Table 4.2, in which the most active members posted at least four threads).

Table 4.2 Plan subscriptions

Price of plan	# of purchasers	Profits generated
0.01	1	0.01
0.1	2	0.2
1.99	183	364.17
9.99	87	869.13
14.99	44	659.56
24.99	15	374.85
29.99	5	149.95
34.99	8	279.92
59.99	3	179.97
69.99	7	489.93
149.99	3	449.7
249.99	1	249.99
Total	359	4,067.28

Profits

When we explored how much profit this forum/stresser generated we found a figure of $4,067.28 per month at its peak. This is actually a low profit margin compared to that generated from other stresser groups, for example, the VSO stresser, which is reported to have made $24,737 profits per month and Lizard stresser around $6,000 per month (Karami, Park and McCoy, 2016). The income of StresserSquadZ may, however, have been small because of the relatively short period that the service operated. The following Figure 4.2 and Table 4.2 show the findings. In Figure 4.2, for example, it is possible to see that many users bought a plan at the launch of the service, but it slows down, then stops almost completely in November when only five members renewed their subscription with no new users joining. Could this have been because other stresser services were taking away the business? In December and January new subscription and renewals began again at a steady pace. It is also possible to see that, except for a few cases, renewals took place in a short time after the initial purchase (this is noticeable in Figure 4.2 by looking at the dots that are under the line).

Once we matched this finding with the price paid by users over time (see Figure 4.2), it was found that higher prices were paid straight away at the first purchase, suggesting that this group was composed of experienced users who already possessed a set of skills necessary to use the tools. Analysis of the prices paid indicate two groups, the amateurs and wannabees and the business offenders. The early birds and users who bought the service after November spent the most money, while between those two sets are few renewals and many trial subscriptions.

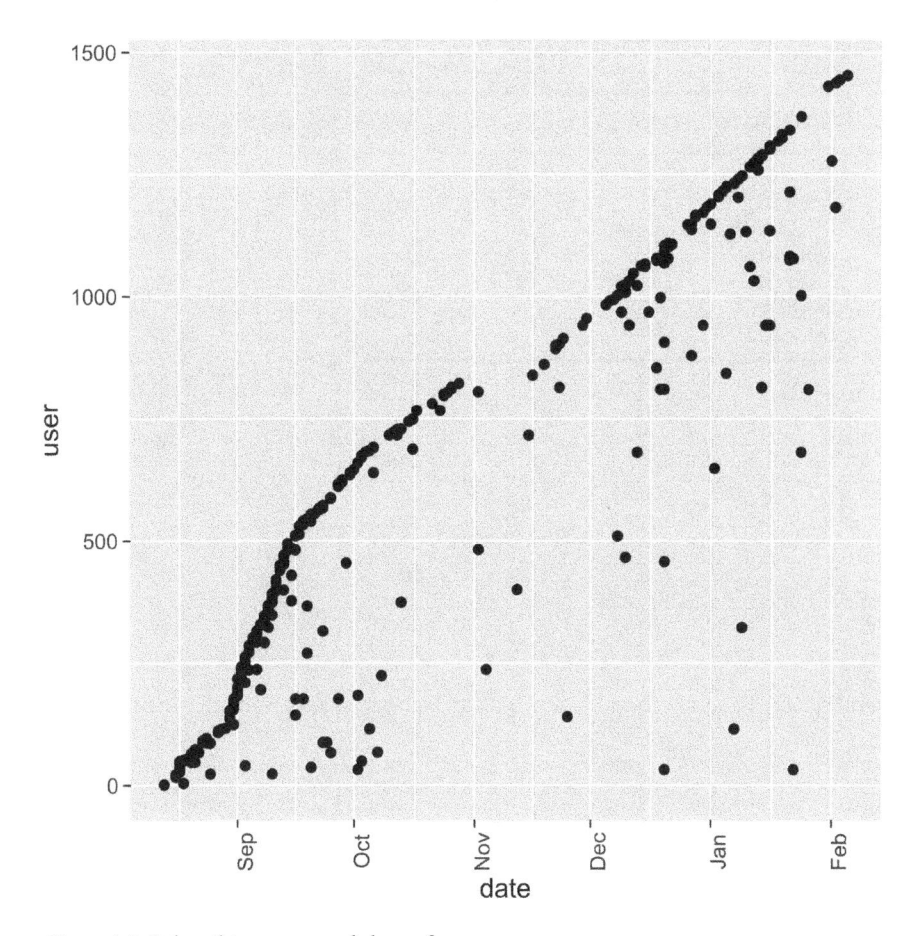

Figure 4.2 Subscribing users and date of payments.

Users activity

An analysis of member's activity and their payment patterns shows that not everyone who subscribed to StressSquadZ could have had an active interest in performing an attack. Alternatively, they may not have wanted to pay to carry one out, and may have simply been curious? In the forum thread, only 127 of the 1,451 (9 per cent) members actively carried out an attack. It appears that while there was only one owner of the forum and two members with administrative powers, another 16 members were very active in replying to forum threads and launching attacks, thus, playing a central role in delivering the stresser. Table 4.3 shows the list of the users who opened more threads in the forum. It was not possible to match the payment data of some users with their forum threads, but the forum data did provide some useful information on tracking down members who posted payment details on threads (not shown here).

Table 4.3 Most active users in the ticket forum

Users	Threads open
Noukie100	14
FantuxModz	13
xxx xxx1	7
danne2	6
a81238208	6
caonimade	5
Kubaa78	4
flipstick	4
DilenXD1	4

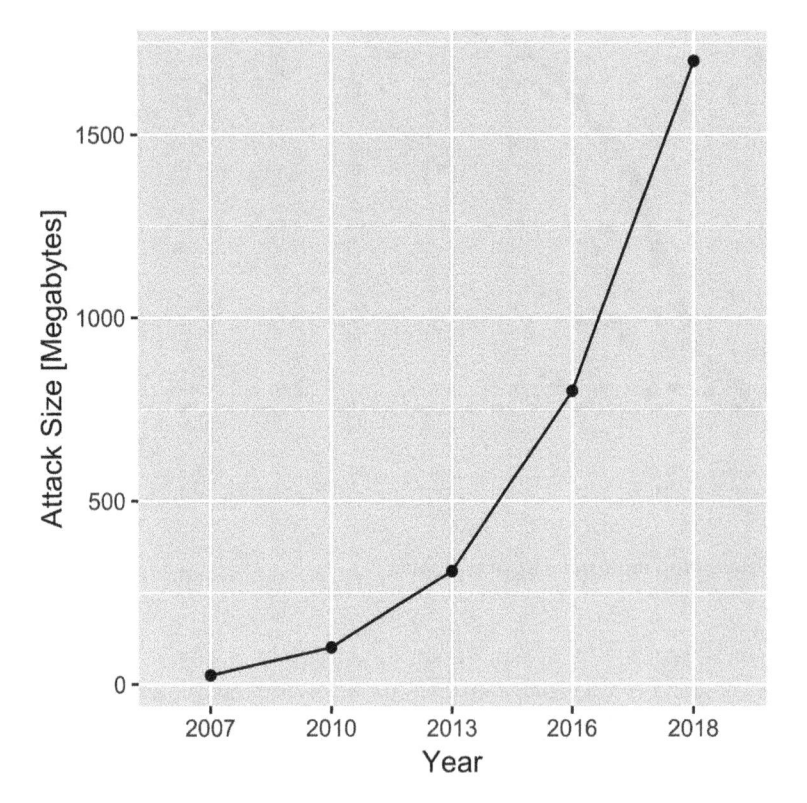

Figure 4.3 Size of DDoS attacks over years.

Discussion and conclusions

The main use of StressSquadZ, it turns out, was mainly without the consent of the website owner and since this constitutes a crime, then the companies or groups (because some are not formally registered as companies) providing stressers are effectively a new form of online organized crime grouping. One solution to reduce DDoS cyber-attacks, therefore, would be to close down the stresser website providers, however, the effectiveness of such an action is not as straightforward as often assumed. When Webstresser.org, the biggest Stresser provider, was shut down by authorities in April 2018 (Kunert, 2018), DDoS attacks reduced by 60 per cent (Cimpanu, 2018). This large reduction was, however, only temporary, because the void created by the takedown was quickly filled by new entrants in the market. Moreover, at the same time, the purpose of some of these attacks must also be considered to differentiate between those seeking to employ DDoS attacks for legitimate purposes such as stress testing, those using them for illegitimate purposes to extort money from victims or damage a system, and those intending to use them to create terror (in the form of fear, uncertainty and distress). In the least case scenario, members and customers of online services such as stressers satisfy their intellectual curiosity without ever consciously causing a broader effect. In the worst-case scenario they give malicious individuals a justification for their violence (and terror). This line of thought not only challenges the more simplistic assumptions about DDoS attacks but also the view that the crime-terror nexus is expanding and that the division between organized crime and terrorism is becoming increasingly blurred. Technology, in brief, relentlessly alters the features of crime and terror.

There were many similarities between the way the stresser was provided and how the online retailers of legal products and services work. Their service differentiation marketing strategy, for example, helped them expand the market and acquire new users and user groups. As observed earlier, they offered a trial period to quickly grab the market and get users acquainted with the service, while also providing higher levels of service for those with advanced skills and needs. This enabled this second group to look for a best buy and attracted users who are usually extremely inelastic in their behaviour, and from what we saw, tend to get more support from the ticket service.[3]

The differential marketing strategy separated the business offenders and sponsored hackers from the amateurs and wannabes, a fact that is represented by the different amounts of revenue attracted. While the amateurs (wannabees and script-kiddies) constituted half (51 per cent) of payments they only reflected a tenth (10 per cent) of the total sums received. The business offenders, on the other hand, constituted two-fifths (43 per cent) of payments, but provided about half of the total profits. The sponsored hackers constituted a much smaller percentage (6 per cent) of the market share, but two-fifths (41 per cent) of all profits, as shown in Table 4.2.

In the case of StressSquadZ, it was possible to see three distinct categories of users/clients. First, there were the amateurs and wannabes who were mainly users who bought the service out of curiosity to try it out, often after becoming interested after discussions in other chat forums. Sometimes they did not really know how to use the service properly, or wished to try it out of curiosity, or to commit small or unique attacks and then stop. These, we argue, were not seriously minded offenders and probably either regarded their use of the stresser as part of a hobby, or as a way of improving their computing skills (i.e. script-kiddies).

These *ingénue* (amateurs and wannabes) contrast with a second group who acted like more serious offenders. These commercial offenders, for want of a better description, knew exactly which kind of service they were after, perhaps because of previous experience and/or their advanced skills. Moreover, they understood how a stresser works and were clearly shopping around for the best value for money. Once they had tried a stresser out under the trial scheme and were happy with it, a number upgraded their plan to the VIP service. These are the groups of people that have the required skillset to carry out organized and terror attacks.

A third category of stresser users was the sponsored hacker. Like a sponsored athlete with sports goods or well-known racing drivers advertising powerful cars, they show to potential users what can be done with the service. They not only demonstrate its potential but also give the illusion of its power, effectiveness and efficiency. But, like the sports industry, the supply of high end products and services is limited, the cost is high and to use a specific product implies that the user needs specific characteristics or features which not everyone possesses. These are the individuals who also expose the stresser sites to broader audiences and markets, but in time, also law enforcement agencies.

To conclude, the findings of this research are not as dramatic as the tropes, rhetoric and cultural hype surrounding organized crime would suggest. Sure, StressSquadZ was a facilitator of DDoS attacks, which can have very serious consequences for victims, but it was only one of a number of different types of online crime groups. There was little evidence that StressSquadZ (or any other booter service) was ever used to deliberately produce the sort of shock terror that a kinetic explosion would. There was equally little evidence of them producing the fear backlash that ultimately shapes the political process. It could be said that this was a low level stresser and could not host such a large attack, but this is simply not the case because this stresser could launch as large an attack as the offender's resources would permit. This analysis indicates that organized cyber-criminals, like many other offending groups online, are adaptive and seek to balance the maximization of profits (proceeds of crime) with the minimization of operating risks (arrest and prosecution). There was no evidence of intent to develop the operations further, or of any involvement with any other organized crime or terror group with a view to expanding criminal activity.

Notes

1 This chapter is based upon research conducted for the TAKEDOWN Project (Horizon 2020, Grant 700688) and the ESRC Transnational Organised Crime (TNOC) research program. It also draws upon the work of the EPSRC CRITiCaL project (EP/M020576/1). The opinions, findings and conclusions expressed in this

chapter, however, are those of the authors' and do not necessarily reflect those of the funding body. This chapter is developed from a paper originally delivered as Musotto and Wall (2018).
2 The internet in Africa and Middle East has not the same internet speed than the internet in Europe, Russia or the USA. Attacks launched from areas with poorer connections result in more limited and less effective disruptions. This lack of speed also raises doubts about the abilities and strategies of attackers, the DDoS malware in this case could have been a 'rebranding' or reuse of an existing tool.
3 Ticket service is an issue tracking system, where a service desk organizes all the problems that arise with products into a specific workflow to get a solution in the most efficient way.

References

Amir, W. (2018), 'Lizard Squad is Alive and Continuing Activities as BigBotPein: Report', *HackRead*, 31 January, www.hackread.com/lizard-squad-is-alive-continuing-activities-as-bigbotpein/ (accessed 15 March 2018).

BBC (2017), 'Ukranian Postal Service Hit by 48-hour Cyber Attack', *BBC News Online*, 10 August, www.bbc.co.uk/news/technology-40886418 (accessed 15 March 2018).

BBC (2018), 'Fake News "Crowding Out" Real News, MPs Say', *BBC News Online*, 29 July, www.bbc.co.uk/news/technology-44995490

Boiten, E. and Wall, D. (2017), 'WannaCry Report Shows NHS Chiefs Knew of Security Danger, but Management Took no Action', *The Conversation*, 30 October, https://theconversation.com/wannacry-report-shows-nhs-chiefs-knew-of-security-danger-but-management-took-no-action-86501.

Cimpanu, C. (2018), 'Maersk Reinstalled 45,000 PCs and 4,000 Servers to Recover From NotPetya Attack', *Bleeping Computer*, 25. www.bleepingcomputer.com/news/security/maersk-reinstalled-45-000-pcs-and-4-000-servers-to-recover-from-notpetya-attack/ (accessed 20 August 2018).

Claburn, T. (2018), 'Sad-sack Anon Calling Himself "Mr Cunnilingus" Online is Busted for DDoSing Ex-bosses', *The Register*, 18 January, www.theregister.co.uk/2018/01/18/it_technician_ddos_former_employer/ (accessed 15 March 2018).

Corera, G. (2017), 'NHS Cyber-attack was "Launched from North-Korea"', BBC, 16 June, www.bbc.com/news/technology-40297493 (accessed 12 September 2018).

Corfield, G. (2017), 'Brit Behind Titanium Stresser DDoS Malware Sent to Chokey', *The Register*, 25 April, www.theregister.co.uk/2017/04/25/british_malware_author_2_years_jail_titanium_stresser/ (accessed 15 March 2018).

Cornell, S.E. (2006, February), 'The Narcotics Threat in Greater Central Asia: From Crime-terror Nexus to State Infiltration?', *China and Eurasia Forum Quarterly*, 4(1): 37–67.

Dishman, C. (2001), 'Terrorism, Crime, and Transformation', *Studies in Conflict and Terrorism*, 24(1): 43–58.

Europol (2015), 'Review 2015', www.europol.europa.eu/content/page/europol%E2%80%99s-priorities-145 (accessed 15 March 2018).

FBI (2017), 'Booter and Stresser Services Increase the Scale and Frequency of Distributed Denial of Service Attacks: Alert Number I-101717b-PSA', *FBI Public Service Announcement*, 17 October, www.ic3.gov/ media/2017/171017–2.aspx (accessed 15 March 2018).

Field, M. (2018), 'WannaCry Cyber Attack Cost the NHS £92m as 19,000 Appointments Cancelled', www.telegraph.co.uk/technology/2018/10/11/wannacry-cyber-attack-cost-nhs-92m-19000-appointments-cancelled/ (accessed 11 October 2018).

Greenberg, A. (2018), 'The Untold Story of NotPetya, the Most Devastating Cyberattack in History', *WIRED*, 22 August, www.wired.com/story/notpetya-cyberattack-ukraine-russia-code-crashed-the-world/

Hall, K. (2016), 'DDoS Script Kiddies are Also… Actual Kiddies, Europol Arrests Reveal', *The Register*, 12 December, www.theregister.co.uk/2016/12/12/europol_arrests_34_ddos_kiddies/ (accessed 15 March 2018).

Hutchinson, S. and O'Malley, P. (2007), 'A Crime–terror Nexus? Thinking on Some of the Links between Terrorism and Criminality', *Studies in Conflict Terrorism*, 30(12): 1095–1107.

Karami, Mohammad, Park, Youngsam and McCoy, Damon (2016), 'Stress Testing the Booters: Understanding and Undermining the Business of DDoS Services', in *Proceedings of the 25th International Conference on World Wide Web*. International World Wide Web Conferences Steering Committee, pp. 1033–1043, https://doi.org/10.1145/2872427.2883004

Kassner, M. (2016), 'The Rising Cost of DDoS', *Data Center Dynamics Magazine*, 22 April, www.datacenterdynamics.com/analysis/the-rising-cost-of-ddos/

Krupp, Johannes, Backes, M. and Rossow, C. (2016), 'Identifying the Scan and Attack Infrastructures behind Amplification DDoS Attacks', *Proceedings of the 2016 ACM SIGSAC Conference on Computer and Communications Security*. ACM: 1426–1437, https://doi.org/10.1145/2976749.2978293

Kunert, P. (2018), 'Webstresser.org Taken Down by Europol Plod and Chums', 25 April, www.theregister.co.uk/2018/04/25/worlds_biggest_ddosforhire_site_shuttered_admins_cuffed/ (accessed 25 October 2018).

Lukes, S. (1974), *Power: A Radical View*, London: Macmillan.

Lukes, S. (2005), *Power: A Radical View* (2nd edition), London: Palgrave Macmillan.

Makarenko, T. (2001), 'Transnational Crime and its Evolving Links to Terrorism and Instability', *Janes Intelligence Review*, 13(11): 22–24.

Makarenko, T. (2002), 'Crime, Terror and the Central Asian Drug Trade', *Harvard Asia Quarterly*, 6(3): 1–24.

Makarenko, T. (2003), 'A Model of Terrorist-Criminal Relations', *Janes Intelligence Review*, 15(8): 6–11.

Makarenko, T. (2004), 'The Crime-terror Continuum: Tracing the Interplay between Transnational Organised Crime and Terrorism', *Global Crime*, 6(1): 129–145.

Makarenko, T. (2012), 'Foundations and Evolution of the Crime–Terror Nexus', in Allum, F. and Gilmour, S. (eds), *Routledge Handbook of Transnational Organized Crime*, London and New York :Routledge.

Morales, C. (2018), 'NETSCOUT Arbor Confirms 1.7 Tbps DDoS Attack; The Terabit Attack Era Is Upon Us', *Arbor Networks*, 5 March, www.arbornetworks.com/blog/asert/netscout-arbor-confirms-1-7-tbps-ddos-attack-terabit-attack-era-upon-us/ (accessed 15 March 2018).

Musotto, R. and Wall, D.S. (2017), 'Modelling Organised Crime Groups and Terrorist Networks. D2.2. TAKEDOWN Understanding Organised Crime Groups and Terrorist Networks, H2020'. Restricted Circulation.

Musotto, R. and Wall D.S. (2018), 'Are Booter Services (Stressers) Indicative of a New Form of Organised Crime Group Online?', UNODC Linking Organized

Crime and Cybercrime Conference, School of Global Studies, Hallym University, Chucheon, South Korea, 7–8 June 2018.
NCA (2017), 'Pathways into Cyber Crime', *National Crime Agency*, www.national crimeagency.gov.uk/publications/791-pathways-into-cyber-crime/file (accessed 15 March 2018).
Nichols, S. (2018), 'Mueller Bombshell: 13 Russian "Troll Factory" Staffers Charged with Allegedly Meddling in US Presidential Election', *The Register*, 16 February, www.theregister.co.uk/2018/02/16/mueller_russians_election_indictment/
Porter, D. (2017), 'How Localgovs Can Guard Against DDOS Stresser Attacks', *Efficient-Gov*, 15 November, https://efficientgov.com/blog/2017/11/15/how-localgovs-guard-against-DDOS-stresser-attacks/ (accessed 15 March 2018).
Schwartz, M.J. (2017), 'Daniel Kaye Charged With DDoS, Blackmail Against Lloyds and Barclays Banks', Information Security Media Group, 31 August, https://goo.gl/3vh9Ds (accessed 15 March 2018).
Shelley, L.I. and Picarelli, J.T. (2002), 'Methods Not Motives: Implications of the Convergence of International Organized Crime and Terrorism', *Police Practice and Research*, 3(4): 305–318.
Shelley, L.I. and Picarelli, J.T. (2005), *Methods and Motives: Exploring Links between Transnational Organized Crime and International Terrorism*, US National Institute of Justice Report.
Shein, E. (2018), 'The Nexus Between Cybercrime and Emerging Global Threats'. 25 October. Cyber Security Hub, www.cshub.com/executive-decisions/news/the-nexus-between-cyber-crime-and-emerging-global-threats (accessed 26 October 2018).
Traynor, I. (2007), 'Russia Accused of Unleashing Cyberwar to Disable Estonia', *Guardian*, 17 May, www.theguardian.com/world/2007/may/17/topstories3.russia (accessed 15 March 2018).
Wall, D.S. (2013), 'Policing Identity Crimes', *Policing and Society*, 23(4): 437–460.
Wall, D.S. (2018), 'How Big Data Feeds Big Crime', *Current History: A Journal of Contemporary World Affairs*, 117(795): 29–34. www.researchgate.net/publication/322399468_How_big_data_feeds_big_crime.
Wolf, K. (2017), 'Cyber Jihadists Dabble in DDoS: Assessing the Threat', *Flashpoint*, 13 July, www.flashpoint-intel.com/blog/cyber-jihadists-ddos/ (accessed 15 March 2018).
Wu, M. and Knoke, D. (2017), 'Dark Networks: The Terror-Crime Nexus', in Koops, J.A. and Biermann, R. (eds), *Palgrave Handbook of Inter-Organizational Relations in World Politics* (pp. 471–484), London: Palgrave Macmillan.

5 The role of information and communication technology (ICT) in modern criminal organizations

Andrea Tundis and Max Mühlhäuser

Introduction

Criminal groups operate illegally through corruption, exploitation, violence and commerce with the aim of obtaining power, influence, and monetary gains. These groups do not always follow a specific structured organization, they can vary from hierarchies to clans, networks, and cells. Crimes usually include drug trafficking, migrant smuggling, human trafficking, money laundering, firearms trafficking, illegal gambling, extortion, counterfeit goods, wildlife and cultural property smuggling (UNUDC, 2017). The large quantity of money involved in all such illegal activities, which poses a growing threat to national and international security, damages legitimate economies, with severe implications for public safety, public health, democratic institutions and economic stability.

Thanks to the continuous evolution of cyber technologies and the growing use of the internet, powerful communication means are developed that make the sharing of information, knowledge and experiences easier. This causes an increasing number of people to move their activities towards cyberspace (Brunst, 2010). However, with the obvious advantages, many failings are emerging.

In the last decades, due to the exploitation of the internet, the development of new computer-based technologies has led to an increased opportunity to conduct criminal activity as well as to spread threats and glorify violence. Internet-based organized crime and cyber terrorism are becoming increasingly relevant and are already gaining more significance when compared to their conventional criminal counterparts (OCC, 2005).

Information technology represents a powerful and effective tool for criminals, for supporting the creation of new criminal scenarios, simplifying the execution of specific illegal activities, and reducing the risk of detection (Tundis *et al.*, 2018). Criminals are becoming, as a consequence, more 'advanced, smart and difficult to be identified' due to the incorporation of cyber techniques into their illicit activities, both for the commission of specific crimes and for their facilitation (Dowson and Omar, 2015). As modern and successful companies move their businesses to the Web to gain advantages in new markets, criminal groups follow suit. Unquestionably, the internet is a useful instrument to support illegal actions because of available mechanisms of anonymity and lack of censorship. Moreover, with a very low level of risk, it provides useful communication channels, it allows criminals to accomplish their goals and encourages malicious actors to exploit the same resources with considerable benefit.

In the following pages the role of information technology is highlighted. To begin with, a description is provided of emerging cyber-criminal scenarios and the evolution of existing ones. Then, current IT-based approaches, which are available to prevent or mitigate cybercrimes for each scenario, are presented (Steven, 2016; Spalek, 2014; Jalil, 2003).

Defacement of governments and public institutions

Public and government institutions, as well as agencies, represent an attractive target for criminals due to the huge amount of public data and information they hold and which can be exploited to achieve illegal objectives. Cyber-criminals hack such systems to access big amounts of data containing confidential and personal information of citizens for political and economic reasons. From a technical point of view, the most common problem is related to the software. The operating systems in these institutions are often outdated, as are the security solutions they rely upon. Moreover, the employees are unaware of new technologies and of new emerging security threats. This combination makes them easy targets for criminal groups (Zaharia, 2017).

The defacement of governmental platforms is a typical case, where the major goal is to take down the entire system or the network by making it unable to operate normally: this causes damage to the organization both economically and financially. The UK National Health Service became a victim of such a crime when the WannaCry Ransom attack was initiated through a simple e-mail that infected the whole network, resulting in devastating consequences (Chen and Bridges, 2017; Hoeksma, 2017). The cyber-criminals demanded money to repair the infected systems, which compromised 2,000 computers, making them unusable for more than one week, and causing huge loss and service disruption.

A similar case relating to government and public institutions, involving *Ransomware*, is described by Nadir and Bakhshi (2018). The attack restricted users from accessing their own computer systems or personal data files, either by locking the system or by encrypting some of the files stored. In this case, the criminals asked for a *ransom* (money or digital currency) in order to decrypt the files and restore access to the system (Pathak and Nanded, 2016). Ransomware attacks can be carried out through e-mail spams, phishing, redirecting the websites to malicious sites and software downloaders (Zahra and Shah, 2017; Sgandurra et al., 2016; Cabaj, Gregorczyk and Mazurczyk, 2018). Ransomware can be classified as crypto-ransomware and locker-ransomware. In the former case, the user's data are encrypted and blocked until a ransom is paid for the decryption. In the latter case, the entire system is locked and the user is unable to access it even if the files are untouched.

Denial of Service (DoS) is a common method of attack to disable or disrupt online operations by flooding the targeted servers with huge number of packets (requests), which ultimately lead to the servers being unable to handle normal service requests from legitimate users. Public and institutional IT platform are nowadays the main target of this type of attack operated by cyber-criminals. The impact of such attacks can be disastrous from both an economic and social perspective as it can cause organizations to suffer from massive losses. An extension of DoS is Distributed-DoS (DDoS), which is typically executed by a so-called botnet (Böck *et al.*, 2018). Malware infections can install silent software on a victim's machine which places it under the control of a remote attacker. There exists a big business in creating botnets for criminal enterprises who can use them to launch DDoS (Cisco Systems, 2004).

Prevention approaches

The most common practices against Ransomware threats are *Encryption, System recovery, Firewalls, Reputation and Trust-based mechanisms*, (NMR, 2017; Pope, 2016). In particular, *encryption* allows encoding messages or information in such a way that only authorized parties can access it. *System Recovery* is a mechanism that can be adopted to avoid data being lost in case of blackout of the system or corruption, whereas the use of *firewalls* and *anti-virus programs* represent the basis of prevention mechanisms. Moreover, *reputation system* and *trust-based frameworks* constitute advanced prevention methods to provide a scalable and a generalized approach for countering different types of misbehaviours resulting from malicious attacks and threats.

Among the existing technical solutions to neutralize DDoS, there are *Blackholing, Intrusion Detection System (IDS), Routers, Firewalls* (Molaviarman, 2017). In particular, *Blackholing* describes the process of a service provider blocking all traffic destined for a targeted enterprise as far upstream as possible by sending the diverted traffic to a 'black hole', where it is discarded in an effort to save the provider's network and its other customers. Possibilities are also offered by *Routers*, centred on *Access Control Lists (ACLs)*. The routers can protect against some DDoS attacks, such as ping attacks, by filtering non-essential and unneeded protocols. *Firewalls* play an important role in any organization's security solution, and although they are not purpose-built DDoS prevention devices, they can be used as complementary prevention mechanisms. Similarly, *Intrusion Detection Systems* are able to offer anomaly-based capabilities to detect external attacks, although they require extensive manual tuning by experts (Sen, 2016).

Other security mechanisms against defacement are based on systems monitoring, that can be associated to IDS to prevent illegitimate users from accessing specific sites (Verma and Sayyad, 2015; Viswanathan and Mishra, 2016).

Auction and trade fraud

Online auction fraud is one of the most commonly reported internet frauds (Mundra, Rakesh, and Ghrera, 2013). It has the highest incidence among reported cyber-criminality. Here, the seller attempts to scam the buyer by providing fraudulent misrepresentation of a product. The auctions are manipulated or the product is not delivered after it has been paid for. It may also happen that the buyer tries to scam the seller.

In the first case, the following may take place. There may be *dummy bidders*: one option for the seller is to outbid the buyer by using dummy bidders that can be achieved with multiple manually managed fake accounts or with bots. There can be *withholding of goods* after their payment. Due to the high possibility of getting their account blocked after the scam, the sellers have to frequently change their fake accounts. *Misrepresentation* can be used to simply boost or overrate the price of a given product, while comments and rating sections can be manipulated as well as the information about the products.

In the second case, where the buyer wants to scam the seller, the following can take place. *Low bid – high bid – not pay*, when the buyer can manipulate auctions. A low bid, followed by a very high bid with another account can be placed. After the auction is finished, the account with the high bid refuses to pay and so the seller is forced to repeat the auction or give the product to the second highest bid, which is the same buyer (Government of Canada, 2017). *Not pay goods* is where the buyer does not pay for delivered goods or claims that the item has not been received (Rampen, 2017). *Switch and return*, is a method whereby the buyer has a broken or malfunctioning product without warranty. As a consequence, a new version of that device is ordered, the broken and the new one are then exchanged and the broken version is sent back, claiming that the product was already broken and that it should be replaced or refunded (Rampen, 2017). *Feedback extortion* is where the buyer receives the products regularly, but refuses to pay the money for the delivered goods, wants the money back or tries to get a discount by blackmailing the seller with negative feedback on the product.

Prevention approaches

Possible counter-measures to prevent or mitigate auction and trade fraud can be achieved through trading platforms, by activating:

- *user verification*, which ensures a higher level of security although requiring a degree of effort and registration delay for the users;
- *captcha queries*, that uses a "challenge-response" test to determine whether or not the user is human.

In cases of *withholding of goods* as well as of *misrepresentation*, the buyer has a variety of options to avoid this scam, such as the use of *payment systems* like credit cards or other systems that allow the dispute of charges. Another way is the use of *trustees*, who receive and keep the payment until buyer and seller confirm the successful exchange of the goods. After the confirmation, the trustee forwards the payment to the seller. The trustee can be represented by the trading platform or a third party. Another opportunity for trustees with human involvement are so-called *smart contracts*. This technology, which is part of cryptocurrencies like Bitcoins and Ethereum, supports the execution of code that is verified by the P2P network. This code can manage crypto wallets and the cash stored on them, which can be used to send money to the seller when both parties have confirmed the trade, like a normal trustee (Juels, Kosba, and Shi, 2016). Another approach, to reduce the risk of being scammed by the seller, consists of buying from sellers in their own country or from countries that have common trade laws or some partnership in law enforcement. Through this, the chance of a successful prosecution of the seller increases. *User verification* is another option especially for sellers, but the buyer can also rely on ratings provided for the seller and the feedback from other users on the respective product, even if this information can also be manipulated by dummy bots or faked comments under the control of the seller.

In the case of sellers being scammed, the risk can be prevented by *user verification* as well as *trustee system*. Furthermore, in the case of *not pay goods* the buyer can be prevented by warranty (Internet Auction Fraud, 2017), whereas in the case of *switch and return*, a good countermeasure consists of storing the *serial numbers* by the buyer.

Advance-fee fraud

Advance-fee fraud is one of the most common trust-based tricks. In this scenario, the scammer promises the victim a large amount of money, which will supposedly be received after the payment of a small fee. If the victim consents to the payment, the scammer continues to bring up more justifications for further requests of money, until the victim refuses to pay.

Specific cases include *The Nigerian Letter*, one of the most lucrative forms of online scams. The victim is persuaded to pay a fee in advance in order to obtain a large amount of money. Between 1–5 per cent of recipients actually reply with varying degrees of involvement (Cukier, Nesselroth and Cody, 2007). In the *dating and romance Scam* online social networks and especially online dating websites are used to develop personal, romantic or sexual relationships with like-minded people. Fraudsters try to earn the trust of their victims by attracting them with romantic and emotional promises. Scammers often use images of models and even artificial intelligence software programs, called Lovebots, are employed in dating and romance scams (Rege, 2013; CyberLover, 2010; FlirtBot, 2010). They operate in chatrooms and dating sites by driving victims into sharing personal data or visiting malicious websites like webcam sites. *Lottery Scam* is an application of advance-fee fraud and affects a large number of e-mail users (Kerremans *et al.*, 2005). This fraud begins with an unsolicited e-mail or phone call claiming that the recipients are the lucky winner of a lottery. When they respond to the fraud message, the scammers ask them for bank account information, for transfer charges or processing fees. After the money is delivered, the scammer either disappears or asks for further funds.

Prevention approaches

In such cases, prevention mechanisms include blocking IP addresses related to specific countries as well as disabling the access to multiple popular platforms. Common strategies and specific mechanisms against advance-fee fraud are:

- *Scambaiting*: this is the process of luring internet scammers into a trap and involves wasting their time, exploiting their resources and raising awareness about online fraud. Baiters try to convince the scammers that they are the perfect innocent victims and appear as a particularly profitable target. They often use a fake identity for this purpose. The scam-baiters organize themselves on various Internet platforms (Thescambaiter, 2017; 419eater, 2017; Scamorama, 2017), where they exchange information about current scams and share their stories within the community (Zingerle and Kronman, 2013).
- *E-Mail Detection*: this approach aims at identifying spam and phishing in unsolicited e-mails. Common e-mail detection tools are ClamAV (ClamAV, 2017), an anti-virus tool that detects malicious software embedded within e-mails, and SpamAssassin (SpamAssassin, 2017), which uses a set of rules and a Bayesian classifier to determine if a message is spam or not. Predominant e-mail authentication approaches are SPF, Sender-ID and DomainKeys (Amin, 2010).
- *Contextual approaches* are very effective for identifying spam. They check the e-mail content against a set of rules or heuristics and assign a probabilistic score to the presence of certain keywords or phrases. Machine learning and hash-based techniques are often applied to obtain a higher accuracy in classifying an e-mail as legitimate or illegitimate.
- *Reputation-based approaches* maintain lists of previously classified senders, categorizing them into 'good' and 'bad', or calculating a level of trust through relationship linkages.
- *Resource-consumption-based approaches* aim to discourage scammers by wasting their time and resources and by increasing their costs related to network bandwidth or latency. HashCash is, for example, a system that requires the senders to solve a cryptographic puzzle before sending an e-mail to a particular recipient.

Identity theft

This consists of illegally using another person's name and personal information in order to obtain money or loans (see Chapter 11). The most common cases of identity fraud are performed through *phishing*, which aims to appropriate information and sensitive data, such as passwords or credit cards details, from the online users (Raffetseder, Kirda and Kruegel, 2007; James, Sandhya and Thomas, 2013). This crime can take place by using mass-generated spam e-mails, containing links to a replication of the trustworthy website, such as online banking. Other techniques for domain masking are misspellings and similar looking characters (e.g. using the number '1' for the lowercase letter 'L'). Furthermore, instant messaging and social networks are often means for malware (SANS Institute, 2007). *Pharming* derives from the words 'farming' and 'phishing'. In this case a cyberattack is used to redirect internet users from legitimate websites to another (malicious) website where login data is demanded from the victim. It is used by malicious actors to elicit information for identity theft. *Call ID Spoofing* involves phishers causing the telephone network to advertise a trustworthy originator of a call when the true originator is themselves. The Caller ID display visualizes a phone number different from that of the telephone from which the call was placed. Phishers use Voice over Internet Protocol (VoIP) numbers, available through retailers such as Skype, to setup a war dialler which is software that sequentially dials phone numbers. When a person answers, they are informed about some kind of fraudulent activities on their credit card or bank account and they are invited to call a phone number to confirm personal data.

Prevention approaches

Typical preventive measures against identity theft are:

- *Phishing detection tools*: they inform the user about possible threats and examine background information, for example by looking up malicious links in a database. TORPEDO (TORPEDO, 2017), a just-in-time and just-in-place tooltip for Thunderbird, Firefox and Google Chrome, displays the URL that is behind a link the user is about to click on and highlights the unique domain in the tooltip.
- *Digital certificates*: security begins with establishing trust between a user and a web site. Digital certificates are a way to establish this trust in the form of an encrypted digital key system. A public and private key structure is established whereby a company has a private key, obtained from a Certificate Authority, and a user who wishes to make secure transactions obtains the corresponding public key from the company.
- *Firewalls*: there are many e-mail firewall products that implement rules to block spam and phishing scams, which are updated as new phishing schemes are found. Not only do they block the spam, but they also verify

the IP numbers and web addresses of the e-mail source and compare them to known phishing sites.
- *Anti-virus*: phishing is typically not spread through computer viruses, but if a device is infected with a worm, this could give the scammer access to personal data of the user. Security best practices suggest that all users should implement an anti-virus product regardless of whether they are concerned or not about phishing or online fraud.
- *Secure e-mail protocols*: there is a push within the industry to modify the existing e-mail transport protocols and include built-in security at this lower level. Validating the identity of the originating sender of a message would go a long way in preventing phishing attacks. Built-in encryption may eliminate the need for using separate encryption methods, allowing transparent authentication for the user.
- *Browser enhancements*: recent versions of Microsoft Internet Explorer, Mozilla Firefox, Google Chrome and Opera offer new security features aimed at controlling phishing attacks and other online fraud. The browsers maintain databases of known phishing sites, where they can look up a site and let the user know of the danger.

Darknet

Darknets are private virtual networks in which users connect only with people they trust. In its most general meaning, a darknet can be any kind of closed and private group of communicating people, but the name is often used for file sharing networks (Vinay, 2017). They can be used for good reasons, such as: (i) to protect the privacy of citizens, which is subject to mass surveillance, (ii) protect dissidents from political reprisals, (iii) spread news of a confidential nature. Nevertheless, they can also be exploited for criminal purposes such as terrorism operations, hacking, fraud, sale of illegal products on crypto-markets, and sharing both legal and illegal files. Internet forums, chat rooms, and other online communication platforms remain a key environment for cyber-criminals, especially for terrorists. These places are enablers for the establishment of virtual criminal communities and groups.

Deep Web refers to net sites which are widely used for underground communication. 'The Onion Router' (Tor) is a free tool specifically conceived to ensure the users' privacy: it is a form of network surveillance that obscures the traffic analysis (Matusitz, 2008). The network traffic in Tor is guided through a number of volunteer-operated servers (called 'nodes'), which encrypt the information. It does not register where the traffic comes from nor where it is heading, thus impeding any tracking. Tor is an ideal resource for group discussions among terrorists and other anonymous communication.

Dark market is used by people who advertise and sell illicit products: drugs, pornography, weapons and unauthorized software services.

Dark forums have the sole purpose of enabling communication. They provide the opportunity for the emergence of a community of like-minded individuals, regardless of their geophysical location. The structure and the organization of dark forums might be very similar to the familiar web forums, but the topics and concerns of the users may vary enormously.

Prevention approaches

Network monitoring has been extensively used for security, forensics and anomaly detection with the main objective of identifying malicious activities based on traffic patterns and to trigger alerts. System monitoring of darknet represents a common method to analyse malicious activities on networks including the internet, which can offer insight on individual cyber-criminal profiles, their connections, behaviours, capabilities, as well as intentions. Through monitoring darknet it is possible to understand (i) the current status of ongoing activities, (ii) the trend in terms of 'products on the market', (iii) how long a product stays on the market, as well as to investigate the origin of products, how such product will be used and so on.

Three main ways to enable monitoring are based on: *Crawlers and Parsers*, *Machine Learning* and *Virtual HUMINTs* (Meegahapola et al., 2017; Nunes et al., 2016; Dragos, 2012).

Crawler and Parsers are programs designed to traverse the website and retrieve HTML documents. Topic based crawlers have been used for specific purposes, where only webpages of interest are retrieved, as well as to collect forum discussions from darknet.

Machine Learning: this is a combination of semi-supervised methods, which work with limited labelled data by leveraging information from unlabelled data, along with supervised methods, that include classification techniques such as Naive Bayes (NB), Random Forest (RF), Support Vector Machine (SVM) and Logistic Regression (LOG-REG).

Virtual HUMINT aims at collecting tactical/operational intelligence from the information generated by members of the virtual communities. It consists of an intelligent virtual identity (avatar) to gain trust from, and create long-term relationships with, the members of the participated/monitored communities, as well as recruit, handle, manipulate and deceit them with the purpose of collecting information. They can interact and develop relationships with criminals and sources from the comfort of their own office or home (Koren, 2015; Magee, 2010; Dhami, 2011). Main elements of virtual HUMINT collection by private companies are of a similar nature: they include the fake ID (the creation of many fake digital personas on many platforms to engage hackers), the joining of a 'gang' (the attempt to gain access to closed forums, chat rooms and cybercrime marketplaces), the bait and switch, as well as flirting and flattering (Sullivan, 2012).

Propaganda

Propaganda is, quite often, based on misleading information, which is used to promote a political cause or point of view (Gold, 2011). Terrorists benefit from propaganda and use different tactics to reach people at a local as well as at the global level. Furthermore, social media platforms enable terrorists to communicate and disseminate information among a wider population. The Internet is an inexpensive and 'anonymous' medium for the distribution of religious, political or ideological messages that can influence and shape the minds of new audiences around the world. User-generated content, such as extremely violent videos and images, can be easily uploaded, are not so difficult to produce and have easy accessibility, with little or no regulations, censorship, or other forms of government control.

Propaganda may manifest itself through the *attraction of like-minded* persons, when the main targets are young males, who are susceptible to manipulation and radicalization by extremist preachers, especially on social media platforms. Social networks play an important role in influencing the behaviour of individuals and their willingness to take part in collective actions because of their socializing, recruitment and decision shaping functions (Passy, 2001). The benefits conveyed by the spiritual leaders for involvement in terrorism are, among other things, a sense of belonging to a strong collective identity, status and power. They promote common knowledge of terrorist ideologies and violence and generate support for their cause within the Muslim communities, for example by exaggerating the external threats from other groups (Chatfield, Reddick and Brajawidagda, 2015).

Terrorists can aim at *deterrence*, when propaganda serves to spread disinformation about governments involved in counter-terrorism, disseminating horrific images through social media platforms. In this case, the main goal is to intimidate Western public opinion and to support the moral legitimacy of terrorist violence (e.g. by reframing suicide attacks as martyrdom operations).

Terrorists are able to deliver threats, such as cyber-fear, which is generated when terrorists threaten a computer attack by pretending to be able to, for example, bring down airliners, disable air traffic control systems, or disrupt national economies by wrecking the computerized systems that regulate stock markets.

Prevention approaches

Many social media websites have policies against content in support of terrorism or violence, but influencers can just open new accounts in case of deletion of their profiles. Prevention of propaganda is typically based on the *monitoring, classification* and *analysis of terrorist communication* over online media in order to prevent and investigate crimes. Such prevention approaches can be implemented in the following ways.

- *Monitoring extremist behaviour on social media*: it is possible to analyse the social networks of suspicious persons by identifying explicit links between them and terrorist groups (Tundis et al., 2018; Tundis and Mühlhäuser, 2017).
- *Keyword- and feature-based analysis of communication*: data mining offers the possibility to evaluate Twitter, dark web forums and other communication mediums through the use of certain keywords and to analyse terrorist communication and writing style (Mahmood, 2012; Abbasi and Chen, 2005). Greetings, signatures, quotes, links and forum messages are used to extract linguistic features and evaluating stylistic details for patterns which are linked to extremist content.
- *Honeypots*: intelligence agents can infiltrate extremist chat rooms or forums by posing as radicals and pretending to have the same violent desires and interests shared by terrorist groups, with the aim of tempting terrorists to reveal themselves.
- *Shut down terrorist websites*: a strategy announced by the US government in 2007 which called for the creation of a blacklist of violent and terrorist-related web sites. This blacklist is meant to be circulated within the public sector, so that computers in schools, libraries and universities are prevented from accessing blacklisted sites. The Counter Terrorism Internet Referral Unit (CTIRU) is in charge of website blocking which was established in 2010 to assess internet content and coordinate removal of inappropriate content.

Terrorist communication

Covert channels are defined as communication resources used to illicitly transfer information in a manner that the security policy of the system breaks (Ezekiel et al., 2005). They operate on top of existing communication resources and embed malicious messages by using different methods. The most common types of covert channels are: *storage covert channels* and *timing covert channels*.

- *Timing Covert Channel* uses a clock or other time measurement to signal the value sent over the channel. The sender manipulates the usage of communication resources conforming to message bits such that the receiver can rectify the message from the communication stream, which can include changing the rate of packet transmission or varying the message sizes according to the message to be transmitted (Cabuk et al., 2004).
- *Storage Covert Channel* is more commonly used than timing covert channels as it is easier to implement. The sender embeds messages of bits in the object values which are read by the receiver. This works by mutual exchange of storage between processes. Resources like physical memory, shared hardware resources, I/O schedulers and queues for shared devices

can be used as storage channels. For example, by taking a look at a printing queue: the higher security process exchanges messages with the lower security processes by sending a 1 or a 0 to the printer queue and the lower security process (the receiver) polls the queue to determine if it is full.

Prevention approaches

Performing a detailed analysis of the system can frequently uncover abnormal behaviour, for example, monitoring running processes, sent messages and newly installed files that are unauthorized. In particular, low security processes have to be monitored to prevent them from accessing higher security resources.

Typical prevention mechanisms include the following:

- *Mandatory Access Controls*: only qualified actors who provide the necessary security attributes can access files and programmes (Zander, Armitage, and Branch, 2007).
- *Shared Resource Overflow* restricts processes by limiting their quota to fill resources queues. Therefore, processes which appear too 'greedy' are detected by the system and are prevented to allocate even more resources. If their quota is full, the requested resource is no longer shared between processes.
- *Bandwidth Reduction*: noise is added to the channel in order to slow down the communication, which makes its use harder.

Prevention mechanisms against *timing covert channels* are:

- *Event-based mathematical models*, which calculate the capacity of covert channels and analyses features like noise, performance and reliability (Shrestha *et al.*, 2016).
- *Fuzzy time*, which randomizes the length of the operating system tick interval and reduces the granularity of the system-wide time register, by hampering their usability measured by increase of noise and reduced throughput (Zander, Armitage and Branch, 2007).
- *Time-deterministic replay*, which can reproduce the execution of a program, including its precise timing, and can be used to reconstruct what the timing of the packets should have been (Chen *et al.*, 2014). Each machine is required to log its inputs, which is examined periodically. Then it is replayed with time-deterministic replay on another machine, using a known implementation of the examined machines software. The packet timing during replay should match any observations during play (e.g. from traffic traces) if no timing covert channel is present. Any significant deviation would be a strong sign of such a channel.

Critical infrastructures sabotage

Sabotage is the action that aims to weaken corporations, industries or infrastructures through subversion, obstruction, disruption or destruction. The accidents at Chernobyl (1986) and Fukushima (2011) showed the world the devastating effects of a critical infrastructure like a nuclear power plant. A successful cyberattack on a power plant is one of the worst-case scenarios when it comes to cyber terrorism. These types of attacks are inherently harder to intercept by over-stretched security forces. Below we present some cases and potential preventive counter-measures.

- *Computer-based technologies*: the case of the attack on a uranium enrichment facility in Iran by the *Stuxnet* worm is the most famous case and the most successful attack on a nuclear facility until now. Here, four different zero-day exploits were used by the programmers to distribute the malware, enter the computer systems of the facility and destroy the enrichment centrifuges (Lindsay, 2013). Some examples (CANPDT, 2017; APS, 2017) include Monju NPP (in 2014), where a worker in the control room infected his computer with a video playback application update. The Hydro and Nuclear Power plant in South Korea was attacked in 2014, most likely by North Korea, targeting the workers of the facility who received infected phishing e-mails. In 2003, a slammer worm crashed the Ohio Nuclear Plant Network, infecting the computer network of the power plant and disabling its safety monitoring system.
- *Cyber-physical-based technologies*: these are advanced technologies which are used to physically perform activities that in the past required the presence of humans. Drones are typical examples, which reach locations that might be dangerous and to perform both passive activities (such as the monitoring) and active actions (for example by launching attacks), with a quasi-absent risk to be caught or identified.

Prevention approaches

Usually, the main weak spot of the NPPs and enrichment facilities are the workers. In most cases the critical systems are not directly connected to the internet, so humans and their equipment have to be used to infiltrate the high security systems. One way to reduce this risk is to draw the attention of the workers to security measures and scan all their equipment containing chips and storage when they enter a high security environment. The parts of the facility that are connected to the internet are much harder to defend because there can always be zero-day exploits that attack unknown weak points in software and hardware. A solution for that could be that power plant companies, countries or other friendly organizations buy the zero-day exploits from black markets or give hackers the legal opportunity to sell the discovered weak points to them. By this the black market prices will grow and the number of security loopholes available to criminals and terrorists will decline. Prices range from a few thousand to a few hundred thousand for general application zero-day exploits and up to a million for SCADA system exploits (BS-SCADA, 2017), but this is a lot of money compared to the income of power producing companies or whole countries.

The main prevention approaches should be based on workers' risk awareness and security measures adopted by internet-connected systems, up-to-date anti-virus software and a strict division among critical and uncritical systems.

Closing remarks

This chapter provided an overview of the role of ICT in modern criminal organizations by discussing specific cybercrime scenarios. Specifically, eight scenarios were presented: defacement of governments and public institutions, auction and trade fraud, advance-fee fraud, identity theft, darknet, propaganda, terrorist communication and critical infrastructures sabotage. For each scenario, some widely adopted prevention approaches and security mechanisms have been described.

In most cases, the counter-measures against cyber-attacks and fraud are too complicated and expensive or need a significant implementation effort. Furthermore, there is often little awareness of the possible threats and, in many cases, security is not seen as a top priority by companies. Issues around freedom of speech and privacy have to be considered when attempts are made to prevent criminals from using the internet or to monitor their actions. The lack of protection against zero-day exploits is still a big problem because they are by definition new and unknown. As cyberspace, its system and related applications become more and more complex, the number of new weak points is increasing and, as a consequence, it is even more complicated to predict, control and manage them.

Furthermore, it is important to highlight that such emerging scenarios are not only enabled by technical factors, such as dematerialization of illegal activities, increased international collaborations and online anonymity (Tundis et al., 2018), but they are also the result of the low level of cooperation among police forces and other law enforcement agencies, the adoption of weak and obsolete communication mechanisms, inconsistency among national and international laws and regulations, as well as absence or low-level involvement of the citizens.

References

Abbasi, A. and Chen, H. (2005), 'Applying Authorship Analysis to Extremist-group Web Forum Messages', *IEEE Intelligent Systems*, 20(5): 67–75.
Amin R.M. (2010), 'Detecting Targeted Malicious Email Through Supervised Classification of Persistent Threat and Recipient Oriented Features', *Doctoral Dissertation*, George Washington University, DC, USA.

APS (2017), www.networkworld.com/article/2217684/datacenter/attacks-on-power-systems-hackers-malware.html (accessed 24 September 2018).

Böck, L., Vasilomanolakis E., Mühlhäuser, M. and Karuppayah, S. (2018), 'Next Generation P2P Botnets: Monitoring under Adverse Conditions', *Symposium on Research in Attacks, Intrusions and Defenses*, Crete, Greece, 10–12 September: 511–531.

Brunst, P.W. (2010), 'Terrorism and the Internet: New Threats Posed by Cyberterrorism and Terrorist Use of the Internet', in *A War on Terror: The European Stance on a New Threat, Changing Laws and Human Rights Implications* (pp. 51–78), New York: Springer.

BS-SCADA (Buying and Selling SCADA) Zero-Days (2017), http://resources.infosecinstitute.com/how-much-is-a-zeroday-exploit-for-an-scadaics-system/#gref (accessed 24 September 2018).

Cabaj, K., Gregorczyk, M. and Mazurczyk, W. (2018), 'Software-Defined Networking-based Crypto Ransomware Detection Using HTTP Traffic Characteristics', *Computers and Electrical Engineering*, 66(c): 353–368.

Cabuk, S., Brodley, C.E. and Shields, C. (2004), 'IP Covert Timing Channels: Design and Detection', *Conference on Computer and Communications Security*, Washington, DC, USA, 25–29 October: 178–187.

CANPDT (Cyber-attacks Against Nuclear Plants: A Disconcerting Threat) (2017), http://resources.infosecinstitute.com/cyber-attacks-against-nuclear-plants-a-disconcertingthreat/#gref (accessed 24 September 2018).

Chatfield, A.T., Reddick, C.G. and Brajawidagda U. (2015), 'Tweeting Propaganda, Radicalization and Recruitment: Islamic State Supporters Multisided Twitter Networks', in *Annual International Conference on Digital Government Research* (pp. 239–249), Phoenix, AZ, USA, 27–30 May.

Chen, Q. and Bridges, R.A. (2017), 'Automated Behavioral Analysis of Malware: A Case Study of WannaCry Ransomware', *IEEE International Conference on Machine Learning and Applications (ICMLA)*, Cancun, Mexico, 19–21 December: 454–460.

Chen, A., Moore, W.B., Xiao, H., Haeberlen, A., Phan, L.T.X., Sherr, M. and Zhou, W. (2014), 'Detecting Covert Timing Channels with Time-Deterministic Replay', *USENIX Symposium on Operating Systems Design and Implementation*, Broomfield, CO, 6–8 October: 541–554.

Cisco Systems (2004), Defeating DDOS Attacks. White paper, https://theswissbay.ch/pdf/Whitepaper/Network/Defeating%20DDoS%20attacks%20-%20Cisco%20Systems.pdf (accessed 24 September 2018).

ClamAV (2017), www.clamav.net/0 (accessed 24 September 2018).

Cukier, W.L., Nesselroth E.J. and Cody, S. (2007), 'Genre, Narrative and the "Nigerian Letter" in Electronic Mail', *Hawaii International Conference on System Sciences*, Waikoloa, USA, 3–6 January: x:1–x:10.

CyberLover (2010), www.telegraph.co.uk/news/uknews/1572077/Cyberlover-flirts-its-way-to-internet-fraud.html (accessed 24 September 2018).

Dhami, M.K. (2011), Behavioural Science Support for JTRIG's (Joint Threat Research and Intelligence Group's) Effects and Online HUMINT Operations. *UK Government Communications Headquarters Report*, www.statewatch.org/news/2015/jun/behavioural-science-support-for-jtrigs-effects.pdf (accessed 24 September 2018).

Dowson, M. and Omar M. (ed.) (2015), *New Threats and Countermeasures in Digital Crime and Cyber, Terrorism*, USA: IGI Global.

Dragos, V. (2012), 'Shallow Semantic Analysis to Estimate HUMINT Correlation', in *International Conference on Information Fusion*, Singapore, 9–12 July: 2293–2300.

Ezekiel, S., Wolfe, J., Trimble, R. and Oblitey W. (2005), 'Covert Storage Channels: A Brief Overview', *Covert Channels Research Group*, www.iup.edu/WorkArea/DownloadAsset.aspx?id=60863 (accessed 24 September 2018).

FlirtBot (2010), www.botlibre.com/browse?id=11547311 (accessed 24 September 2018).

Gold, S. (2011), 'Terrorism's "Invisible" Propaganda Networks', *Engineering and Technology*, 6(7): 58–61, August.

Government of Canada (2017), *On-line Shopping Fraud: From a Buyer or Seller's Point of View*, www.rcmp-grc.gc.ca/scams-fraudes/shopmagasinage-eng.htm (accessed 24 September 2018).

Hoeksma, J. (2017), 'NHS Cyberattack May Prove to be a Valuable Wake up Call', *BMJ: British Medical Journal*, 35, BMJ Clinical Research, United Kingdom.

Internet Auction Fraud (2017), www. fbi.gov/scams-and-safety/common-fraud-schemes/internet-auction-fraud (accessed 24 September 2018).

Jalil S.A. (2003), *Countering Cyber Terrorism Effectively: Are We Ready to Rumble?*, Washington: US System Administration, Networking and Security Institute (SANS).

James, J., Sandhya, L. and Thomas, C. (2013), 'Detection of Phishing URLs Using Machine Learning Techniques', in *Conference on Control Communication and Computing*, December: 304–309.

Juels, A., Kosba A. and Shi, E. (2016), 'The Ring of Gyges: Investigating the Future of Criminal Smart Contracts', *ACM SIGSAC Conference on Computer and Communications Security*, Austria, Vienna, 24–28 October: 283–295.

Kerremans, K., Tang Y., Temmerman, R. and Zhao G. (2005), 'Towards Ontology-based E-mail Fraud Detection', *Portuguese Conference on Artificial Intelligence*, Covilha, Portugal, 5–8 December: 106–111.

Koren, D. (2015), 'Virtual HUMINT: Conducting Human Intelligence Operations in the Virtual Environment', *Master's Thesis. Naval Postgraduate School*, http://hdl.handle.net/10945/56397 (accessed 24 September 2018).

Lindsay, J.R. (2013), 'Stuxnet and the Limits of Cyber Warfare', *Security Studies*, 22(3): 365–404.

Magee, A.C. (2010), 'Countering Nontraditional HUMINT Collection Threats', *International Journal of Intelligence and CounterIntelligence*, 23(3): 509–520.

Mahmood, S. (2012), 'Online Social Networks: The Overt and Covert Communication Channels for Terrorists and Beyond', in *Conference on Technologies for Homeland Security (HST)* (pp. 574–579), Waltham, MA, 13–15 November.

Matusitz, J. (2008), 'Cyberterrorism: Postmodern State of Chaos', *Information Security Journal: A Global Perspective*, 17(4): 179–187.

Meegahapola, L., Alwis, R., Heshan, E., Mallawaarachchi, V., Meedeniya, D. and Jayarathna S. (2017), 'Adaptive Technique for Web Page Change Detection using Multi-threaded Crawlers', in *International Conference on Innovative Computing Technology(INTECH)*, London, United Kingdom, 16–18 August: 120–125.

Molaviarman (2017), *An Overview of DDoS And Prevention Mechanisms*, www.molaviarman.net (accessed 24 September 2018).

Mundra, A., Rakesh, N. and Ghrera, S.P. (2013), 'Empirical Study of Online Hybrid Model for Internet Frauds Prevention and Detection', *Conference on Human Computer Interactions (ICHCI)*, Chennai, India, 23–24 August: x:1–x:7.

Nadir, I. and Bakhshi, T. (2018), 'Contemporary Cybercrime: A Taxonomy of Ransomware Threats and Mitigation Techniques', *Conference on Computing, Mathematics and Engineering Technologies (iCoMET)*, Sukkur, Pakistan, 3–4 March: x:1–x:7.

NMR (No More Ransom), (2017), www.nomoreransom.org/en/prevention-advice.html (accessed 24 September 2018).

Nunes, E., Diab, A., Gunn, A., Marin, E.. Mishra, V., Paliath, V., Robertson, J., Shakarian, J., Thart, A. and Shakarian, P. (2016), 'Darknet and Deepnet Mining for Proactive Cybersecurity Threat Intelligence', in *Conference on Intelligence and Security Informatics*, Arizona, USA, 27–30 September: 7–12.

OCC (Organized Crime and Cybercrime) (2005), www.crimeresearch.org/library/Cybercrime.htm (accessed 24 September 2018).

Passy, F. (2001), 'Socialization, Connection, and The Structure/Agency Gap: A Specification of The Impact of Networks on Participation in Social Movements', *Mobilization: An International Quarterly*, 6(2): 173–192.

Pathak, D.P. and Nanded, Y.M. (2016), 'A Dangerous Trend of Cybercrime: Ransomware Growing Challenge', *International Journal of Advanced Research in Computer Engineering and Technology (IJARCET)*, 5(2), Behopal, India: 371–373.

Pope, J. (2016), 'Ransomware: Minimizing the Risks', *Innovations in Clinical Neuroscience*, 13(11): 37–40.

Raffetseder, T., Kirda, E. and Kruegel, C. (2007), 'Building Anti-Phishing Browser Plug-Ins: An Experience Report', in *Workshop on Software Engineering for Secure Systems Workshop*, Minneapolis, Minnesota, 20–26 May: x:1–x:6.

Rampen, J. (2017), 'eBay Buyer Scams: 4 Frauds Sellers Need to Watch out for', www.mirror.co.uk/money/ebay-buyer-seller-scams-fraud-5552823 (accessed 24 September 2018).

Rege, A. (2013), 'A Criminological Investigation of Online Dating Crimes', *APWG eCrime Researchers Summit*, San Francisco, CA: 1–9. DOI:10.1109/eCRS.2013.6805773

SANS Institute (2007), 'Phishing: The Analysis of a Growing Threat', in *Security Essentials Certification (GSEC) Practical*, version 1.4b, SANS Institute, www.innovateus.net/science/what-are-different-types-phishing-attacks (accessed 24 September 2018).

Scamorama (2017), www.scamorama.com (accessed 24 September 2018).

Sen, J. (2016), 'A Survey on Reputation and Trust-Based Systems for Wireless Communication Networks', *Journal HIT Transaction on Electronics, Communication, Computers and Networking*, 1(2): 92–111.

Sgandurra, D., Muñoz-González, L., Mohsen, R. and Lupu, E.C. (2016), 'Automated Dynamic Analysis of Ransomware: Benefits Limitations and Use for Detection', Computing Research Repository (*CoRR*), E-print Archive, Cornell University, Ithaca, NY (USA), 1–12.

Shein, R. (2004), *Zero-Day Exploit: Countdown to Darkness*, Massachusetts, USA: Syngress.

Shrestha, P.L., Hempel, M., Sharif, H. and Chen, H.-H. (2016), 'An Event-Based Unified System Model to Characterize and Evaluate Timing Covert Channels', *IEEE Systems Journal*, 10(1): 271–280.

Spalek, B. (2012), 'Community-Based Approaches to Counter-Terrorism', in Spalek, B. (ed.), *Counter-Terrorism*, London: Palgrave Macmillan.

SpamAssassin (2017), http://spamassassin.apache.org/ (accessed 24 September 2018).

Steven, P. (2016), *Crime Prevention: Approaches, Practices, and Evaluations* (9th edn), New York: Routledge.

Sullivan, P.J. (2012), *Redefining Human Intelligence for the Modern Age*, Master's Thesis. American Military University.

Thescambaiter (2017), www.thescambaiter.com (accessed 24 September 2018).

TORPEDO (2017), *TOPERDO Tooltip Powered Phish Detection*, www.secuso.informatik.tu-darmstadt.de/de/secuso/forschung/ergebnisse/torpedo/ (accessed 24 September 2018).

Tundis, A., Bhatia, G., Jain, A. and Mühlhäuser, M, (2018), 'Supporting the Identification and the Assessment of Suspicious Users on Twitter Social Media', *IEEE International Symposium on Network Computing and Applications* (NCA), Cambridge, MA, 1–3 November, pp. x:1–x:10.

Tundis, A., Huber, F., Jäger, B., Daubert, J., Vasilomanolakis, E. and Mühlhäuser, M. (2018), 'Challenges and Available Solutions Against Organized Cyber-crime and Terrorist Networks', in *WIT Transactions on the Built Environment*, 174: 429–441, DOI:10.2495/SAFE170391

Tundis, A. and Mühlhäuser, M. (2017), 'A Multi-language Approach Towards the Identification of Suspicious Users on Social Networks', *International Carnahan Conference on Security Technology (ICCST)*, Madrid, Spain, 23–28 October, pp. x:1–x:6. DOI:10.1109/CCST.2017.8167794.

UNUDC (United Nations Office on Drugs and Crime) (2017), www.unodc.org/unodc/en/organized-crime/intro.html (accessed 24 September 2018).

Verma, R.K. and Sayyad, S. (2015), 'Implementation of Web Defacement Detection Technique', *Journal of Innovations in Engineering and Technology (IJIET)*, 6(1): 134–140.

Vinay, S. (2017), *What is the Darknet, and How Will it Shape the Future of the Digital Age*, www.abc.net.au/news/2016-01-27/explainer-what-is-the-dark-net/7038878 (accessed 24 September 2018).

Viswanathan, N. and Mishra, A. (2016), 'Dynamic Monitoring of Website Content and Alerting Defacement Using Trusted Platform Module', in *Emerging Research in Computing, Information, Communication and Applications* (pp. 117–126), Singapore: Springer.

Zaharia, A. (2017), 'What is Ransomware and 15 Easy Steps to Keep Your System Protected', https://heimdalsecurity.com/blog/what-is-ransomware-protection/#ransomwaretargets (accessed 24 September 2018).

Zahra, A. and Shah, M.A. (2017), 'IoT Based Ransomware Growth Rate Evaluation and Detection using Command and Control Blacklisting', *IEEE International Conference Automation and Computing* (ICAC), Huddersfield, UK, 7–8 September: x:1–x:6.

Zander, S., Armitage, G. and Branch, P. (2007), 'Covert Channels and Countermeasures in Computer Network Protocols', *IEEE Communications* Magazine, 45(12): 136–142.

Zingerle, A. and Kronman, L. (2013), 'Humiliating Entertainment or Social Activism? Analyzing Scambaiting Strategies Against Online Advance Fee Fraud', *International Conference on Cyberworlds*, Yokohama, Japan, 21–23 October: 352–355.

419eater (2017), www.419eater.com (accessed 24 September 2018).

6 The rise of low-tech terrorist attacks in Europe

Andrew Monaghan

Introduction

This chapter analyses major terrorist attacks in Europe since 2004. During that time there have been numerous acts of political violence against Europe's civilian, military/security and police forces, but this work focuses mostly on those major incidents where more than ten civilians died due to the actions of the individuals or groups.

Terrorism is a contested concept and even the United Nations has not yet been able to decide upon any legally binding and final series of words which have the force of law. Indeed, the *Routledge Handbook of Terrorism Research* has an impressive 261 alternative definitions of terrorism, an entire book devoted to untangling this Gordian Knot (Schmid, 2012). However, a workable solution can be attained by alighting upon 'terrorism as a tactic', whereby:

> Terrorism as a tactic is employed in three main contexts: (i) illegal state repression, (ii) propagandistic agitation by non-state actors in times of peace or outside zones of conflict and (iii) as an illicit tactic of irregular warfare employed by state- and non-state actors.
>
> (Ibid.: 159)

This more tactical assessment of terrorism will be used as the benchmark throughout the remainder of the chapter.

Fifteen major terrorist incidents in Europe since 2004 will be detailed and scrutinized in this work, to reveal how the *modus operandi* of the perpetrators have dramatically changed in the last decade. There has been a shift away from bombings and hijackings of aeroplanes, towards a more low-tech approach, particularly mass-shootings, stabbings and vehicular assaults on urban people.

The chapter analyses these trends through the eyes of Routine Activities Theory, which believes that motivated criminals use the everyday pastimes of city populations to choose soft targets for their assaults, as they are relatively unprotected by police and security officers.

Finally, options are discussed about how governments, intelligence staff and the police can deal with this rapidly emerging, and increasingly deadly, adoption of low-tech assault tactics.

Recent trends in European terrorism

In the European Union's 28 countries (soon to be 27), the number of failed, foiled or completed terror plots has fluctuated: in 2014 (226), 2015 (193), 2016 (142) and 2017 (205); as for arrests for suspected terrorism the numbers are: 2014 (774), 2015 (1,077), 2016 (1,002) and 2017 (1,219) (Europol, 2018).

Since 2004 Europe has experienced 15 major terrorist incidents. Ten of these instances of terrorism involved some form of radicalized Islamic extremists, four were claimed by one of the branches of Al-Qaeda and six by Islamic State. Three involved local separatist movements and two were conducted by right-wing/nationalist extremists. Five of the assaults were carried out by lone-wolf operators, while the remaining ten involved a plot of two or more antagonists, with the most complex involving numbers in the high-teens.

The first three major terror assaults since 2004 were all bombings: the Madrid train bombings in March 2004 (Rose, Murphy and Abrahms, 2007), where 192 were killed and over 2,000 injured; July 2005 in London, where 56 died from four bombs, including the four perpetrators and over 700 were injured on three underground trains, and one bus (Drury, Cocking and Reicher, 2009); and in 2011, 14 were killed by a bomb on the Minsk Metro in Belarus, with over 200 injured (May, 2011). Before these three incidents, from December 1988 to February 2001, all six previous major attacks in Europe involved explosions.

Following the three consecutive bombings from 2004–2011, of the remaining 12 major terrorist incidents in Europe, only four contained explosive devices as part of the perpetrator's *modus operandi*. One of these, the Norway attacks by Anders Behring Breivik, which took place on 22 July 2011, began with a car bomb outside government offices in Oslo, which resulted in eight killed and ten hospitalized with serious injuries and then concluded with a mass shooting at Utoya island, 30 km northwards, where 69 were shot dead and a further 56 hospitalized with severe injuries (Thoresen *et al.*, 2012). The remote island was hosting a summer camp for the Norwegian Labour Youth movement, and the perpetrator was a right-wing nationalist who is a representative of the classic 'lone-wolf' terrorist-operative type. Lone-wolves are incredibly difficult for the authorities to intercept before they begin their attack, as there are no communications between cell members to monitor and act upon (Nesser, 2012). It should be noted however that the term lone-wolf has attracted criticism from a group of survivors of terrorism, who contend that it glorifies and glamourizes the perpetrator. Survivors are running a social medial campaign under the hashtag #WordsMatter (Davis, 2018), challenging the media nomenclature used in reporting these issues.

Bullets and bombs

In January 2015 two gunmen, the Kouachi brothers, attacked the HQ of the French satirical magazine Charlie Hebdo (which had previously published cartoons about Muslim preachers), while a further attacker shot a policeman and then took hostages in a kosher supermarket. The incidents took place over a five-day period, including a man-hunt for the terrorists and resulted in 20 dead, including the three perpetrators and 22 injured. Claiming allegiance to Al-Qaeda, all three attackers were born and raised in France, the two brothers of Algerian origin and the other of Mali ethnic origin (Chrisafis, 2015).

The next event was the Volnovakha bus attack in the Ukraine on 13 January 2015, when Russian separatists fired rockets at a bus which had stopped at a checkpoint in the eastern province of Donetsk. Twelve bus passengers were killed, and 18 others injured during the attack (BBC News, 2017).

On 9 May 2015, a shootout occurred in the town of Kumanova, near the Kosovo border, between Macedonian police officers and National Liberation Army (NLA) suspects. During this police raid eight officers were killed and ten militants; a further 37 police were injured (AFP, 2015).

A further 'mixed' *modus operandi* terror-attack took place in Paris on 13 November 2015, when three suicide bombers detonated bombs outside of the Stade de France. Here, coordinated multiple attacks were launched by terrorists claiming to be members of Islamic State in Iraq and Syria (ISIS). The three suicide bombers detonated devices outside the stadium while France were playing an international football match against Germany. This resulted in four dead, including the three bombers (CNN, 2018). In the shooting incidents, 39 were killed outside various cafes, bars and restaurants. A suicide bomber blew himself up inside the restaurant Comptoir Voltaire, injuring one patron; three gunmen burst into the Bataclan concert venue, where Eagles of Death Metal were playing a gig. They used assault rifles to shoot and kill 89 people there. During a subsequent assault by the police, one gunman was shot dead and two blew themselves up using suicide-bomb vests. A total of 130 people was killed during this plethora of incidents and around 400 injured, about a quarter of them seriously (ibid.). This series of terrorist attacks on the same day represents the deadliest that France has experienced in its history (Sputniknews, 2018).

On 22 March 2016 three coordinated bomb attacks in Belgium, two at Brussels airport in Zaventem and one at Brussels Metro station, killed 32 people, along with the three perpetrators; around 200 civilians were wounded in the attacks. ISIS claimed responsibility for these attacks stating that they were revenge for Belgium's participation in fighting against the Islamic State 'government' in Syria and Iraq (Dearden, 2017).

'The ultimate mowing machine …'

As part of its English language agitprop internet drive, al-Qaeda in the Arabic Peninsula (AQAP), launched a webzine called 'Inspire' in 2010. This e-zine, which has since led to prosecutions in the UK and US for its possession, was started with the intention of being a self-help manual for aspiring jihadis in Western countries, furnishing articles with instructions on how supporters can adopt effective 'terror tactics' and build low-cost, low-tech devices for use against those nations who were part of the US-led Coalition fighting the various branches of Al-Qaeda, or ISIS (Black, 2013). The intention was to provide an online and updated version of 'The Anarchist Cookbook', the infamous work by William Powell (1971), still available in print and as a Public Domain online download. The book was planned to be part of the counter-culture resistance movement:

> This book is for the people of the United States of America.… The Anarchist Cookbook is not a revolutionary book, just as a gun cannot shoot … if the people of the United States do not protect themselves against the fascists, capitalists and communists, they will not be around much longer.
>
> (Powell, 1971: 27)

Its four chapters were on drugs; electronics, sabotage and surveillance; natural, non-lethal and lethal weapons, and finally explosives and booby traps.

AQAP is based in Yemen, where a bitter civil war has been fought for years, and where Saudi Arabia has intervened militarily against the Houthis, a powerful rebel-group backed by Iran, and Zaydis Shia in nature; based in the north of the country (Salisbury, 2015). The predominantly Saudi Sunni (Salafi) Wahabi government's opposition to the Houthis, has been countered by support from predominantly Shia Tehran. The situation in Yemen continues to deteriorate, with the country enduring a major famine in 2018 as the main port, Hodeidah (held by the Houthi since 2014), has faced an air-bombardment from the Saudis (Borger, 2018).

In Yemen, an anarchic failed state is caught between a Saudi-Iranian proxy-war. It is the poorest country on the Arabic peninsula but also the second most populous, and AQAP has been ceded fertile ground to grow and prosper there (ibid.). The current leader of AQAP is its co-founder Qasim al-Raymi (Counter Extremism Project, 2018).

The second internet edition of AQAP's 'Inspire' e-zine featured an article entitled, 'The Ultimate Mowing Machine', in which the writer recommended the use of a pick-up truck to create a 'mowing machine, not to mow grass but mow down the enemies of Allah' (CNN Wire Staff, 2010). The target countries for these vehicular improvised Weapons of Mass Destruction (WMD's) included those which supported the:

> ... Israeli occupation of Palestine, the American invasion of Afghanistan and Iraq or countries that had a prominent role in the defamation of Muhammad.
>
> (Ibid.)

The article went on to recommend using a four-wheel drive pick-up truck in order:

> To achieve maximum carnage, you need to pick up as much speed as you can while still retaining good control of your vehicle in order to maximize your inertia and be able to strike as many people as possible in your first run.
>
> (Ibid.)

After laying out the approach for creating the maximum civilian casualties for the vehicular terror-assault, *Inspire* then continues in another article to recommend the use of guns in an attack:

> For this choose the best location. A random hit at a crowded restaurant in Washington, DC at lunch hour, for example, might end up knocking out a few government employees.
>
> (Ibid.)

Many of the *Inspire* articles clearly targeted individual 'lone-wolf' operators. The long-term strategy marks a shift from group-instigated complex plots, towards trying to empower the individual operative to be able to contribute to the cause in an effective and deadly manner. In the same edition of Imagine another article explains how pressure-cooker bombs can be used to devastating effect. These Improvised Explosive Devices (IEDs), encased in kitchen utensils packed with nails, are then detonated by the bomber. The first edition of *Inspire* had an article titled 'Make a Bomb in the Kitchen of your Mom', and the second edition gave the following chilling instructions:

> The pressurized cooker should be placed in crowded areas and left to blow up. More than one of these could be planted to explode at the same time. However, keep in mind that the range of the shrapnel in this operation is short range so the pressurized cooker or pipe should be placed close to the intended targets....
>
> (Ibid.)

Fruit of the poison tree ...

Home-made pressure cooker shrapnel IED devices were used at the US Boston Marathon bombings in 2013, resulting in three dead at the event and 260 injured (McPhee, 2018). Those responsible were the Tsarnaev brothers,

Muslim immigrants from the former Soviet republic of Kyrgyzstan, arriving in 2002 (biography.com, 2014). The deadliest case study of the deployment of pressure cooker bombs was at the Ariana Grande concert bombing in 2017 at the Manchester Arena, which resulted in 23 dead (including the bomber) and 800 received either physical or psychological injuries (MEN, 2018). The bomber was UK citizen Salman Abedi 22, who was in Libya in 2014 with his brother, and left as an evacuee, as that country became engulfed in the violent civil war that followed the collapse of the Gaddafi regime in 2011 (The Week, 2018).

On 14 July 2016, while the streets of the south-western city of Nice were crowded with French citizens celebrating Bastille Day, a lone terrorist drove a 19-tonne truck into them causing carnage. A grim total of 87 celebrants were mown-down and killed (including the perpetrator), while a further 450 were injured. The plans fomented in the article in AQAP's 2010 edition of *Inspire*, 'the ultimate mowing machine' had come to pass, on a mass-murder scale in Nice on France's national day. The attacker was a 31-year-old Tunisian man resident in France, and ISIS claimed responsibility for the incident, saying it was a response to their call-to-arms for jihadis throughout the world to fight against the US-led Coalition that was advancing against the Islamic State 'government', with its putative capital in Mosul, captured in 2014, and lost in July 2017 (Bergen, 2017; Burke, 2017).

Terror-cells throughout Europe and radicalized lone-wolf operators now no longer needed to have read *Inspire* online. The publicity surrounding the Nice attack, which reverberated worldwide on TV stations, radio networks, newspapers and social media posts, revealed how a determined, organized and single-minded operator, could acquire the means (trucks, small vans and even cars), to execute a simple low-tech plan which would have lethal consequences on unsuspecting civilian targets.

In contrast, the difficulties for those involved in bomb-making and deployment are many: acquiring the chemicals to manufacture home-made IEDs and suicide-vest bombs; the danger of being snooped-on while downloading instructions about how to build and detonate explosive devices; the problem of finding a safe-house where the materials could be stored, prepared and assembled; the inherent risks of the terrorists blowing themselves up as they constructed and transported their devices, and finally the possibility of security personnel intercepting the terrorist/s while delivering and transporting the IED to the target. In comparison, the ease and simplicity of hiring (or hijacking) a truck, car or van, and driving to the selected location before accelerating and driving at the civilian targets, such as those out enjoying the Bastille Day celebrations in Nice, are stark.

There is an old aphorism that states that the definition of stupidity is to keep repeating something that has failed. Terrorists who saw the success of the Nice truck attack in July 2016 were quick to desist from older, less successful methods, and adopt the more simple and successful approach by turning vehicles into mobile WMDs. This had a much smaller chance of prevention and detection of the plot, or failure due to the IED blowing-up the terrorist too early or failing to explode after being planted at the desired location.

Routine activities theory

A paradigm shift in the way terrorist attacks were being implemented had taken place. The movement by terrorist organizations to low-tech methods of attack, e.g. knives in mass-stabbing incidents or the use of vehicular WMDs, is a response to the range of increased security measures undertaken by governmental authorities. For instance, against the purchase of chemical precursors for bomb-making. A typical home-made IED will contain gasoline, propane and ammonium nitrate, the latter of which can be purchased easily as chemical fertilizer at garden centres, although not all fertilizers are made from ammonium nitrate (Rowan, 2010).

There is also the increasing surveillance of terrorist organizations' attempts to plan sophisticated bombing attacks by intelligence organizations like MI5 and Europol, and the increased communications monitoring of the internet to detect terrorists downloading instructions for bomb-making; or watching radicalizing videos posted by ISIS or Al-Qaeda.

Routine Activities Theory entails the re-interpretation and application of ideas developed by Park and Burgess (2012) in their classic study of the social ecology of crime in the city of Chicago. Their research findings are salient to the understanding of recent terrorist attacks in Europe due to shifting levels of 'public guardians'. Following the nine major consecutive bombing terror attacks, from the Pan Am flight 103 bombing over the UK in December 1988, to the Minsk Metro bombing in April 2011, it can be legitimately argued that the plethora of counter-measures undertaken by state and international intelligence and law enforcement authorities has increasingly choked-off the opportunities for terrorists to be able to plan, prepare, construct and successfully orchestrate attacks involving explosive devices. The 'public guardians' had become such a forceful and effective presence that the opportunities for a successful attack involving IEDs were severely retarded. Improvements in airport scanners, searches, detection and security devices all played their part. As did the significant expansion of the budgets, personnel, and technological/digital effectiveness of internet and mobile phone monitoring by organizations like the new Department of Homeland Security (DHS) in the US and MI5, after 9/11 and the July 2005 London bombings. In the UK, MI5, the Government Communication Headquarters (GCHQ) in Cheltenham and the Secret Intelligence Service (SIS), have undergone a profound and effective enlargement. Funding for all three comes from the Secret Intelligence Account (SIA), which has been at the level of £2 billion a year from 2011, £1.8 billion in 2015–2016, with a projected rise to £2.3 billion per year by 2021–2022 (MI5, 2018). MI5 currently employs 4,000 staff and spent 63 per cent of its entire budget in 2015–2016 on international counter-terrorism.

In the US, the budget for homeland security rose even more proportionately, from $19.5 billion in 2002, to $40,952,727 billion in 2016 (Homeland Security, 2011).

A hostile environment for terrorists

In addition to the increased spending on law enforcement and security intelligence undertaken by many Western powers since the 9/11 attacks and the London bombings of July 2005, the ability of terrorists to strike at high profile targets such as domestic and international aircraft flights has been severely restricted. Airport security has been significantly enhanced and made extremely difficult for terrorist groups to beat. Such security is comprised of two main types, the standardized physical screening processes which all passengers must navigate before boarding a plane, and the elevated risk-screening measures to which a certain type of passenger is subjected, say those from certain countries or from specific ethnic origins or religions (Alards-Tomalin *et al.*, 2014). The former involves luggage X-rays and metal detecting sensors, while the latter involves the much more intrusive and invasive pat-downs or even strip searches by airport security staff.

There have been several foiled terrorist plots against domestic and international flights recently. They include: Richard Reid, 'the Shoe-Bomber' who made a failed attempt to bring down a transatlantic jet in 2001 with a pair of IED's (Nesser, 2012). Reid was prevented from lighting the fuses in the Pentaerythritol Tetranitrate (PETN) hidden in his shoes by airline passengers and crew; there was also the liquid-bomb plot in the UK in 2006, which encompassed 18 attackers from an Al-Qaeda terror-cell, carrying liquid explosives disguised as personal drinks onto seven transatlantic flights from the UK to the US and Canada (Gardham, 2009). An estimated 5,000 passengers and crew would have been killed, along with a similar number of people underneath the falling wreckage. This threat has been neutralized by the imposition of restrictions on the amount (100ml maximum), type and nature of carry-on liquids at airport security checks (Bunker, 2017).

A security alert in March 2017 resulted in a ban on carry-on laptops/personal electronic devices in the passenger cabins of aircraft in both the US and UK. This followed an explosion on the Somali owned Daallo Airlines Flight 159 based in Dubai in February 2016, caused by a carry-on electronic device such as a laptop, tablet-computer or portable games console (ibid.). Such devices can still be checked into the cargo-holds or aircraft, due to the difficulty of triggering them by remote-timer or radio/mobile signals.

These counter-measures involved the use of increasingly sophisticated and effective airport security checks and intelligence techniques. The UK government stated its intention to employ a multi-layered approach to aircraft/airport security, that involved boosting the use and efficiency of body-scanners and explosive trace detection equipment as hard security measures; and the deployment of increased passenger profiling and 'watchlists' to intercept high-risk passengers who might attempt a terrorist attack (House of Commons Home Affairs Committee, 2010).

All these measures only relate to pre-departure screening of passengers. Further anti-hijacking tactics of planes in-flight included the covert deployment of 'sky marshals' among passengers, and increased fortification of doors to the cockpit to resist unauthorized entry (Meurant, 2013).

The ever more sophisticated and ubiquitous presence of airport security measures and pre-flight intelligence has severely constricted the opportunities for terrorists to succeed in plots against domestic and international airline flights. But, when one door closes, another opens.

The opening door

AQAP's *Inspire* web-magazine laid out how 'softer' targets could be hit by radicalized jihadi's in foreign countries. The lack of public guardians attributed by Park and Burgess (2012) in Chicago's high-crime 'zone of transition' is readily applicable to this shift in recent European terrorists' *modus operandi*. The image of balloon filled with air is relevant. When the authorities tightened their fist around one segment of the terrorist balloon, another expands commensurately to accommodate the displaced air. Hence, the difficulty of getting hold of guns in certain countries, the high-risk of failure of attacks aimed at hijacking and bombing aeroplanes, and the dangers and difficulties of planning, constructing and executing home-made IEDs/pressure cooker bombs, all led terror-plotters to adapt their tactics. The instructions contained within AQAP's *Inspire* e-zine and the devastating 'success' of the Nice truck attack in July 2016, proved a valuable roadmap for the new strategy for political violence.

Significantly, the absence of 'public guardians' is one of the key determinants of why the vehicular assault on large numbers of urban civilians works so well. In the UK, all you need to hire a vehicle is a photo-ID driving license, or paper license from before 31 March 2000. The hiring company may ask for a code with the photo-ID licence, but only to check online if there are any penalty points on the licence which do not show on the card (GOV.UK, 2015). However, medium weight and heavier weight vehicles can only be driven by those who possess the approved categories on their licence (C, C1, CE and C1E). These categories have Maximum Authorised Mass (MAM)[1] limits, which stretch from 750 kg for the smallest, to 12,000 kg for the largest (GOV.UK, 2018).

A similar lax hiring situation was exploited by the perpetrator of the Nice truck attack in July 2016. Mohamed Lahouaiej-Bouhlel had hired the 19 tonne refrigerated white cargo truck in Laurent-du-Var, just outside of Nice. Three days later the truck was used in the attack, which killed 87 (including the terrorist), in a 15-minute frenzy of smashing into pedestrians on the sidewalks (Reuters, 2016). Furthermore, terrorists can easily bypass such shallow vehicle hire restrictions by simply hijacking the vehicle instead.

The minimal security checks involved in hiring a heavy-weight vehicle provide those plotting to use them as vehicular WMDs with fertile opportunities for acquiring the means to carry out an attack, alongside the almost total lack of public guardians at the chosen site. All that is needed is a driving license with the required category on it, and then the murder-device can be accelerated into the selected targets. Although there may be a few police or security guards mingling among the crowds at the target-site, they are ineffective in stopping any class of vehicle, from car, van, large van or truck, from scything down dozens of pedestrians.

Cohen and Felson (1979) further developed the ideas of Park and Burgess (2012), into the more complete Routine Activities Theory when they analysed rising crime levels in many US cities in the 1970s. In addition to the lack of public guardians in certain spaces where people lived everyday aspects of their urban lives, they also highlighted the contribution which two other important factors could make: the presence, or lack thereof, of motivated offenders and second, the presence of suitable targets.

> ... despite their great diversity, direct-contact predatory violations share some important requirements which facilitate analysis of their structure. Each successfully completed violation minimally requires an offender with both criminal inclinations and the ability to carry out those inclinations, a person or object providing a suitable target for the offender, and absence of guardians capable of preventing violations.
> (Cohen and Felson, 1979: 590)

The core of Routine Activities Theory is the existence of the right physical, social and economic environment for predatory criminals to exploit, alongside the right timing. When their three key elements are all present and overlapping: motivated offenders, a lack of public guardians and plenty of easy victims; this is what Cohen and Felson (1979) termed the convergence of spatial (or city ecology) and temporal (in terms of timing) factors. When the presence of motivated offenders, easy victims and the lack of public guardians all overlap simultaneously in time and space in urban areas, then criminals and terrorists are presented with a perfect 'Goldilocks Zone' in which to operate. This is a term drawn from the Planetary Sciences, focused on the narrow range of space in solar systems for habitable planets to be situated (Rampino and Caldeira, 1994).

Motivated aspiring terrorists

The salience of Cohen and Felson's (1979) urban Routine Activities Theory model to the shifting *modus operandi* of European terrorist activities in the last decade is, boldy stated, that extremist radicalization of fanatical individuals into motivated terrorist offenders has been exacerbated by many recent historical events. Here, Routine Activities Theory reveals some parallels with the Rational Choice criminological theory, as an aetiology for understanding the drivers of terrorist behaviours (Crenshaw, 1981). The adoption of low-tech terror tactics is analogous to the selection of a criminal methodology which produces the greatest 'cost benefit calculations' for the participants, an entirely rational personal equation about the relative chance to succeed or fail. The presence of large numbers of easy victims in urban areas during holidays, festivals or sporting events, has provided terrorists with the greatest opportunity for slaying civilians in an indiscriminate vehicular assault. This is a kind of anti-Utilitarian approach (Mill, 2016), whereby the most death and carnage is to be inflicted for the least risk and cost to the terror-plotter.

However, many recent historical events could be interpreted in a different manner to the promulgation of this Routine Activities Theory/Rational Choice Theory to the rise of low-tech tactics. Such occurrences can be perceived to have alternatively promoted an intense visceral anger among radical Islamic terrorists towards those Western states which have been blamed for orchestrating various outcomes. These furious responses among individuals and groups fall more within structural and psychological theories as drivers of terrorist actions (ibid.). Foreign interventions in countries like Afghanistan, Iraq and Syria etc., can be seen to have caused a far more emotional response among those affected: hatred, anger, the desire for retribution, justice and reparations, these are all instead seen as the sources of terrorist motivations. Salient historical events include:

- The US-led Coalition/s invasions of both Afghanistan and Iraq; the proxy-war fought between the US ally (Sunni) Saudi Arabia and (Shia) Iran via their interventions in civil-war torn Yemen. Resentment against Western 'Crusaders' killing Muslims has multiplied and fuelled hatred, inspiring many to try to join local resistance groups, or launch terrorist attacks to punish those countries involved (Warrick, 2015).
- The lack of any coherent and pragmatic plans for governing Afghanistan and Iraq after the Taliban (under Mullah Omar), and Ba'athist regimes (under Saddam Hussein), were ousted. Fanatics and radical Islamic groupings flourished in the anarchic regions of these post-regime change states (ibid.).
- Tensions in the Middle East between the US's regional ally Israel, and theocratic Shia Mullah governed, Iran (Kaye, Nader and Roshan, 2011).
- Civil war in the Syria of incumbent dictator Bashar al-Assad, whose Ba'athist regime resorted to the use of terror weapons against its own population, using chemical weapons (chlorine gas) and barrel-bombs (The Economist, 2013).
- The rapid rise of the 'Caliphate' declared by Islamic State in large sections of Iraq and Syria, exemplified by the capture in 2014 of its capital city Mosul from Iraq, under the leadership of Abu Bakr al-Baghdadi, the self-declared Caliph (Warrick, 2015). This led to a sudden influx of radicalized foreign jihadis into Islamic State controlled territories, to aid the

fight for the Caliphate and its yearning vision of the restoration of a mythical seventh-century utopia; harking back to a medieval theocratic rule embodied by Sharia Law, based on the principals of Islamic jurisprudence. This has become known as the 'Frozen Time' hypothesis (Ruggiero, 2017b), which inspired many Islamic radicals to become supporters, jihadis or foreign terrorists. Hence:

> ... sharia guides all aspects of Muslim life, including daily routines, familial and religious obligations, and financial dealings. It is derived primarily from the Quran and the Sunna – the sayings, practices, and teachings of the Prophet Mohammed. Precedents and analogy applied by Muslim scholars are used to address new issues. The consensus of the Muslim community also plays a role in defining this theological manual.
>
> (Johnson and Sergie, 2014)

- The exodus of many of those who survived the fall of Islamic State's Caliphate after the loss of Mosul in July 2017. This represents a 'reverse diaspora' in which battle-hardened ISIS fighters attempted, and often succeeded, in making their way back undetected to their original countries. In the UK, this has led to an estimated 425 jihadis covertly returning, out of total known contingent of 850, including 100 women and 50 children, the largest contingent of any European country. Beyond Europe even more have returned: to Turkey (900), Tunisia (800) and Saudi Arabia (760) (Dearden, 2017). The security threats from these unwelcome homecomers are both shrouded and potentially lethal.
- The adoption of the internet to spread the propaganda of right-wing nationalism or fundamentalist Islam; by Al-Qaeda (Afghanistan, Northern Pakistan and Yemen, etc.) (Burke, 2017); Islamic State (Syria and Iraq); Hamas (Palestinian Territories/Gaza) and Hezbollah, centred in southern Lebanon (Laqueur and Schueftan, 2016). Such agitprop propaganda includes: a series of grizzly videoed decapitations of Western Christian captives, with either long-knives or short hacking tools, like those carried out by 'The Beatles',[2] the four young British ISIS recruits who are alleged to have carried out 27 beheadings while masked and commentating over their recordings of the murders (Sommerville, 2018); the e-zine *Inspire* published by AQAP since 2010 (CNN Wire Staff, 2010); recordings of training videos for domestic and foreign jihadis; various 'victories' for the organiZations, such as the declaration of the Caliphate by Abu Bakr al-Baghdadi from the minbar[3] of the Grand al-Nuri mosque in Mosul, with its famous leaning minaret, shortly after its capture in 2014[4] (CBS News, 2017).

Easy victims

The second of Cohen and Felson's (1979) three Routine Activities Theory determinants, in terms of their spatial and temporal overlap, is the presence of numerous easy victims. In their thesis, crowds of urban populations and the businesses they frequent, provide a panoply of targets for criminals to victimize. In the application of Routine Activities Theory to terrorism, the same factor is apparent. For example, in the Bastille Day attack in Nice in July 2016, the attacker drove his large cargo truck down the pavements for 2 km, which were crowded with civilians flocking to the city centre to enjoy the festivities in the restaurants, bars and cafes. Eighty-six pedestrians were killed and the only barrier the driver faced was swerving to avoid some police cars that were blocking access to the centre of Nice (Bergen, 2017; Reuters, 2016). People were scythed-down like grass stalks in this realization of AQAP's 'ultimate mowing machine' (CNN Wire Staff, 2010). The attack finished when police shot the attacker dead as he emerged with a pistol from the truck's cab.

A new twist on the terrorist exploitation of a plenitude of soft-human targets came in the following major terrorist incident in Europe, the Munich shopping mall shooting on 22 July 2016, only eight days after the Nice truck attack. Here, an 18-year-old lone-wolf nationalist German-Iranian man, shot dead nine people, wounded 16 others and finally killed himself (Associated Press, 2016). The Bavarian mall was crowded with shoppers at the time. The date was exactly five years on from when another right-wing nationalist, Anders Breivik, killed 77 people in Norway.

There are some contradictory facts when gun laws in Germany are considered following the Munich mass shooting. On the one hand, the country has the fourth highest level of gun-ownership in the world (two million Germans own 5.5 million firearms, out of a total population of 80 million), but it also has some of the strictest gun laws (Anderson, 2016).

The aetiological elements that helped spawn the Nice truck attack and then the Munich shopping mall mass shooting, both fit comfortably within Cohen and Felson's (1979) Routine Activities Theory hypothesis of three overlapping factors: motivated offenders, easy targets and an absence of public guardians; although the Nice attack was executed through the use of a vehicular WMD, while Munich involved a firearm.

In 2017 terrorists begin to successfully combine these different tactics for indiscriminate mass-attacks, but with vehicles and knives rather than guns, in the London Bridge attack.

An absence of public guardians

On the evening of 19 December 2016, Anis Amri, a Tunisian, drove a hijacked truck through Berlin's Breitscheidplatz market vendors and visitors, killing 11 and injuring over 50. He had earlier shot dead the Polish driver of the truck. After fleeing the scene, he was finally shot dead at a routine police check in Italy (Chase, 2017). As a consequence of this attack, which exploited the lack of public guardians in these urban spatial and temporal events, when 2,600 Christmas markets opened in Germany a year later, many concrete barriers had been placed around them, and significantly more security staff were present (Alkousaa, 2017).

Eight people were killed and 48 injured, including four police officers, by three terrorists in a combined assault in London on the evening of Saturday 3 June 2017. The three perpetrators were later shot dead by armed police in the Borough Market area of London, taking the total death-toll to 11. The attackers had crashed their van and then abandoned it, after they had used it to mount the pavement on London Bridge and smash into the pedestrians in their path. All three fled the scene with 30 cm long pink ceramic knives tied to their wastes and headed to Borough Market before they were killed by armed police, who fired 46 shots at the three men (BBC News, 2018).

Khuram Butt, Rachid Redouane and Youssef Zaghba were the three terrorists, and the numbers of dead would have been much higher had they managed to hire a 7.5 tonne truck, which they failed to pick up from a rental company as they had not presented the necessary payment details. They resorted to using a smaller Renault van instead. When police raided a flat used by the three as a safe-house, they discovered a copy of the Quran opened on a page about martyrdom (Symonds, 2017). Three victims died during the vehicular assault on London Bridge, and the other five civilians killed were people out and about on the streets and in the bars and restaurants of Borough Market. Later, four Molotov cocktails were found unused, stashed in the back of the crashed van (ibid.).

The three overlapping elements, spatially and temporally, of Cohen and Felson's (1979) Routine Activities Theory can be exposed in the London Bridge attack. First, motivated radicalized Islamic jihadis; second, the unprotected and unaware crowds of pedestrians and shoppers on the bridge and in the market area; third, the lack of public guardians present to deter attacks. Ordinary people, going about their quotidian evening leisure activities provided all the victims needed for a small terrorist cell to conduct a deadly twin method low-tech attack.

Europe's last major terrorist incident unfolded in a series of connected events in Catalonia which resulted in 16 dead civilians, eight dead attackers, and over 150 injured victims. On 16 August 2017, three jihadis blew themselves up accidentally, at their HQ/bomb factory in Alcanar, a few kilometres down the Mediterranean coast from Cambrils. The cell's leader, Moroccan imam Abdelbaki Es Satty, was one of those killed. Police found 120 gas cannisters in the wreckage of the house and the explosion forced the remaining members of the terror-cell to resort to vehicular assaults as an ad hoc back-up plan. On 17 and 18 August 2017 a white van, driven by Younes Abouyaaqoub, 22, was driven down Las Ramblas, a pedestrianized avenue in Barcelona, in the late afternoon. The driver aimed to hit the many tourists and locals in the area, killing 14. He eventually abandoned the vehicle and fled on foot. He then hijacked a car, stabbing the driver to death and drove off with the dead man in the back seat, before abandoning the car and being shot dead on 21 August 2017. Eight hours later, in the town of Cambrils, 100km down the coast, a black Audi A3 car ploughed into pedestrians, killing one. Five terrorists wearing fake suicide belts jumped out of the car, which had crashed and overturned. Four were shot dead at the scene, and the other shot dead later after a chase (BBC News, 2017).

The Catalonia attacks revealed the risks of premature self-annihilation when plotters attempted to construct home-made IEDs. Also, the presence of motivated attackers in a terror-cell under the command of their radical imam ringleader. Finally, the lack of meaningful security barriers or public guardians in the bustling urban streets of Barcelona/Cambrils. All three elements feature in the core of Routine Activities Theory. Furthermore, it shows how AQAP's 'ultimate mowing machine' could still reap a significant death-toll, despite being used in haste as a desperate improvised back-up plan once the terror-cell's main tactic had literally been blown sky-high. The effectiveness of their move towards more low-tech tactics, from more complex and technological ones like bomb-making, is evident. The easy source of victimization for terrorists includes: shoppers, festival-celebrants, holiday-makers and those enjoying every day urban leisure pursuits like café's, restaurants, concerts and drinking with friends in the streets.

'Hybrids' and low-tech terror tactics

The move by European terrorist organizations towards using simple, effective and more deadly methods in the last decade, allows us to consider the relevance of the postulation that organized crime has been collaborating with terror networks. Does a European crime-terror nexus exist (Basra and Neumann, 2016)?

The primary aspiration of organized criminal networks is to enhance and secure the streams of profits from activities such as: people trafficking and smuggling, modern slavery, illegal drug production and their import/export, illicit drug supply down to street-level dealers and sales to individual consumers, prostitution and sex workers, cybercrime and fraud, both online and offline. In contrast, terrorist organizations' goals and methods are very discreet from this, with their aims far more ideological and political, to be achieved through the application of indiscriminate attacks upon ordinary citizens (Campbell, 2014). This can be either state sponsored violence, or aggression from more demotic sources.

Evidence corroborates Campbell's (2014) assertion that the two illegal entities, organized crime and terrorist organizations, are separate entities in their compositions, goals, strategies and tactics. Where is the financial gain for the sponsoring body, when a large truck is hijacked, driven to a crowded inner-city area and used as a vehicular WMD? The facilitation of indiscriminate attacks on urban pedestrians, either crushed to death or after suffering lethal impact-traumas from the vehicle, indubitably generates no financial inducements for organized crime. Indeed, the converse is far more likely. Business activities and the footfall of customers pursuing shopping and leisure pastimes often falls dramatically in the location where the terrorist attack occurred. For example, the number of tourists who went to Tunisia in 2014 was 7.4 million, while in 2015 the figure nosedived to 5.3 million following the deaths of 39 tourists (30 from the UK) after a mass shooting on the beachfront at Sousse. The figure rose to 7.1 million in 2017 as the memories of the 2015 incident faded, and new security measures were implemented (Amara, 2018).

Visitor numbers to central London tourist attractions fell by 17 per cent between May 2017 and mid-September 2017, compared with the same period in 2016 (Hornall, 2017). This followed the terrorist incident at London Bridge/Borough Market in June 2017 in which 11 died, including the three perpetrators.

The number of visitors to Turkey, which were 36.8 million in 2014, subsequently crashed to 25.3 million in 2016 following the failed coup attempt against President Erdogan's regime in that year (Anadolu Agency, 2018). The increasingly authoritarian president has labelled those who participated in the abortive attempt to overthrow the government in Ankara as members of a terrorist organization (Fethüllahist Terrorist Organisation – FETÖ). Within 24 hours of the coup attempt, 265 were killed, including 47 innocent civilians and over 100 plotters, according to president Erdogan (Worley, 2016).

The economic effects of state sponsored violence on their own citizens can be equally calamitous. Annual Gross Domestic Product (GDP) growth in China was 7.9 per cent in 1980, 3.8 per cent in 1990, and 8.4 per cent in the year 2000 (*Guardian*, 2012). On 4 June 1989 the Communist regime ordered the Peoples Liberation Army (PLA) into Tiananmen Square to clear out predominantly student democracy protesters, resulting in the deaths of an estimated 10,000 people. This barbarous example of state terrorism and repression against its own civilian population, concluded with the bayoneting to death of the wounded and the hosing of burnt human remains down the square's drains (Lusher, 2017). Unsurprisingly, the numbers of US tourists to China crashed by 80 per cent immediately following the massacre (Kramer, 1990).

Political violence from terrorists frequently leads to a massive decline in business in the affected city, region or country. This is the case for both legitimate business interests like shops, tourist attractions and the leisure and hotel business, and for illegitimate enterprises, such as drug sales, pickpocketing, visits to prostitutes and sex workers or unlicensed gambling. Less visitors and customers in the 'black economy', like their legal counterparts, are bad for profits. Consequently, the participation, financing, or facilitation of terrorist activities and attacks is fundamentally inimical to the raison d'etre of organized criminal networks, whose primary goal is to maintain and enhance profit streams from their fomenting of the black economy.

The 'hybrids' thesis is further weakened when the ideas of Ruggiero (2017a) are applied to the recent low-tech terror tactics being employed in Europe. The social configurations within the binary criminal/terrorist organizations are entirely discreet. While terrorist groups require tight-knit homogenous memberships to successfully execute their plots, the reverse is true of organized crime gangs. When a terror-cell plans to carry out an attack and attempts to carry it out, an ideological consensus among the groups members is vital to preserve their mutual loyalty, commitment, secrecy and the viability of the operation. However, membership of organized criminal networks is far more heterogeneous in composition. They usually collaborate in an ad hoc manner, with the aim of jointly ensuring mutual profits for the disparate but overlapping elements (ibid.). Criminal gangs and their affiliates are only bound together loosely and temporally by their common greed for illicit profits. They have created a mutually beneficial *modus vivendi*.

Many of the low-tech terror assaults like the Nice truck attack, the Munich shopping centre mass shooting or the Berlin Christmas market attack, were carried out by 'lone-wolves'. Such single operations, often by people who are relatively unknown to the authorities or even total 'clean-skins',[5] puts them completely outside of the active cooperating participants of criminal networks. The lone-wolf may have an ideological commitment to the terrorists' cause, but they are frequently acting unilaterally when they plot and execute their low-tech indiscriminate attacks on civilians. Using trucks, cars and vans to unleash carnage on urban pedestrians by turning them into vehicular WMDs, puts them completely outside the milieu of criminal gangs, whose separate memberships work together for mutual profit. Lone-wolfs are isolated, singular and while frequently taking their philosophical and ideological cues from the online propaganda of a terrorist organization, are not actively collaborating with them. Nor do they seek any financial profit from their actions, their goal is the furtherance of radical political or religious objectives, including their own possible 'martyrdom' for the cause (Campbell, 2014; Ruggiero, 2017b).

The only credible support for the existence of a crime-terror nexus in Europe lies in the concept that members of both organizations have transferable skills, which can be used productively as a member of either group (Ruggiero, 2017a). These might include security skills, operational tactics in avoiding detection by security forces and fundraising activities to boost the financial resources of the group. There is evidence that members of both crime and terror groups have crossed-over from one to another at some point. However, this does not mean that they are currently active in both at the present, merely their trajectory involved an earlier affiliation with the now abandoned former criminal/terror entity (Basra and Neumann, 2016).

Conclusion

The challenges that governments, intelligence services and the police face by the changing tactics employed by European terrorists are profound, including:

- Home-made pressure cooker IEDs rammed with nails and fertilizer;
- Hired or hijacked lorries and vans used to mow down pedestrians;
- Gun or knife wielding lone-wolves or terror-cells, who commit indiscriminate mass-shootings and stabbings in busy urban areas;
- The increased radicalization of Islamic fanatics fed an online diet of English language propaganda advocating revenge, punishment or retaliation against Western powers who are perceived to be existential threats to Muslims, or to areas controlled by Al-Qaeda or Islamic State;
- The online publication of instructions on how to plan, construct and execute terror assaults using low-tech means;
- The returning jihadi diaspora that have fled ISIS controlled lands in the fallen Caliphate surrounding Mosul, battle-hardened and trained in combat.

What can the intelligence services and police do about the threats posed by the successful adoption of low-tech tactics by European terrorists?

Earlier, the image of a fist squeezing a balloon filled with air was used to help explain the changing tactics employed by terrorists. When airport and airline security tightened, plotters moved onto more viable targets, namely civilians going about their daily lives or routine activities. This provided fertile ground for motivated offenders to victimize people using low-tech but devastating new approaches. The attraction for terror-plotters was augmented by the relative absence of public guardians to protect unsuspecting crowds at festivals, markets, tourist locations or celebrations.

So far, the policy of governments, intelligence agencies and police forces has appeared to be reactive. Installing concrete bollards to protect Christmas markets the following year, or erecting Vehicle Security Barriers (VSBs) on bridges, after the latest atrocity (Edwards, 2017). However, this perception does not take account of the large number of failed and foiled plots which are stopped, which provided the bulk of the 1,219 arrestees in the 28 EU countries in 2017 (Europol, 2018). But, the statement issued by the Provisional Irish Republican Army (PIRA) in 1984 after the Grand Hotel Brighton bomb which failed to kill UK Prime Minister Margaret Thatcher,[6] remains disturbingly apposite:

> Today we were unlucky, but remember, we only have to be lucky once; you will have to be lucky always.
>
> (MacGuill, 2014)

For terror-plotters there are undoubtedly plenty of new soft targets in urban spaces, filled with potential victims whom the motivated offenders can easily prey upon without worrying too much about the presence of a police deterrence.

It is certainly true that Europe's police have enhanced their capabilities in terms of the rapid deployment of armed-response squads when an assault is underway, thus significantly reducing the number of potential victims, but again, this is a reactive measure, merely limiting the damage.

Politicians have protected themselves and other high-risk/visible targets with the use of 'Rings of Steel' and 'Rings of Concrete', but such measures may have led to a state of 'splintered-urbanism', whereby the great and the good are predominantly safe behind their fortified barriers. The rest of the urban population remains vulnerable to low-tech terror assaults as they go about their daily routine activities (Coaffee, 2004).

Notes

1 MAM refers to maximum loaded weight of the vehicle, also known as Gross Vehicle Weight (GVW).
2 Another term objected to by the #WordsMatter campaign, for glamourizing terrorist cells.
3 A flight of steps/platform for Imams to address Islamic worshipers in mosques.
4 ISIS blew up the 800-year-old building before the city was recaptured by Iraqi forces in 2017.
5 Terrorists entirely unknown to the police and intelligence services.
6 The bomb did kill five, including a Conservative MP, and injured 34 others.

References

AFP (2015) 'Armed Clashes on Macedonia-Kosovo Border: Five Police Killed', *Telegraph*, 10 May 2015.

Alards-Tomalin, D., Ansons, T.L., Reich, T.C., Sakamoto, Y., Davie, R., Leboe-McGowan, J.P. and Leboe-McGowan, L.C. (2014), 'Airport Security Measures and Their Influence on Enplanement Intentions: Responses from Leisure Travelers Attending a Canadian University', *Journal of Air Transport Management*, 37: 60–68.

Alkousaa, R. (2017), 'Germany's Christmas Markets Open Under Tight Security a Year After Attack', *Reuters*, https://uk.reuters.com/article/uk-christmas-season-germany/germanys-christmas-markets-open-under-tight-security-a-year-after-attack-idUKKBN1DR2HE (accessed 3 September 2018).

Amara, T. (2018), 'Tunisia Sees Record Tourist Numbers in 2018 as Attack Effect Fades', *Reuters*.

Anadolu Agency (2018), 'Turkey Expects 40 Million Tourists from Abroad in 2018: Experts'.

Anderson, A. (2016) *Five Things to Know about Guns in Germany*, www.thelocal.de/20160616/five-things-to-know-about-guns-in-germany-us-gun-control-laws (accessed 16 August 2018).

Associated Press (2016) *Police Hunt for Motive in Munich Shooting that Killed 9*, www.foxnews.com/world/police-hunt-for-motive-in-munich-shooting-that-killed-9 (accessed 15 August 2018).

Basra, R. and Neumann, P.R. (2016), 'Criminal Pasts, Terrorist Futures: European Jihadists and the New Crime-terror Nexus', *Perspectives on Terrorism*, 10(6): 25–40.
BBC News (2017), 'Barcelona Attacks: What We Know So Far', *BBC News*.
BBC News (2018), 'London Attack: What Happened', *BBC News*.
Bergen, P. (2017), *Truck Attacks – A Frightening Tool of Terror, With a History*, www.cnn.com/2016/07/14/opinions/truck-attacks-tactic-analysis-bergen/index.html (accessed 1 August 2018).
biography.com (2014), *Dzhokhar Tsarnaev Biography*, www.biography.com/people/dzhokhar-tsarnaev-21196765 (accessed 12 August 2018).
Black, I. (2013), 'Inspire Magazine the Self Help Manual for al Qaida Terrorists'.
Blighty, *The Economist* (2013), 'The Vote of Shame'.
Borger, J. (2018), 'Deadly Yemen Famine Could Strike At Any Time, Warns UN Boss', *Guardian*.
Bunker, R.J. (2017), *Laptop Bombs and Civil Aviation: Terrorism Potentials and Carry On Travel Bans*, http://trendsinstitution.org/wp-content/uploads/2017/07/Bunker-Laptop-Bombs-and-Civil-Aviation-Working-Paper-July-2017-Final.pdf (accessed 4 August 2018).
Burke, J. (2017), 'Rise and Fall of Isis: Its Dream of a Caliphate is Over, So What Now?', *Observer*.
Campbell, L. (2014), 'Organized Crime and National Security: A Dubious Connection?', *New Criminal Law Review: In International and Interdisciplinary Journal*, 17(2): 220–251.
CBS News (2017), *Iconic Mosque where ISIS Leader Declared Caliphate Destroyed*, www.cbsnews.com/news/iconic-al-nuri-mosque-mosul-destroyed/ (accessed 26 August 2018).
Chase, J. (2017), *A Year on From Terror Attack, Berlin Christmas Market Opens Calmly Germany News and In Depth Reporting from Berlin and Beyond DW 27.11.2017*, www.dw.com/en/a-year-on-from-terror-attack-berlin-christmas-market-opens-calmly/a-41547811 (accessed 13 September 2018).
Chrisafis, A. (2015), 'Charlie Hebdo Attackers: Born, Raised and Radicalised in Paris', 12 January.
CNN (2018), *2015 Paris Terror Attacks CNN*, https://edition.cnn.com/2015/12/08/europe/2015-paris-terror-attacks-fast-facts/index.html (accessed 10 July 2018).
CNN Wire Staff (2010), *New Issue of Magazine Offers Jihadists Terror Tips – CNN.com*, www.cnn.com/2010/WORLD/meast/10/12/mideast.jihadi.magazine/index.html (accessed 12 June 2018).
Coaffee, J. (2004), 'Rings of Steel, Rings of Concrete and Rings of Confidence: Designing out Terrorism in Central London Pre and Post September 11th', *International Journal of Urban and Regional Research*, 28(1): 201–211.
Cohen, L.E. and Felson, M. (1979), 'Social Change and Crime Rate Trends: A Routine Activities Approach', *American Sociological Review*, 44(4): 588–608.
Counter Extremism Project (2018), *Al-Qaeda in the Arabian Peninsula (AQAP)*, www.counterextremism.com/threat/al-qaeda-arabian-peninsula-aqap (accessed 22 June 2018).
Crenshaw, M. (1981), 'The Causes of Terrorism', *Comparative Politics*, 13(4): 379–399.
Davis, C. (2018), 'No 'Lone Wolf': Media Urged to Take Care Over Terrorism Vocabulary'.

Dearden, L. (2017), *Over 400 Isis Jihadis have Already Returned to the UK*, www.independent.co.uk/news/uk/home-news/isis-british-jihadis-return-uk-iraq-syria-report-islamic-state-fighters-europe-threat-debate-terror-a8017811.html (accessed 30 August 2018).

Drury, J., Cocking, C. and Reicher, S. (2009), 'The Nature of Collective Resilience: Survivor Reactions to the 2005 London Bombings', *International Journal of Mass Emergencies and Disasters*, 27(1): 66–95.

Edwards, T. (2017), 'London Attack: Safeguarding our Bridges', *BBC News*.

Europol (2018), *EUROPEAN UNION TERRORISM SITUATION AND TREND REPORT 2018 (TESAT 2018)*, www.europol.europa.eu/activities-services/main-reports/european-union-terrorism-situation-and-trend-report-2018-tesat-2018 (accessed 15 September 2018).

Gardham, D. (2009), 'Airline Terror Trial The Bomb Plot to Kill 10,000 People Telegraph'.

GOV.UK (2015), *Hiring a Vehicle*, www.gov.uk/government/news/hiring-a-vehicle (accessed 17 July 2018).

GOV.UK (2018), *Vehicle Weights Explained*, www.gov.uk/vehicle-weights-explained (accessed 12 August 2018).

Guardian (2012), *China GDP: How it has Changed Since 1980*, www.theguardian.com/news/datablog/2012/mar/23/china-gdp-since-1980 (accessed 23 June 2018).

Homeland Security (2011), *DHS Budget*, www.dhs.gov/dhs-budget (accessed 1 August 2018).

Hornall, T. (2017), 'Record Number of Tourists Visit UK Despite Terror Attacks in 2017', *Independent (Online)*, 26 December.

House of Commons Home Affairs Committee (2010), *Home Affairs Committee 9th Report. Counter-Terrorism Measures in British Airports*, www.publicinformationonline.com/download/15178 (accessed 13 April 2018).

Johnson, T. and Sergie, M.A. (2014), 'Islam: Governing Under Sharia', *Council on Foreign Relations*.

Kaye, D.D., Nader, A. and Roshan, P. (2011), *Israel and Iran: A Dangerous Rivalry*, RAND National Defense Research Institute Santa Monica, CA, www.dtic.mil/dtic/tr/fulltext/u2/a554597.pdf (accessed 7 September 2018).

Kramer, C. (1990), 'China After Tiananmen Square', *New York Times*.

Laqueur, W. and Schueftan, D. (2016), *The Israel-Arab Reader: A Documentary History of the Middle East Conflict: Eighth Revised and Updated Edition*, London: Penguin.

Lusher, A. (2017), *At Least 10,000 People Died in Tiananmen Square Massacre, Secret British Cable Alleges*, www.independent.co.uk/news/world/asia/tiananmen-square-massacre-death-toll-secret-cable-british-ambassador-1989-alan-donald-a8126461.html (accessed 18 August 2018).

MacGuill, D. (2014), *30 Years Ago Tonight, the IRA Tried to Murder Margaret Thatcher*, www.thejournal.ie/brighton-bomb-margaret-thatcher-ira-1718475-Oct2014/ (accessed 14 April 2018).

May, M. (2011), *How to Deal with Belarus? New Approaches in EU–Belarus Relations* DEU.

McPhee, M. (2018), *Whoever Built the Boston Marathon Bombs is Still on the Loose, Able to Kill Again*, www.newsweek.com/2018/01/19/boston-marathon-bomb-maker-loose-776742.html (accessed 13 July 2018).

MEN (2018), *Manchester Terror Attack*, www.manchestereveningnews.co.uk/all-about/manchester-terror-attack (accessed 19 May 2018).

Meurant, G. (2013), *Airport, Aircraft, and Airline Security*, London: Elsevier.

MI5 (2018), *People and Organisation MI5 The Security Service*, www.mi5.gov.uk/people-and-organisation (accessed 12 July 2018).

Mill, J.S. (2016), 'Utilitarianism', *Seven Masterpieces of Philosophy*, New York: Routledge, pp. 337–383.

Nesser, P. (2012), 'Research Note: Single Actor Terrorism: Scope, Characteristics and Explanations', *Perspectives on Terrorism*, 6(6): 61–73.

Park, R.E. and Burgess, E.W. (2012), *The City*, Chicago: University of Chicago Press.

Powell, W. (1971), *The Anarchist-Cookbook*, http://archive.org/details/anarchist-cookbook-william-powell_201609 (accessed 6 March 2018).

Rampino, M.R. and Caldeira, K. (1994), 'The Goldilocks Problem: Climatic Evolution and Long-term Habitability of Terrestrial Planets', *Annual Review of Astronomy and Astrophysics*, 32(1): 83–114.

Reuters (2016), 'Timeline: The Bastille Day Attack in Nice', *Reuters*.

Rose, W., Murphy, R. and Abrahms, M. (2007), 'Does Terrorism Ever Work? The 2004 Madrid Train Bombings', *International Security*, 32(1): 185–192.

Rowan, K. (2010), *How Do Fertilizer Bombs Work?*, www.livescience.com/6413-fertilizer-bombs-work.html (accessed 18 March 2018).

Ruggiero, V. (2017a), *Dirty Money: On Financial Delinquency*, Oxford: Oxford University Press.

Ruggiero, V. (2017b), *TAKEDOWN: Understand the Dimensions of Organised Crime and Terrorist Networks for Developing Effective and Efficient Security Solutions for First-line-practitioners and Professionals*, London: Albawaba (London) Ltd, https://search.proquest.com/docview/1788434372 (accessed 3 February 2018).

Salisbury, P. (2015), *Yemen and the Saudi-Iranian "Cold War"*, The Royal Institute of International Affairs, http://gateway.proquest.com/openurl?url_ver=Z39.88-2004&res_dat=xri:policyfile&rft_dat=xri:policyfile:article:00173947 (accessed 17 February 2018).

Schmid, A.P. (2012), 'The Revised Academic Consensus Definition of Terrorism', *Perspectives on Terrorism*, 6(2).

Sommerville, Q. (2018), 'Face to Face with "the Beatles", the Isis Torture Squad', *The Observer*, 12 August.

Sputniknews (2018), *Deadliest Terrorist Attacks in France: From Charlie Hebdo to Champs Elysees*, https://sputniknews.com/europe/201803231062841974-deadliest-terrorist-attacks-france/ (accessed 11 September 2018).

Symonds, T. (2017), 'London Attackers 'Planned to Use Lorry''', *BBC News*.

The Week (2018), *Salman Abedi: Manchester Bomber Rescued by Royal Navy Prior to Attack*, www.theweek.co.uk/95452/salman-abedi-manchester-bomber-rescued-by-royal-navy-prior-to-attack (accessed 17 April 2018).

Thoresen, S., Flood Aakvaag, H., Wentzel-Larsen, T., Dyb, G. and Kristian Hjemdal, O. (2012), 'The Day Norway Cried: Proximity and Distress in Norwegian Citizens Following the 22nd July 2011 Terrorist Attacks in Oslo and on Utøya Island', *European Journal of Psychotraumatology*, 3(1): 1–11.

Warrick, J. (2015), *Black Flags: The Rise of ISIS*, New York: Anchor.

Worley, W. (2016), 'Prime Minister Says 265 People Killed in Attempted Military Coup, Including at Least 100 "Plotters"', *Independent (Online)*, 16 July.

7 Global system dynamics in the relationships between organized crime and terrorist groups[1]

Inmaculada Marrero Rocha

Introduction

As stated by the Secretary General of the United Nations:

> Terrorism and transnational organized crime are distinct phenomena, have different ways of working and aims, and are addressed through different international legal frameworks. Despite the differences, for the past 15 years the General Assembly and the Security Council have been considering how terrorists interact with transnational organized crime groups because such interactions are increasingly affecting international peace and security.
>
> (UN Secretary General, 2015: 1)

However, the relationship between organized crime and terrorism is not a new issue and has been widely analysed by different disciplines, such as sociology, criminology, political science and security studies (Ruggiero and Leyva, 2017; Ruggiero, 2019). Relations between ethno-nationalist terrorist groups or extremist ideologies with organized crime groups with a strong national identity have had a very important place in the research agenda (Shelley and Picarelli, 2005; Stohl, 2008). Research has broadly addressed the similarities and differences between criminal violence and political violence, examining the organizational characteristics of those who practice them, the particularities of their respective memberships and the nature of the activities they carry out (Sanderson, 2004). Both types of groups, despite mainly limiting their activity to national contexts, have been able to develop a degree of internationalization necessary to progress in their illegal businesses and in their political goals, respectively. In the past, however, the two types of organizations have lacked a worldwide joint strategy (Schmid, 1996).

The evolution of relational networks

More recently, efforts have been made to understand the new types of relationships between terrorist groups and organized crime groups, as both seem to become increasingly complex and heterogeneous, to attract a diversity of actors and to establish direct connections among them (Hutchinson and O'Malley, 2007). Most recent studies aim to offer models that explain the new relational dynamics between the two, while assessing the nature, intensity and consequences of the links established (Makarenko, 2004; De Boer and Bosetti, 2015; Kessels and Hennessy, 2017). These explanatory models have been developed following specific cases of collaboration between terrorism and organized crime, cases that occurred in various regions. Such collaboration, however, appears to go beyond, for example, the exchange of arms for drugs between the Irish Republican Army (IRA) and the Revolutionary Armed Forces of Colombia (FARC), or the training in handling explosives offered by Euskadi Ta Askartasuna (ETA) to the FARC in exchange for drugs (EU Parliament, 2012: 22). Other examples include the collaboration in heroin trafficking aimed at securing funds, during the Kosovo conflict, between the Albanian Mafia and the Kosovo Liberation Army (Proksik, 2017). But also the exchange of drugs for weapons between criminal organizations such as the Calabrian 'Ndrangheta or the Neapolitan Camorra and Islamist terrorist cells based on Italian territory (Curtis and Karacan, 2002).

The new connections also transcend the specific exchange of tactics that took place in past decades, such as the use of terrorism by criminals who tried to intimidate institutions and citizens for political ends. Examples of this were the murders of judges Giovanni Falcone and Paolo Borsellino, in 1992, at the hands of the Sicilian mafia, or the series of attacks perpetrated by the Medellín drug cartel in reaction to the Colombian government's policies regarding the extradition of drug traffickers to the US at the end of the 1980s. Also, groups regarded as terrorist, such as the Kurdish Workers' Party (PKK), the Corsica National Liberation Front (FLNC) or the Irish National Liberation Army (INLA), among others, have carried out conventional criminal activities, such as theft, extortion, arms or drug trafficking to obtain resources (Roth and Sever, 2007; Curtis and Karacan, 2002).

The links between organized crime and terrorist groups that are now reported and documented seem to be so profound that they blur the borders that have always existed between the two, especially when terrorist groups continuously participate in large-scale criminal activities and criminal groups adopt terrorist tactics or rely on the activities of the former with which they come to share objectives (Stohl, 2008). These complex networks manifest themselves in different ways depending on the geographical context and the political, social and economic conditions of the area in which they take shape. Therefore, the analysis of the international dynamics and their evolution can be crucial for an understanding of the new crime-terror nexus.

The international system has acquired great complexity in terms of the participation of violent non-state actors (VNSA). Currently, ethno-nationalist terrorist groups or extremist political ideologies, which we could call 'classic', coexist with new terrorist organizations that have overcome the state logic and manifest a vocation for international expansion, thanks to the global nature of their objectives. Such organizations challenge the state monopoly in international relations and have redesigned their relations with other VNSAs. In the case of organized crime, the "classic" criminal groups have expanded their international reach, adapting to the global expansion of commerce and designing global operating strategies. They have thus overcome the limits of traditional local activity, that now they may share with smaller groups, while growing more flexible and adapting to the global world.

The following sections deal with some aspects of the evolution of the international system that have favoured the transformation of the crime-terror nexus. Attention is given to the proliferation of private actors that condition, redesign and multiply the processes of international relations in order to achieve their objectives, even if these are contrary to the principles and norms of international law and of domestic legislations. The analysis will also cover the possibilities offered to illegal and violent actors by the globalization process in terms of information, communication and transport, which condition their objectives and spaces of action. Finally, the focus will be on the development of armed conflict and the opportunities this offers to redefine the relations between terrorist groups and organized criminals. In places where violence has become a permanent feature, different relational networks with civil society and greater opportunities to collaborate with other groups have been established, due to the absence of authorities that control the basic institutions of the state, monopolize the use of force and guarantee the safety of citizens.

Privatization of international relations and violent non-state actors

The incessant privatization of international relations has moved individual lives away from tribal, local or national contexts onto the global scene. Change has not only affected access to information and relationships between people and authorities, but has also contributed to the creation of an international public opinion. Individuals are now the targets of decisions or actions taken by the authorities of foreign states, international organizations and private actors or conglomerates (Gill, 1995; Adamson, 2005). Privatization also encouraged certain groups to identify and articulate objectives and demands in the international sphere, outside state jurisdictions, at times addressing interlocutors other than states.

In previous periods, the arena of international relations was characterized by alliances between states, and conflicts were essentially motivated by territorial conquest (Bull, 2012). Thus, the centrality of the state as an actor of international relations has been, until relatively recently, indisputable. Any non-state actor that could influence an international process, in a direct or indirect way, was subject to the designs and interests of the states. But, from the end of World War II, the increase in categories and number of actors in international relations, whose origins date from the late nineteenth century and early twentieth century, accelerated. At first, with the appearance of international organizations and, later, of non-central governments, there was an increase in public actors derived from the States; later, non-central governments began to take an interest in international affairs and to perceive the advantages of participating in them, coordinating or complementing state action (Arts, Noortmann and Reinalda, 2001; Duchacek, 1990; Frieden, 1999).

The actors involved in private initiative whose main objective is profit have also proliferated, for example, international corporations as well as non-governmental organizations. Undoubtedly, these new entities have reduced the role of the state, but their activities have always been subject to state conditions and to the norms of international law and the internal law of states (Risse-Kappen, 1995).

Simultaneously, with the appearance of new legal actors, organized crime groups with a strong national identity emerged, whose activities were previously linked to a certain territory, although their business had an international significance. In the same way, terrorist groups arose whose ideological foundations had an ethno-nationalist or ideologically extremist base and whose goals were focused on provoking a separatist or secessionist process within a state or a change in the political and governmental structures of a country (Williams, 2008). The progressive privatization of international relations has not only led to the emergence of illegal actors but has also benefited their participation in international affairs from two different points of view.

In the first place, it has allowed them to proliferate, escaping progressively from state control and participating, increasingly, in a more autonomous way, in more complex schemes of coexistence and collaboration and/or conflict with other legal and illegal actors. And, second, the interdependence between public and private actors of the international system has allowed them to internationalize their strategies, objectives and activities more and more, as well as to expand the geographical contexts in which they operate until they acquire a global dimension (Keohane, 2002).

Currently, the internationalization of terrorism and organized crime outweighs the need to obtain shelter or military material in other states, as did the "classic" terrorist groups, or to trade illegal products in nearby markets, as organized crime used to do. Now, many violent non-state actors want to influence the international system and condition international processes because their objectives and interests cannot be met within a state framework. Thus, the international logic, marked by a strong inter-state dimension, has been replaced by an increasingly internationalized and global logic, in which private actors seek to condition international governance, even if their participation is illegal, lacks legitimacy and is prosecuted by law (Mulaj, 2010).

Groups of organized criminals, while not renouncing national attachment, have become more independent than public actors, since the global dimension of their activities makes them evade state control, and their relations with the state, regardless of their nature, are less decisive for the development of their activities. They do not use the international system to achieve their national objectives, but formulate their objectives at the global level and interact with many other private actors to achieve them throughout the world (Edwards and Gill, 2004; Berdal and Serrano, 2002). In this way, for the VNSA, the state ceases to be a framework for action and aspirations to become a useful space in which to develop activities in the most advantageous political, economic and social conditions (Galeotti, 2014).

In the case of terrorist groups, the abandonment of the state logic has been even more radical. Instead of ethno-nationalist terrorist groups or extremist ideologies, which pursue a separatist process or a change in the structures of governments, there are now groups with global aspirations whose goal is to influence global governance (Sandler and Siqueira, 2006; Lutz and Lutz, 2013; Clauset and Young, 2005). These new organizations, which are devoted to global terrorism, have proliferated, especially since the attacks of 11 September 2001, thanks to the groups derived, split or sponsored by Al-Qaeda, the rise of the self-styled Islamic State of Iraq and the Levant, and the activation of sympathetic groups and individuals, in different geographical areas, willing to carry out terrorist activities on their behalf (Lia, 2007). Unlike the classic terrorist groups, global terrorism challenges the borders established by the Western powers, aims to reconfigure global hegemonic relations and develops its political project in the states in which it has managed to establish itself (Martini, 2016; Rougier, 2008).

Globalization and decentralization

The globalized international system ceases to be a set of states/societies and comes to be understood as a single unit of analysis, a global social system, where an international division of labour is in place and opportunities and development are unequal (Wallerstein, 2013). The expansion of economic liberalism worldwide has influenced the cooperation activities of the VNSA and their organizational schemes have been adapting at the same time as the international system evolves. In this globalized international system, both organized crime and terrorist groups adapt their behaviours and activities in order to participate and gain a place within the world system, taking advantage of the regulatory frameworks and institutions that states have created to liberalize world trade and capital movements (Martínez Vela, 2001). As a result, states have embarked on important cooperation processes with the objective of overcoming the negative consequences of the expansion of markets and the great advances in the field of communications and the transmission of information that blur state borders and facilitate illegal VNSA participation. The latter benefit from the 'world-system' by mocking the state authority and that of other public actors such as international organizations (Ibáñez, 1999).

Among the opportunities offered by the global-world system to these illegal and violent groups is, first of all, access to the different state jurisdictions, thanks to increased mobility and advanced transport facilities. These groups, therefore, are not required to respect national and international standards that might hinder the achievement of their objectives. Second, the global system provides violent groups with the opportunity to maximize their economic benefits or political objectives, to adapt to, and take full advantage of, the logistical, political, socio-economic and cultural circumstances of each of the geographic areas in which they operate. Irrespective of the modus operandi and the type of society in which they operate, in the end it is difficult to determine the legality or illegality of their acts, although the purpose of these actions, which in principle may be of a legal nature, is to achieve objectives that in themselves are illegal. In this type of contexts, the processes of cooperation among VNSAs proliferate, and the nature and intensity of their contacts or links will be determined by the facilities offered by the different geographical areas in which they occur. In short, the process of globalization offers them greater flexibility and anonymity in the establishment of cooperation, as well as better opportunities to escape from national and international jurisdictions (Dishman, 2005).

Traditionally, organized crime and terrorism have been deeply rooted in certain societies and the scope of their activities depended on their relations with state authorities. Thanks to the consequences of globalization, both the criminal organizations that continue to maintain centralized and hierarchical structures and others that are smaller and have more horizontal organizational schemes adapt their operation to the characteristics of a globalized society. Organizations that practice global terrorism do so in the same way (Passas, 2003). Flexibility and decentralization, therefore, become key variables for the choice of the most appropriate economic and political contexts, as well as the most advantageous regulatory framework, in which organizations can operate.

The process of globalization has made obsolete the image of organized crime as structured hierarchies that use threats and violence to acquire or maintain control of illegal markets and obtain profits (Reuter, 2009). Currently, participation in more flexible and smaller criminal structures is expanding, as is the growth of 'disorganized' groups. Such new structures are capable of identifying the opportunities offered by cooperation with other groups, including those who practice political violence. The geographical expansion of the activities carried out by traditional criminal organizations and by other more flexible and less vertical groups forces all to improve their military capabilities, infrastructures and contacts with other VNSAs (Varese, 2011; Albanese, 2000).

However, decentralization does not mean the total absence of hierarchy, but rather a more flexible type of organization that facilitates the planning of more global objectives. Likewise, the organizational flexibility to which VNSAs now tend does not require that a large number of members establish themselves in a given territory. Organizations with broad memberships and centralized structures can cooperate with others that are smaller or larger, depending on the potential profits to be made in certain areas. The volatility of illegal markets has led organized criminals to establish new "joint ventures" with organizations linked to global terrorism: the latter have taken over the monopoly of force and political control of certain territories, which are usually the places of origin or transit of the merchandize in which criminal organizations trade. The groups that maintain a decentralized structure and participate in a wide network of possible partners and businesses are better able to evade detection and extend their survival (Pearson, Akbulut and Lounsbery, 2017). And, although decentralization may entail risks in terms of communication and coordination, it offers greater protection to the leaders of these criminal and terrorist groups. In addition, decentralization does not prevent the launch of high-impact terrorist attacks and large-scale organized crime operations that affect different regions and countries. In fact, the flexibility of the alliances and the decentralization of their activities have facilitated the connection through networks between criminal groups and terrorist groups in areas such as Iraq, Syria, Libya or Mali and Afghanistan, among others (Abadinsky, 2012; Qin, Xu, Hu, Sageman and Chen, 2005).

The decentralization and flexibility of organized crime and terrorism makes it possible for many groups to change the nature of their activities and gain greater visibility, thus renouncing their traditional adherence to secrecy. When the hierarchical order is blurred and members are de-localized, the micro-identities of a religious, ethnic and cultural nature do not hamper cooperation, on the contrary, the activities and objectives of each group blend together and the exchange of membership is facilitated (McLauchlin, 2018). Some studies show that a very high percentage of individuals arrested or convicted in Europe for jihadist terrorism have a criminal record. But, in the trans-Sahara area, the transfer of membership has been documented even for mutual assistance and support between criminal and terrorist groups. A study carried out in 2016 by the *International Centre for the Study of Radicalization and Political Violence* (Basra, Neumann and Brunner, 2016) shows that the convergence between these criminal and terrorist organizations is creating a more hybrid profile of members, who may belong to both types of organizations (Bloom, 2017). The phenomenon of criminals who become terrorists is not recent, but it does seem to have increased because the jihadist narrative offers criminals the possibility of redemption, while allowing them to continue carrying out criminal activities under religious legitimation (Mishali-Ram, 2018). The criminals who join the ranks of terrorist groups offer knowledge on access to weapons, logistical and operational capabilities and familiarity with the use of violence, which result in greater possibilities of obtaining funds for the financing of the terrorist organization.

In conclusion, organized crime and terrorist groups are able to adapt both their organizational structures and their activities to international markets (Ibáñez and Sánchez, 2015). Whether economic profit is the main purpose, as in the case of organized crime, or only an instrument to achieve political-ideological objectives, as supposedly in the case of terrorist groups, both violent organizations end up operating as illegal multinational companies intent at increasing benefits and reducing risks, and seeking ways to circumvent international and internal laws that hinder their activities. Countering the efforts of states and international organizations to fight terrorism and organized crime, economic and technological globalization offers these groups opportunities to collaborate, to secure funds, to access new territories and refine their ability to achieve objectives.

Armed conflict, organized crime and terrorism

The collaboration between organized crime and terrorism has also gained momentum thanks to the opportunities offered by the evolution of international conflict. Changes in the global dynamics of conflicts resulting in the drastic reduction of inter-state wars and the parallel increase in internal armed conflicts have left states without a monopoly in the use of violence. Most of the current armed conflicts take place within the borders of a state and 'infect' neighbouring countries. They tend to have an asymmetric nature, because they involve governmental and non-governmental forces, sometimes with a high participation of private actors (Kaldor, 2013; Pearlman and Cunningham, 2012; Pettersson and Wallensteen, 2015). An example of this is the increase in transnational insurgent movements, which recruit volunteers from countries across the world, who join local militias as foreign fighters (Malet, 2010). Moreover, the warlords are strengthened in situations of prolonged conflict and become interlocutors of international institutions (Deng et al., 2010; Salehyan, Siroky and Wood, 2014), as are groups of international terrorists or organized criminals that challenge the role of states in war situations (García Segura and Rodrigo, 2008; Bozeman, 2015).

The objectives and needs of organized crime and terrorist groups can converge, but can also change if new networks are formed. This will depend on the political, economic and social situation of the states in which the groups operate. In relatively stable contexts, where state authorities continue to monopolize the use of violence, the behaviour of VNSAs is very different from that which occurs in unregulated violent contexts. In other words, context determines the nature and intensity of the activities of the VNSAs, along with the relations such actors establish with the authorities and with the inhabitants of specific localities.

In territories characterized by socio-political and economic stability, where institutions control the use of force and the rule of law prevails, the relations between organized crime and terrorism are subject to a series of limitations. In such territories, organized criminals use violence as a supplementary instrument to boost their business opportunities within the system, while terrorists manifest through violence their intention to destroy the system. Here, the relationships between the two are highly conditioned by state control and the vigilance of civil society (Ruggiero, 2019).

By contrast, territories lacking effective authority and governance, where legitimacy is weak and the control of borders inadequate, offer safe havens for a variety of VNSAs and the development of links among them (Di John, 2010). Here, the terror-crime nexus tends to be more intense due to state control deficits and lack of civil and political rights (Buzan, 2008).

The levels of fragility of states can vary. In some situations, institutions are weak and security functions are insufficient, although the necessary services to the population may be provided. In other situations, institutions are unable to guarantee the security of the population and the control of their resources, at least in a large part of the territory, so that other private actors take on these functions (Djurdjevic-Lukic and Dimitrijević, 2010). Here, organized crime can have access to the legitimate economy, or even to the political apparatus, especially in situations of economic deregulation that encourage the elite to act illegally. Dissident groups, in their turn, embrace violence, form terrorist organizations and connect with global violent actors with a view to demolishing governments and states.

In territories where conflict has led to the disintegration of the state, private actors take over its institutions and functions, remodelling them according to their own interests. In such territories, organized crime and terrorism may stipulate agreements based on the joint use of violence and the spread of fear. They may also forge links with the weak political authorities of the place, which normally owe their survival to the support received by the international community (see the examples of the government of Kabul in Afghanistan and the Government of National Agreement in Libya). In this type of situation, hybrid forms can take shape in which the violence characterizing, respectively, organized crime and terrorism converge and amalgamate. The two may still maintain their own purposes, although these may be shared and interchanged.

Failed states, where the crime-terror nexus is strong, pose a serious danger to neighbouring regions (Varese, 2011). The terrorist groups which accumulate finances through participation in large-scale criminal activity can expand their operations and migrate to different parts of the planet. The relationships established between these two types of VNSA may lead to strategic action, whereby some territories are designated as places of production, others as illegal transit routes, while the clientele may be constituted by entire regions or the entire world. In some contexts, VNSAs will further destabilize already unstable governments, while in others they will appropriate resources and affect the economic, political and social life of populations (Schneckener, 2009).

In Europe, the cooperation between criminals and terrorists has important effects from several points of view. In the first place, Europe becomes the main recipient and consumer of illegal products, with the consequences in social, health, security and human rights that this entails (Wrench, Rea and Ouali, 2016; Sagramoso, 2001; Savona, Riccardi and Berlusconi, 2016). Second, opportunities open for the implantation in European territory of cells and terrorist groups (Hafezi, Jones and Walker, 2018). Third, the recipient territories of illegal products also welcome cooperation between terrorist groups and groups of criminals that provide continuity to the collaboration process that has been initiated between VNSAs in peripheral regions. An example of this is the agreements between Italian mafia groups and groups of criminals and terrorists operating in the North African regions (European Parliament, 2012).

The cooperation between the VNSAs, therefore, has consequences not only in the territories in which it is initiated, but also in various other places. This explains the international concern about regions such as the Trans-Sahara, which has become the best example to explain the circumstances surrounding this model of cooperation among VNSAs. It is true that contraband from the rest of the African continent has always been an activity developed by the Libyan border communities under the informal consent and control of the Gaddafi government. However, since the fall of the regime and the spread of conflict and violence that continues to plague the country, the volume of smuggling of cigarettes, drugs, weapons and migrants has increased exponentially (Shelley and Melzer, 2008). According to a report by *The Global Initiative Against Transnational Organized Crime* (2015), due to the conflicts in Libya and Mali, the criminal economy in the trans-Sahara region has expanded while smuggling routes, protected by terrorist groups, have multiplied. Terrorist groups such as Ansar-Eddine, Boko Haram and Ansar-al Sharia have strengthened ties with criminal organizations in the area and have helped to increase their illegal business in places such as Mali, Nigeria and now reach North Africa. Likewise, the kidnapping of Westerners has become an important means of financing terrorist groups (Martinez and Boserup, 2017; Alda and Sala, 2014). Countries such as France, Germany and Italy, among others, have paid millions of dollars to free their nationals held by these groups, who use the services of criminal groups to execute the kidnappings and to guard the victims, and who in turn collaborate with tribal militias or clans that are related to members of terrorist organizations and members of criminal organizations (Taras and Gangulu, 2015).

Partnerships

In the trans-Sahara region, the VNSAs have members with very similar profiles, which has led not only to the exchange of membership but also to the hybridization of their behaviour. These groups are able to participate in acts of criminal or political violence indistinctly, even if their actions are justified on the basis of the ideals or objectives originally held by the organization by which they were recruited (Lakhani, 2018). Therefore, while the membership is interchangeable, the very ambivalence of the violent activities contributes to the hybridization of the two types of violent groups. The report prepared by Shaw and Mangan in the *United States Institute of Peace* (2014), based on information gathered from 200 interviews conducted in Libya, includes ongoing episodes of collaboration between terrorist and criminal groups in the planning and execution of interconnected trafficking operations of immigrants, arms, drugs and other goods, with local and tribal militias also participating (Shaw and Mangan, 2014). The terrorist organization Al-Qaeda in the Arab Maghreb controls much of the illicit activities in the Sahel, while the Libyan terrorist group Al-Mourabitun, led by Mokhatr Belmokhtar, dominates the trafficking of cigarettes and cocaine in Africa. One of the most lucrative activities seems to be the trafficking in migrants. The European agency Frontex estimates that 60 per cent of the migrants who cross the Mediterranean illegally do so through Libya, and that the trafficking in people along the coasts of North Africa produces annual profits in the region of $255–323 million for Libyan participants alone (FRONTEX, 2017). In this lucrative activity, nomadic tribes, such as the Tuareg or the Tebu, collaborate with organized crime in the management of African migrants and their transfer to the Tunisian or Libyan territory, while terrorist groups continue to exert strict control along these routes and enjoy their part of the profits.

Further partnerships

The close collaboration between terrorist groups and organized crime in the trans-Sahara regions has not only contributed to increasing the volume of trafficking in people arriving in Europe, it has also attracted well-established criminal groups from other regions, such as the Latin American drugs cartels, who have appreciated the advantages of changing their transportation routes. In recent years, a route for cocaine smuggling from Colombia has been established in Guinea-Bissau that leads to the rest of Africa and Europe, and it is estimated that it generates profits of between ten and 20 million dollars a year (just for the groups that participate in the zone of the Sahel, Algeria and Libya) (Vernaschi, 2010; Shaw and Mangan, 2014). The trafficking in drugs that takes place in this area, in addition to the participation of organized crime groups from the region and Latin America, also relies on the intervention of terrorist groups such as Al-Qaeda in the Arab Maghreb and even Hezbollah (Shaw, 2012). In short, the hybridization among VNSAs has generated an industry of 'criminal protection', making the most of the situation of transition and violence in Libya and the Sahel, and establishing a model of criminal governance thanks to the collaboration of armed actors throughout the entire trans-Saharan zone (Comolli, 2018). VNSAs are increasingly able to get the products and people they traffic to the Libyan coast and the border areas, from where they move them mainly to Europe, hence their cooperation with criminal and terrorist organizations that operate in Europe.

Iraq and Syria have become emblematic examples thanks to the business opportunities that have been generated for groups of organized criminals, derived from the financing needs of the self-proclaimed Islamic State, which appropriates the necessary resources of these countries to carry out and practice its political-religious project. Likewise, the Al-Qaeda-dependent organization in Syria, Al-Nusra, has created an entire criminal industry profiting from the assets of Al-Qaeda's ideological legitimacy and its support among citizens of many regions (Clarke, 2018). The traffic in energy resources, such as oil, or in works of art, needs the collaboration of organized criminals capable of placing these products on the market (Brodie and Sabrine, 2018). The same happens when it comes to the execution of kidnapped foreigners. In Syria, groups that practice global terrorism have come to monopolize political-military activity and criminal activity, getting their members to become both fighters of a cause and bandits to obtain resources (Steenkamp, 2017; Normark, Ranstorp and Ahlin, 2017). The collaboration between the criminal gangs and the terrorist organizations that operate there is situated in a kind of black hole in which the politico-ideological objectives of terrorism are diluted in a continued exercise of criminal violence (Kalyvas, 2015).

Hybridization, in sum, implies cooperation or assimilation of the practices of different groups, regardless of the respective objectives and identities. Criminals manage to increase their businesses because of the control that terrorists exert over certain populations and territories (Omelicheva and Markowitz, 2018). Terrorist groups, moreover, while offering criminals security in some areas, utilize part of the profits obtained from criminal activity to provide some services to local populations (Piazza and Piazza, 2017). On the other hand, criminal groups supply terrorist groups with weapons and money to pay their fighters (Shelley, 2004). Sure, terrorist groups seek to change the political and social life of specific territories, while organized crime has no such ambition. Yet, criminal groups find in areas controlled by terrorist violence the connivance necessary for the continuation and consolidation of their illegal businesses (Gendron, 2017).

In conclusion, we are witnessing a new stage in the development of international relations in which cooperation between VNSAs is increasing. This is particularly the case in contexts characterized by armed conflict and in post-conflict fragile states, where disorder and violence are the best allies. If this cooperation manages to perpetuate the fragility of states and violence, greater profits and impunity will ensue (Kalyvas, 2015).

Note

1 This work has been funded by European Project TAKEDOWN (Understand the dimensions of organized crime and terrorist networks for developing effective and efficient security solutions for first-line-practitioners and professionals (2016–2019)) 700688-H2020 FCT-162015 and the Spanish Ministry of Economy and Competitiveness and the European Regional Development Fund (MINECO/FEDER) within the framework of the Research Project with Reference DER2015-63857-R.

References

Abadinsky, H. (2012), *Organized Crime*. Cengage Learning, www.cengage.co.uk/ (accessed 13 October 2018).

Adamson F.B. (2005), 'Globalisation, Transnational Political Mobilisation, and Networks of Violence', *Cambridge Review of International Affairs*, 18(1): 31–49.

Albanese, J.S. (2000), 'The Causes of Organized Crime: Do Criminals Organize Around Opportunities for Crime or do Criminal Opportunities Create New Offenders?', *Journal of Contemporary Criminal Justice*, 16(4): 409–423.

Alda, E. and Sala, J. (2014), 'Links Between Terrorism, Organized Crime and Crime: The Case of the Sahel Region', *Stability: International Journal of Security and Development*, www.stabilityjournal.org/articles/10.5334/sta.ea/ (accessed 27 June 2019).

Arts, B., Noortmann, M. and Reinalda, B. (eds) (2001), *Non-state Actors in International Relations*, Farnham: Ashgate Publishing.

Basra, R., Neumann, P.R. and Brunner, C. (2016), 'Criminal Pasts', *Terrorist Futures: European Jihadists and the New Crime-Terror Nexus*, London: The International Centre for the Study of Radicalisation and Political Violence.

Berdal, M.R. and Serrano, M. (eds) (2002), *Transnational Organized Crime and International Security: Business as Usual?*, Boulder: Lynne Rienner Publishers.

Bloom, M. (2017), 'Constructing Expertise: Terrorist Recruitment and "Talent Spotting" in the PIRA, Al Qaeda, and ISIS', *Studies in Conflict and Terrorism*, 40(7): 603–623.

Bozeman, A.B. (2015), *Conflict in Africa: Concepts and Realities*, Princeton: Princeton University Press.

Brodie, N. and Sabrine, I. (2018), 'The Illegal Excavation and Trade of Syrian Cultural Objects: A View from the Ground', *Journal of Field Archaeology*, 43(1): 74–84.

Bull, H. (2012), *The Anarchical Society: A Study of Order in World Politics*, London: Macmillan International Higher Education.

Buzan, B. (2008), *People, States and Fear*, Boulder: Lynne Rienner.

Clarke, C.P. (2018), 'The Financing of Armed Groups in Conflict', *Armed Conflict Survey*, 4(1): 22–35.

Clauset, A. and Young, M. (2005), 'Scale Invariance in Global Terrorism', *arXiv preprint physics/0502014*.

Comolli, V. (ed.) (2018), *Organized Crime and Illicit Trade: How to Respond to This Strategic Challenge in Old and New Domains*, London: Palgrave Macmillan.

Curtis, G.E. and Karacan, T. (2002, December), 'The Nexus Among Terrorists, Narcotics Traffickers, Weapons Proliferators, and Organized Crime Networks in Western Europe', in *The Library of Congress, December*, www.loc.gov/rr/frd/pdf-files/WestEurope_NEXUS.pdf (accessed 16 September 2018).

De Boer, J. and Bosetti, L. (2015), 'The Crime-conflict "Nexus": State of the Evidence', *Occasional Paper*, 5, 9.

Deng, F.M., Kimaro, S., Lyons, T., Rothchild, D. and Zartman, I.W. (2010), *Sovereignty as Responsibility: Conflict Management in Africa*, Washington: Brookings Institution Press.

Di John, J. (2010), 'Conceptualizing the Causes and Consequences of Failed States: A Critical Review of the Literature', *Revista de estudios sociales*, (37): 46–86.

Dishman, C. (2005), 'The Leaderless Nexus: When Crime and Terror Converge', *Studies in Conflict and Terrorism*, 28(3): 237–252.

Djurdjevic-Lukic, S. and Dimitrijević, V. (2010), 'Human Security and Peacebuilding in the Western Balkans', in *Transnational Terrorism, Organized Crime and Peace-Building* (pp. 17–37), London: Palgrave Macmillan.

Duchacek, I. (1990), 'Perforated Sovereignties: Towards a Typology of New Actors in International Relations', *Federalism and International Relations: The Role of Subnational Units*, 1(2).

Edwards, A. and Gill, P. (eds) (2004), *Transnational Organised Crime: Perspectives On Global Security*, London: Routledge.
EU Parliament's Committee on Civil Liberties Justice and Home Affairs Report (2012), 'Europe's Crime-Terror Nexus: Links between Terrorist and Organised Crime Groups in the European Union, PE 462.503, 2012', www.europarl.europa.eu/document/activities/cont/201211/20121127ATT56707/20121127ATT56707 EN.pdf (accessed 15 September 2018).
Frieden, J.A. (1999), 'Actors and Preferences in International Relations', *Strategic Choice and International Relations*: 39–76, http://scholar.harvard.edu/files/jfrieden/files/actprefir.pdf (accessed 13 October 2018).
FRONTEX, European Border and Coast Board, Risk Analysis (2017), http://frontex.europa.eu/assets/Publications/Risk_Analysis/Annual_Risk_Analysis_2017.pdf (accessed 12 September 2018).
Galeotti, M. (2014), *Global Crime Today: The Changing Face of Organised Crime*, London: Routledge.
García Segura, C. and Rodrigo, A. (eds) (2008), *La seguridad compartida. Nuevos desafíos, amenazas y conflictos armados*, Madrid, Tecnos.
Gendron, A. (2017), 'Criminality, Terrorism and the Changing Nature of Conflict: The Dynamics of the Nexus between Crime and Terrorism', in *The Palgrave Handbook of Security, Risk and Intelligence* (pp. 315–333), London: Routledge.
Gill, S. (1995), 'Globalisation, Market Civilisation, and Disciplinary Neoliberalism', *Millennium*, 24(3): 399–423.
Hafezi, N., Jones, K. and Walker, C. (2018), 'Criminal Prosecutions for Terrorism Financing in the UK', *The Palgrave Handbook of Criminal and Terrorism Financing Law* (pp. 967–993), London: Palgrave Macmillan.
Hutchinson, S. and O'Malley, P. (2007), 'A Crime–terror Nexus? Thinking on Some of the Links between Terrorism and Criminality', *Studies in Conflict Terrorism*, 30(12): 1095–1107.
Ibáñez, J. (1999), 'La realidad de la globalización. Procesos, factores y actores de un incipiente sistema global', https://minerva.usc.es/xmlui/bitstream/handle/10347/8176/03.rips1-1.pdf?sequence=1&isAllowed=y (accessed 17 September 2018).
Ibáñez Muñoz, J. and Sánchez Avilés, C. (eds) (2015), *Mercados ilegales y violencia armada: Los vínculos entre la criminalidad organizada y la conflictividad internacional*, Madrid: Tecnos.
Kaldor, M. (2013), *New and Old Wars: Organised Violence in a Global Era*, New Jersey: John Wiley & Sons.
Kalyvas, S.N. (2015), 'How Civil Wars Help Explain Organized Crime – and How They Do Not', *Journal of Conflict Resolution*, 59(8): 1517–1540.
Keohane, R.O. (2002), 'The Globalization of Informal Violence, Theories of World Politics, and the "Liberalism of Fear"', *Dialogue IO*, 1(1): 29–43.
Kessels, E. and Hennessy, O. (2017, February), 'Examining the Nexus between Terrorism and Organized Crime: Linkages, Enablers and Policy Implications', in *Talking to the Enemy* (pp. 233–254), Baden-Baden: Nomos Verlagsgesellschaft mbH & Co, KG.
Lakhani, S. (2018), 'Extreme Criminals: Reconstructing Ideas of Criminality Through Extremist Narratives', *Studies in Conflict and Terrorism*: 1–16, www.tandfonline.com/doi/full/10.1080/1057610X.2018.1450613 (accessed 13 October 2018).
Lia, B. (2007), *Architect of Global Jihad: The Life of Al-Qaida Strategist Abu Mus' Ab Al-Suri*, London: Hurst.

Lutz, J. and Lutz, B. (2013), *Global Terrorism*, London: Routledge.

Makarenko, T. (2004), 'The Crime-terror Continuum: Tracing the Interplay between Transnational Organised Crime and Terrorism', *Global Crime*, 6(1): 129–145.

Malet, D. (2010), 'Why Foreign Fighters? Historical Perspectives and Solutions', *Orbis*, 54(1): 97–114.

Martínez Vela, C.A. (2001), 'World Systems Theory', *Engineering System Division*, 83: 1–5.

Martinez, L. and Boserup, R.A. (2017), 'Beyond Western Sahara, the Sahel-Maghreb Axis Looms Large', in *Global, Regional and Local Dimensions of Western Sahara's Protracted Decolonization* (pp. 144–163), New York: Palgrave Macmillan.

Martini, A. (2016), 'Global Terrorism as a Threat to the International Order. The Islamic State Case', *Relaciones Internacionales*, (32), www.relacionesinternacionales.info/ojs/article/download/708/480.pdf (accessed 13 October 2018).

McLauchlin, T. (2018), 'The Loyalty Trap: Regime Ethnic Exclusion, Commitment Problems, and Civil War Duration in Syria and Beyond', *Security Studies*, 27(2): 296–317.

Mishali-Ram, M. (2018), 'Foreign Fighters and Transnational Jihad in Syria', *Studies in Conflict and Terrorism*, 41(3): 169–190.

Mulaj, K. (ed.) (2010), *Violent Non-State Actors in World Politics*, New York: Columbia University Press.

Normark, M., Ranstorp, M. and Ahlin, F. (2017) 'Financial Activities Linked to Persons from Sweden and Denmark Who Joined Terrorist Groups in Syria and Iraq During the Period 2013–2016: Report Commissioned by Finansinspektionen', Swedish Defense University.

Omelicheva, M.Y. and Markowitz, L. (2018), 'Does Drug Trafficking Impact Terrorism? Afghan Opioids and Terrorist Violence in Central Asia', *Studies in Conflict and Terrorism*: 1–23.

Passas, N. (2003), 'Cross-border Crime and the Interface between Legal and Illegal Actors', *Security Journal*, 16(1): 19–37.

Pearlman, W. and Cunningham, K.G. (2012), 'Nonstate Actors, Fragmentation, and Conflict Processes', *Journal of Conflict Resolution*, 56(1): 3–15.

Pearson, F.S., Akbulut, I. and Olson Lounsbery, M. (2017), 'Group Structure and Intergroup Relations in Global Terror Networks: Further Explorations', *Terrorism and Political Violence*, 29(3): 550–572.

Pettersson, T. and Wallensteen, P. (2015), 'Armed Conflicts, 1946–2014', *Journal of Peace Research*, 52(4): 536–550.

Piazza, J.A. and Piazza, S. (2017), 'Crime Pays: Terrorist Group Engagement in Crime and Survival', *Terrorism and Political Violence*: 1–23.

Proksik, J.J. (2017), 'EULEX and the Fight Against Organised Crime in Kosovo: What's the Record?', *Trends in Organized Crime*, 1–25, www.altmetric.com/details/27574735 (accessed 13 October 2018).

Qin, J., Xu, J.J., Hu, D., Sageman, M. and Chen, H. (2005, May), 'Analyzing Terrorist Networks: A Case Study of the Global Salafi Jihad Network', *International Conference on Intelligence and Security Informatics*, Berlin, Heidelberg, Springer: 287–304.

Reuter, P. (2009), 'Systemic Violence in Drug Markets', *Crime, Law and Social Change*, 52(3): 275–284.

Risse-Kappen, T. (1995), *Bringing Transnational Relations Back In: Non-State Actors, Domestic Structures and International Institutions* (Vol. 42), Cambridge: Cambridge University Press.

Roth, M.P. and Sever, M. (2007), 'The Kurdish Workers Party (PKK) as Criminal Syndicate: Funding Terrorism through Organized Crime, a Case Study', *Studies in Conflict and Terrorism*, 30(10): 901–920.

Rougier, B. (2008), 'Le jihad en Afghanistan et l'émergence du salafisme-jihadisme', in *Qu'est-ce que le salafisme?* (pp. 65–86), Paris: Presses Universitaires de France.

Ruggiero, V. (2019), 'Hybrids: On the Crime-Terror-Nexus', *International Journal of Comparative and Applied Criminal Justice*, 43(1): 49–60.

Ruggiero, V. and Leyva, R. (2017), 'Organised Crime and Terrorist Networks: Literature Exploration and Open Access Bibliography', www.researchgate.net/publication/312525743_Organized_Crime_and_Terrorist_Networks_Literature_Exploration_and_Open_Access_Bibliography (accessed 13 October 2018).

Sagramoso, D. (2001), *The Proliferation of Illegal Small Arms and Light Weapons in and Around The European Union: Instability, Organised Crime and Terrorist Groups*, London: Saferworld and Center for Defense Studies.

Salehyan, I., Siroky, D. and Wood, R.M. (2014), 'External Rebel Sponsorship and Civilian Abuse: A Principal-agent Analysis of Wartime Atrocities', *International Organization*, 68(3): 633–661.

Sanderson, T. M. (2004), 'Transnational Terror and Organized Crime: Blurring the Lines', *SAIS Review of International Affairs*, 24(1): 49–61.

Sandler, T. and Siqueira, K. (2006), 'Global Terrorism: Deterrence Versus Pre-emption', *Canadian Journal of Economics/Revue Canadienne d'économique*, 39(4): 1370–1387.

Savona, E.U., Riccardi, M. and Berlusconi, G. (eds) (2016), *Organised Crime in European Businesses*, London: Routledge.

Schmid, A.P. (1996), 'The Links between Transnational Organized Crime and Terrorist Crimes', *Transnational Organized Crime*, 2(4): 40–82.

Shaw, M. (2012), 'Leadership Required: Drug Trafficking and the Crisis of Statehood in West Africa', *Policy Brief*, (37): 1–6.

Shaw, M. and Mangan, F. (2014), *Illicit Trafficking and Libya's Transition. Profits and Losses*, Peaceworks, United States Institute of Peace, www.usip.org/sites/default/files/PW96-Illicit-Trafficking-and-Libyas-Transition.pdf (accessed 16 September 2018).

Schneckener, U. (2009), 'Spoilers or Governance Actors? Engaging Armed Non-state Groups in Areas of Limited Statehood', *SFB- Governance Working Paper Series*, (21): 1–36.

Shelley, L. (2004), 'The Unholy Trinity: Transnational Crime, Corruption, and Terrorism', *Brown J. World Affairs*, 11: 101–111.

Shelley, L.I. and Melzer, S.A. (2008), 'The Nexus of Organized Crime and Terrorism: Two Case Studies in Cigarette Smuggling', *International Journal of Comparative and Applied Criminal Justice*, 32(1): 43–63.

Shelley, L.I. and Picarelli, J.T. (2005), 'Methods and Motives: Exploring Links between Transnational Organized Crime and International Terrorism', *Trends in Organized Crime*, 9(2): 52–67.

Steenkamp, C. (2017), 'The Crime-conflict Nexus and the Civil War in Syria', *Stability: International Journal of Security and Development*, 6(1).

Stohl, M. (2008), 'Networks, Terrorists and Criminals: The Implications for Community Policing', *Crime, Law and Social Change*, 50(1–2): 59–72.

Taras, R. and Ganguly, R. (2015), *Understanding Ethnic Conflict*, London: Routledge.

The Global Initiative Against Transnational Organized Crime (11 May 2015), *Libya: A Growing Hub for Criminal Economies and Terrorist Financing in The Trans-Sahara, Policy Brief*, http://globalinitiative.net/wp-content/uploads/2015/05/2015-1.pdf (accessed 17 September 2018).

UN Secretary-General (20 May 2015), *Report of the Secretary-General on the Threat of Terrorists Benefiting from Transnational Organized Crime*, S/2015/366, www.refworld.org/docid/5587db984.html (accessed 27 August 2018).

Varese, F. (2011), *Mafias on the Move: How Organized Crime Conquers New Territories*, Princeton: Princeton University Press.

Vernaschi, M. (2010), 'The Cocaine Coast', *The Virginia Quarterly Review*, 86(1): 43.

Wallerstein, I. (2013), WorldSystem Analysis. *Sociopedia.isa*, 1–8, www.sagepub.net/isa/resources/pdf/World-Systems%20analysis.pdf (accessed 12 October 2018).

Williams, P. (2008), 'Violent Non-state Actors and National and International Security', *International Relations and Security Network*, Zurich, Center for Security Studies, 25: 1–21.

Wrench, J., Rea, A. and Ouali, N. (eds) (2016), *Migrants, Ethnic Minorities and the Labour Market: Integration and Exclusion in Europe*, Berlin: Springer.

8 Understanding the crime-terrorism nexus through a dynamic modelling approach

Florian Huber, Bernhard Jäger, Ido Erev, Doron Cohen, Sergio Bianchi and Matteo E. Bonfanti

Introduction

Europe is facing an increasing number of individuals who are becoming radicalized and recruited for terrorist attacks. In order to be able to fight violent radicalization and terrorism, we need to better understand the pathways of radicalization, the social, psychological and economic dimensions of violent extremism, and the options for de-radicalization or counter-terrorism.

Violent extremism and terrorist networks are very much based on ideology and identity, and social marginalization and institutional change were identified as main drivers of engagement (Kruglanski *et al.*, 2009). Research has shown that the form of organization is fundamentally changing. While previously centralized organizations were dominating the field, today the networks of cells, which act more or less autonomously, are the main form of organization. To some extent, the development is facilitated by digital communication technologies and the possibility to easily train members of terrorist networks to become experts for encryption and secure communication (McDonald, 2013; Whiteside, 2016).

Previous research has also shown that contexts as well as places and situational dynamics, including societal structures, play a crucial role in successfully fighting terrorist networks. By taking contextual and situational parameters seriously, the H2020-Project TAKEDOWN[1] developed a new approach as part of the research, which resulted in a dynamic cube for analysing and assessing cases or organized crime, violent extremism and terrorism. This chapter provides an elaboration of the concept and the logic of the cube, which serves as the entry point for developing a practical tool devised by the TAKEDOWN Project.

The following section highlights the principal framework of the Cube Model. Section 3 presents the model concept and elaborates on how it can be practically applied. Section 4 applies the model on three selected cases from the domain of violent radicalization, extremism or terrorism. Section 5 outlines several options for further applications of the model such as the nexus of organized crime and terrorism or the evaluation of counter-measures. The chapter finally closes with concluding remarks.

Framework

Previous research has shown that the impact of different approaches to fight terrorist networks tend to be sensitive to the nature of the environment, the places, the context and the situation. For example, a hard-line approach of massive drone attacks on terrorists in Pakistan was found to be effective in reducing terror-related incidence rates and lethality of terrorist attacks (Johnston and Sarbahi, 2016), but the same approach was not effective at all (and even counterproductive, i.e. Ganesh, 2015) when implemented in Yemen. In a similar manner, a gentle strategy (i.e. a soft, 'conciliatory' approach) appears to be highly effective in a project in Saudi Arabia aimed at de-radicalizing citizens that are Islamist extremists (see Rabasa et al., 2010), but many believe that this gentle strategy was not very effective in de-radicalizing and reintegrating Islamic extremists in Yemen (Rabasa et al., 2010).

The proposed model tries to clarify this picture by building on the situational crime prevention (SCP) approach (Smith, 2016). It aims at reducing the number of criminal events and hence puts its focus on limiting the opportunities for crimes by analysing crime events as well as the environments in which these events take place. The SCP approach has been criticized for not addressing underlying drivers such as social inequality and for including the risk of displacing criminality. Nevertheless, measures are based on five basic principles: increasing effort, increasing risk, reducing reward, reducing provocation, and removing excuses, and due to their potential for practical implementation, they are applied by law enforcement agencies and other governmental and non-governmental stakeholders.

The aim of developing the proposed Cube Model was to provide a new, dynamic approach that provides quick decision support to then be transferred into actual technological tools for law enforcement agencies and practitioners.

Model concept

This section highlights the process through which the Cube Model was developed and explains how it works from a conceptual point of view.

Model development

As part of the research in the TAKEDOWN project, a thorough literature review was conducted and presented in a public report.[2] As a further basis, a comprehensive analysis of existing models was conducted, which concluded with a detailed requirements specification for the model creation presented in Table 8.1 below.[3]

The Cube Model is based therefore on the findings from the literature review and the analysis of existing models. Based on these findings, three main themes were abstracted and transferred into a model, where they were placed along the axes of a cube in order to allow the allocation of cases based on these three main themes.

Understanding the crime-terrorism nexus 119

Table 8.1 Requirements for the model development

Model requirement	Level	Effect(s)
Operational under uncertainty	Structural	Expand user horizon
Dynamic-friendly	Structural	Avoid reification
		Methodological indistinctiveness
Universally adapational	Structural	Multi-stakeholder friendly
		Target-oriented
Self-learning	Functional	Cross-fertilization
		Ongoing reassessment
Self-reflective	Functional	Structural sensitiveness
		Social embeddedness
Fundamental rights abiding	Normative	Legitimacy
		Social acceptance

Explaining the Cube Model

The model is conceptualized as a three-dimensional (cube) space, which consists of the following dimensions: (1) Expected benefits from joining; (2) Exit costs; (3) Indistinguishability from others or obscurity to outsiders. Figure 8.1 provides a visualization of the Cube Model. The details on the themes or axes are elaborated in detail below.

The dimension along the Y-axis captures the subjective benefit from joining a TN activity. High values imply that joining maximizes expected utility. Low values imply that joining is likely to reflect a mistake. Part of this mistake can be a reflection of a tendency to neglect rare events (Barron and Erev, 2003). Most previous analyses assume high values along this dimension and pay limited attention to mistakes (see Abrahms, 2008; Spencer, 2006).

The dimension along the X-axis captures the costs of exiting the TN environment. High values (the right-hand side in Figure 8.1 cube) reflect situations in which the effort to leave is very costly. An extreme example involves Europeans that join ISIS in Syria, knowing that if they will try to leave they risk either being shot by ISIS forces or by the forces that fight ISIS, or being prosecuted in their home countries for their former affiliation.

The dimension along the Z-axis captures the ability of the stakeholders (that try to fight the TN activities) to distinguish between members of the organizations/networks and people that are not involved in the illegal activity. High value (the far side of the cube) captures situations in which the stakeholders cannot distinguish between members and non-members. Furthermore, one could also refer to the distinction between 'radicals', who are distinguishable due to appearance and behaviour and recruiters or financiers of terrorism, who act in the dark and are not distinguishable from others.

Although the TAKEDOWN model is basically conceptualized and visualized as a three-dimensional space, case-driven applications of the model also

120 *Florian Huber* et al.

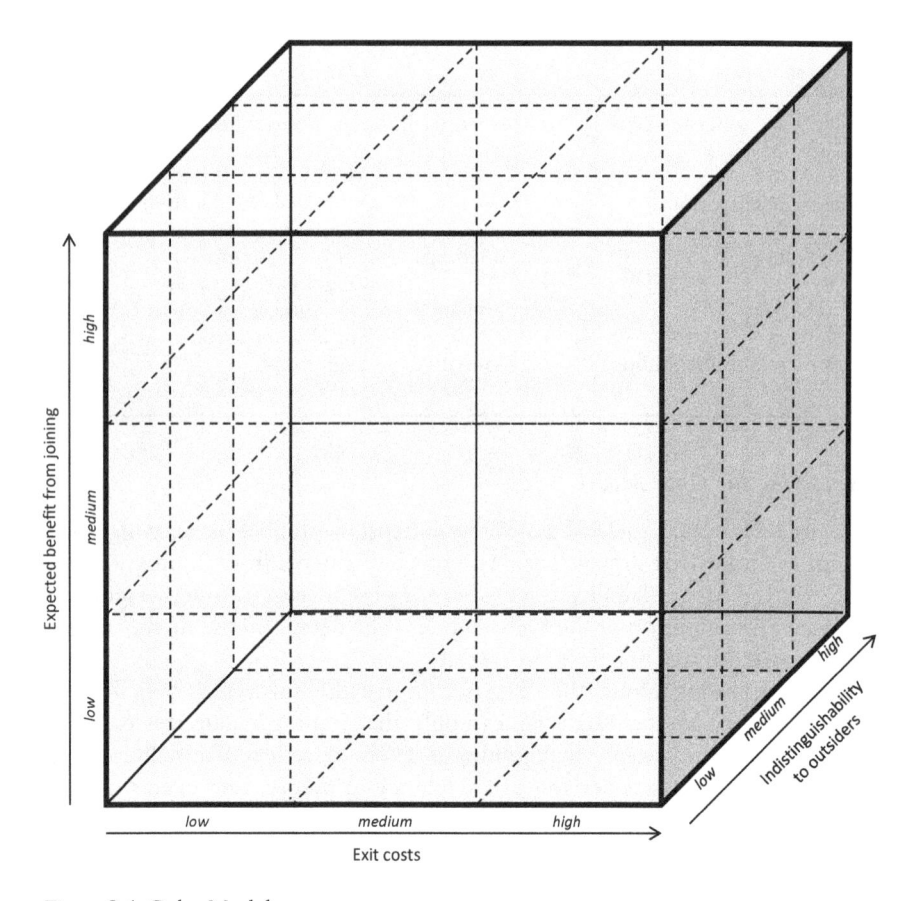

Figure 8.1 Cube Model.

include time as a fourth dimension. It plays for example a crucial role as a factor for tracing and visualizing the movement of a case within the cube over time.

Moving risks in the Cube

Counter-Violent-Extremism practices should always try to relocate an individual or a group towards a segment in the cube, where the risk of active involvement in terrorist attacks is lowest, and effective counter-measures are cheapest and most efficient (see Table 8.2).

Naturally, it is easier (and cheaper) to prevent illegal activity in the bottom-left corner of the cube. When the illegal activity reflects a mistake that can be easily corrected (exit costs are low) and the stakeholders can detect each activity, gentle enforcement can be enough. In such cases, gentle

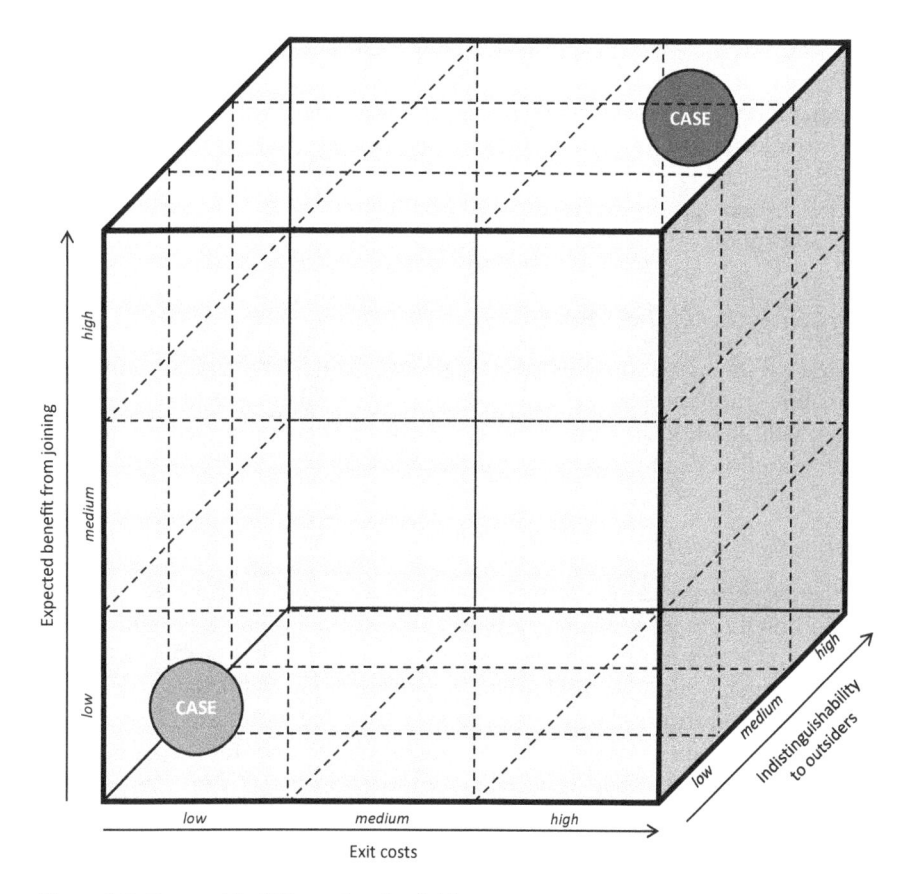

Figure 8.2 Cases with different levels of risk.

enforcement will not only be more effective, but is also expected to be cheaper and more efficient (Frey, 2007).

The incidences in the top-right corner in the cube are much more difficult to address. Thus, when the stakeholders can affect the location of the TN risk, they should try to move it to the bottom-left corner. Effective interventions often involve the expected benefit dimension. For example, providing the population with good education and attractive, official career options, is known to reduce the tendency to join TN (Frey, 2007; Frey and Luechinger, 2002; see also Rabasa *et al.*, 2010).

Moving a TN incidence along the exit cost dimension is more difficult. Exit costs are particularly large when the TN develops within a close-knit neighbourhood or in a religious organization. One possibility is relying on interventions that reduce exit costs (while also reducing the benefits dimension indirectly by influencing the target's immediate surroundings) (Frey, 2007). One example for a response that reduces exit costs is the

122 *Florian Huber* et al.

implementation of principal witness programs using strong incentives. This approach was found to be highly successful in the past (i.e. Wilkinson, 2000).

Decreasing indistinguishability is often a technological task, but it can also be done indirectly. For example, principal witness programs, when successful, can provide authorities with detailed information regarding the TN, reducing indistinguishability of its members (Wilkinson, 2000). However, when stakeholders cannot move the risk, they should find the best strategy that the current location of a case offers.

Applying the Cube Model

Against the background of the concept of the Cube Model, this section highlights how the Cube Model can be applied for analysing cases of organized crime, radicalization and terrorism. Three real cases were selected for demonstration purposes and the analysis is presented below.

Case analysis matrix

As the model – when transformed into a practical tool for risk assessment of cases – intends to provide practical use for practitioners and law enforcement agencies, it needs to provide the possibility to easily include new cases. Also, it has to quickly allow the analysis of cases through pre-defined categories and their allocation in the three-dimensional space. Therefore, a dedicated 'case categorization matrix' was created for structuring the cases for the analysis and the allocation in the model. The case categorization matrix therefore provides a justification for the allocation of a particular case in the model.

The categorization matrix consists of five main factors following the traditional situational crime prevention concepts: (1) Environments; (2) Actors/Key Players; (3) Facilitating conditions; (4) Murderous weapons and tools, and (5) Targets. These factors are divided into 36 parameters, and the parameters are structured into 121 variables, which allow a detailed categorization of cases.[4] The more information on a case is available, the more precise its location in the Cube Model can be established. Furthermore, new information on a case can be added continuously and in a replicable manner. Hence, the matrix and the model are conceptualized as a living framework that allows the user to revise and adapt the position of cases in the cube based on the information that is available.

In order to highlight the practical application of the concept and framework, the following section presents the outcomes of the matrix-based analysis of three exemplary cases related to radicalization, terrorism and organized crime and locates these cases in the Cube Model.

Allocation of three exemplary OC and TN cases

Case 1: terrorism

SHORT SUMMARY

On the morning of 25 July 2016, Adel Kermische, a 19-year-old Algerian who grew up in a housing project in France, entered a Normandy church with another attacker, where he forced Father Jacques Hamel, 86, to his knees and slit his throat. The attackers were armed with knives, and wore fake bombs and explosive belts. The two attackers were shot dead by police as they emerged from the church. Kermische had a relatively comfortable non-religious family background – his mother was a teacher and an elder sister was studying medicine. Media interviews with family and friends indicated a very rapid progress towards radicalization, starting in January 2015. By March 2015 Kermische was arrested for trying to travel to Syria. He was sent back to France, where he was given conditional parole awaiting trial. In May 2015, Kermische tried to enter Syria again. He was charged and returned to France where he was held in preventive custody for ten months. A psychological examination was carried out between October 2015 and February 2016, outlining his frail psychological state. Kermische's family said that he regularly visited hospital since the age of six, after suffering deep depressions and 'other mental problems', with suicidal tendencies documented in his file. For this reason, the psychological assessment, carried out in prison, stated that he was not fully compatible with the conditions of custody. Based upon that and the hearing of Kermische, who recognized his faults in front of the judge and promised to change, after a careful assessment with Kermische's family, the judge granted Kermische an alternative to imprisonment (house arrest), with the 'supervision and support' of his close family, and the support of the local social welfare institutions. The judge investigated also the availability of the family to support the rehabilitation programme, as usual in these cases and imposed a mandatory psychological treatment as part of his bespoke rehabilitation program. As for security concerns, the judge ordered Kermische to wear an electronic tag (preventive security measure which implies police surveillance). The tag was deactivated on the day of the attack.

Against the decision of the surveillance judge (a judge presiding over the conditions imposed on sentenced offenders), there was the opposition of the public prosecutor who considered the judiciary control as not adequate due to the context and history of the case. He stated that despite the fact that the offender showed repentance, the risk of reoffending was very high. While at home, Kermische was able to use Chatogram, an encrypted chat from Telegram, which was not monitored from the surveillance service. Through this application, he came across his accomplice and they planned the attack in a spontaneous manner. In this case, almost all relevant stakeholders were involved: Prosecutors, judges, investigators, prison staff, welfare officers, and

124 *Florian Huber* et al.

police responsible for the execution of alternative measures, as well as the local welfare services, including psychological support. Common to other cases of radicals who passed to terrorism, all known to the police or intelligence, the risk prioritization and the efficacy of the surveillance measures represented the weak point of the program.

OUTCOME OF MAIN COUNTER-MEASURES

The response from authorities to Kermische journey towards violence was contradictory, because, on the one hand, they stopped the fulfilment of his dream to go to Syria; but on the other hand, they offered him another chance to return to his old life, but he has rejected, thus keeping exit costs relatively low. However, this facilitated Kermische's bid to pretend to become a soldier of ISIS, as forgiving measures were ambiguous towards his main motivation – he perceived high benefits from joining ISIS and nothing to gain from the alternative offered by the authorities (his old lifestyle). Accepting suicide as a preferred way of action (he had suicidal tendencies) annulled the effectiveness of the soft measures.

The main conclusion related to the model could be: when one has relatively low exit costs (one's own death as the aspired outcome of behaviour), has high benefits from joining and is low on indistinguishability (but not low enough), policy and actions should either target the benefits dimension effectively (affect the motivation), or implement a better surveillance policy that aims to contain the threat and reduce risks. A proper balance between the necessary rehabilitation measures and corresponding security measures was not in place. The risk reduction strategies needed to be better targeted in relation to the level of the threat, as highlighted by the public prosecutor office in the specific case.

HYPOTHESIZED LOCATION IN THE MODEL

As for Case 1, the expected benefits from joining were seen as rather high, because the person involved expected that joining the terrorist network would solve his personal and mental problems. Due to the close family ties and the probation given by the authorities, the exit costs would have been rather low before the attack was launched. The perpetrator was known to the authorities and even spent time in prison, and as the family knew about his increasing tendencies of radicalization, he ranked low regarding obscurity and indistinguishability to outsiders (even if the authorities underestimated his degree of radicalization that finally led to the attack).

The analysis and the facts-based interpretation regarding the location of the case on each of the three axes results in the visualized model in Figure 8.3.

Table 8.2 Allocation based on the case analysis

Model dimension	Hypothesized location and justification
Expected benefits from joining	high (ISIS related activity appeared to him as a solution to his depression and mental problems)
Exit costs	low (the close family tried to prevent him and the authorities gave him another chance)
Indistinguishability to outsiders	low (spent time in prison, was monitored by French security organizations, and was supposed to be under electronic-ankle bracelet restrictions)

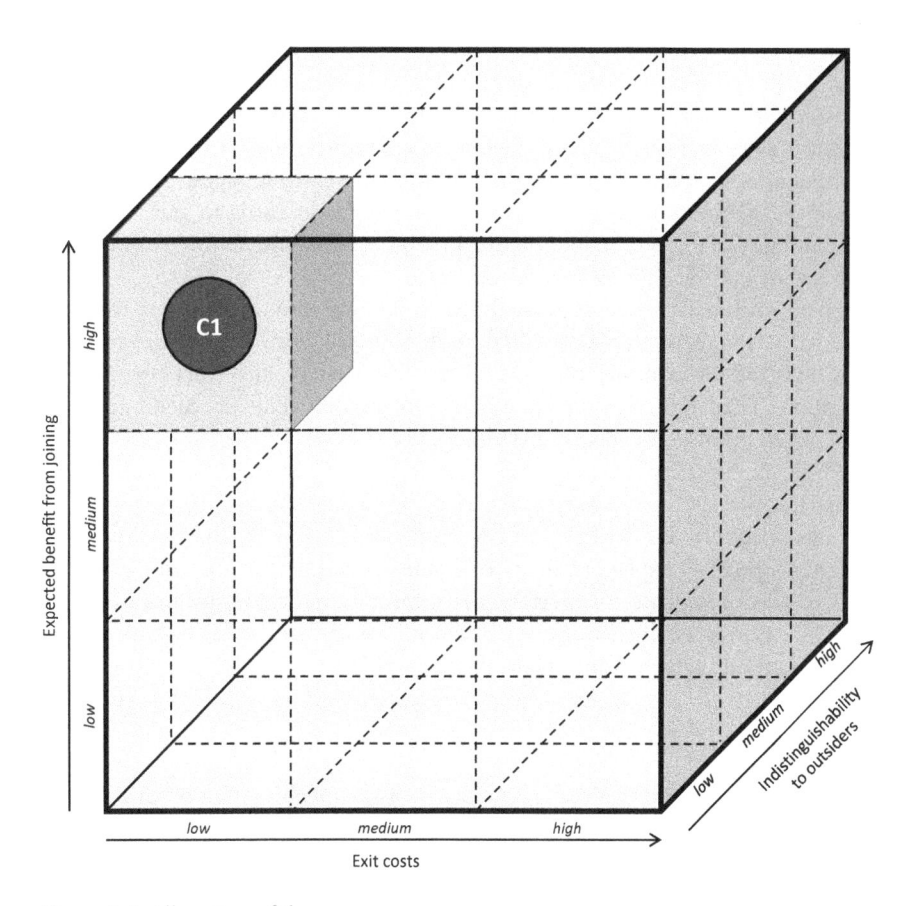

Figure 8.3 Allocation of the case.

Case 2: organized (cyber)crime

SHORT SUMMARY

In August 2016, the Office of the Attorney General of Switzerland filed an indictment in accelerated proceedings against three suspected members of a ring specializing in the fraudulent misuse of credit card data for commercial gain. One of these three members was Farid Essebar, a Moroccan/Russian national known in cyberspace as Diabl0. This was the first time that an indictment was filed for a global phishing case in Switzerland.

The three defendants were charged with computer fraud for commercial gain and multiple counts of attempted computer fraud. The Office of the Attorney General of Switzerland accused the defendants of unlawfully obtaining the data, worldwide, of at least 133,600 credit cards (3,602 of which were Swiss credit cards). The defendants operated from October 2009 until their arrests in 2014 and 2015. They obtained the credit card data by carrying out phishing attacks, using spoof e-mails, websites and text messages.

The perpetrators used the illegally obtained credit cards to purchase services and goods for themselves or third parties or had money unlawfully paid to them via various money transferrals.

These criminal proceedings qualified as a pilot case, as this was the first time in Switzerland that individuals not physically present in the country were charged of criminal offences. The three defendants were arrested in Bangkok (Thailand) and extradited to Switzerland. The proceedings were fast-tracked and the defendants pleaded guilty.

However, in October 2016, the Swiss Federal Criminal Court refused to accept the charges in summary proceedings for a lack of jurisdiction regarding the acts committed abroad by the foreign perpetrators to the detriment of foreign victims. It explained in its oral substantiation that the conviction of such acts would equate to interference in foreign matters under international law. The Office of the Attorney General of Switzerland then had to release the accused individuals from pre-trial custody.

OUTCOME OF MAIN COUNTER-MEASURES

Initially, the Attorney General of Switzerland was of the opinion that, due to the provisions of the Cybercrime Convention in conjunction with Article 6 Swiss Criminal Code (jurisdiction under state treaty obligation), Switzerland is also responsible for dealing with crimes committed abroad by foreign nationals against foreign victims. It was argued that this applies all the more as the charges considered only those states that had previously confirmed not to request extradition. However, as previously noted, the Swiss Federal Criminal Court did not follow this argumentation.

This case underscores how difficult it is to use national responses to counter transnational crimes committed in cyberspace, and was a big blow for

Understanding the crime-terrorism nexus 127

the Attorney General of Switzerland. One representative of the Attorney General of Switzerland stated that one is effectively trying to carry out a legal process of tomorrow with the means of yesterday.

One of the main challenges is to identify phishing offenders: it is very difficult to attribute phishing activities to specific individuals, especially when they are operating rather carefully, as the three people in this case. Moreover, requests for legal support from other countries and/or multinational companies (e.g. internet companies with headquarters in the US) take a long time to be accepted and processed. Such investigations are incredibly cumbersome. For example, just the printed version of a Facebook-profile of one of the perpetrators of this case consisted of over 29,000 pages.

It does not come as a surprise therefore that the Attorney General of Switzerland ceases the investigations in 75 per cent of its phishing cases after not being able to identify specific perpetrators or unsuccessfully requesting support from other countries and/or companies.

HYPOTHESIZED LOCATION IN THE MODEL

Due to the large gains that can be (and actually were) acquired, the expected benefits from joining can considered as being rather high. At the same time, the exit costs are rather low, because the criminals operate from different countries and if they manage to not leave digital traces, they can disappear and remain anonymous. Additionally, after being arrested in Thailand and brought to custody in Switzerland, the main suspect was even released and was able to leave the country. In contrast, the indistinguishability to outsiders was high, because of the global distribution of the OC group members, the covered operations in cyberspace and the use of middlemen when physical presence was needed.

The analysis and the facts-based interpretation regarding the location of the case on each of the three axes results in the visualized model in Figure 8.4.

Table 8.3 Allocation based on the case analysis

Model dimension	Hypothesized location and justification
Expected benefits from joining	high (the main motivation for the perpetrators seemed to be financial benefits)
Exit costs	low (when the case would have remained uncovered, he might have had the chance to disappear; he was also freed from the charges made in Switzerland)
Indistinguishability to outsiders	high (the group operated mainly in cyberspace, was based in Thailand and consisted of individuals of different nationalities; they also often used middlemen when obtaining cash-outs)

128 *Florian Huber et al.*

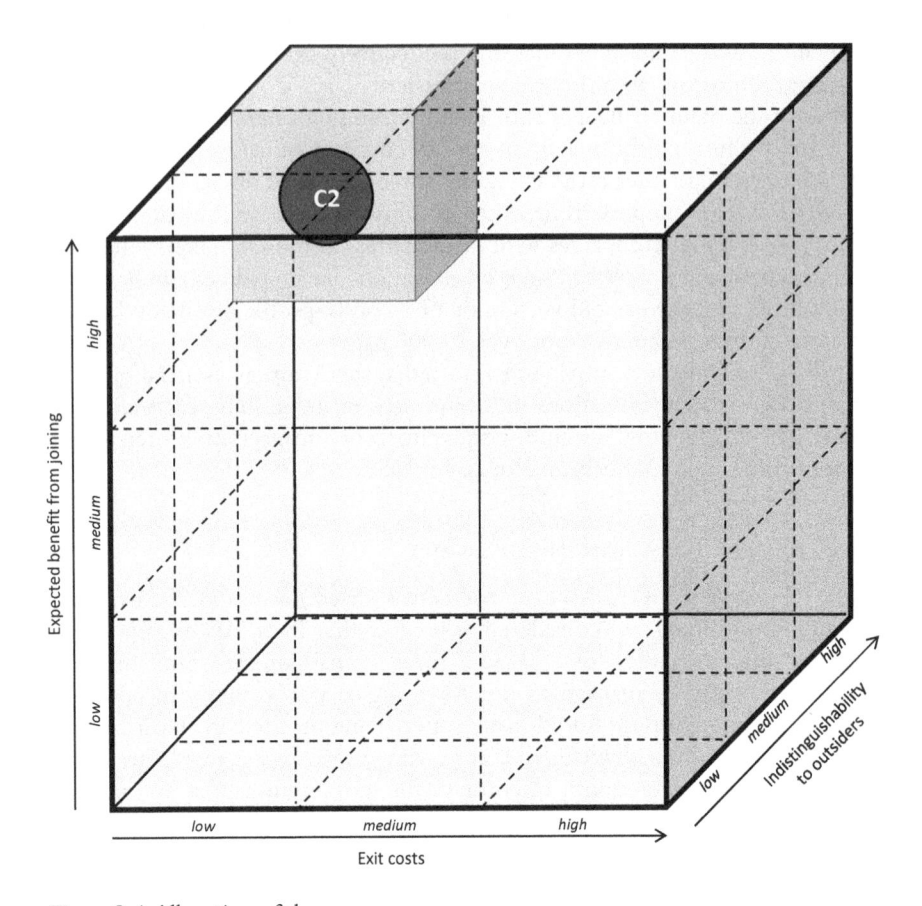

Figure 8.4 Allocation of the case.

Case 3: radicalization

SHORT SUMMARY

Sandra, a young girl, born in Morocco, of Moroccan citizenship, legally resident in Spain (Gandia, Valencia) initiated a process of radicalization of her religious and political beliefs. A student at a local high school, she started to defend and support ISIS in social networks. She decided she wanted to emigrate and marry a mujahidin, therefore she contacted people who informed her that she needed to go to Syria through Istanbul.

Upon her return to Spain, she started to disseminate propaganda of ISIS and calling for the jihad with even more vehemence. She talked with several people of her wish to move to Syria and encouraged other people to do so. She manifested her intention to contribute with money. Her parents opposed her decision, refused to let her go to a conflict zone and insisted that she

Understanding the crime-terrorism nexus 129

continue her studies in Morocco, ignoring that her contacts with ISIS were, in fact, in Morocco.

OUTCOME OF MAIN COUNTER-MEASURES

She was convicted for collaboration with TN. She was sentenced to five years imprisonment, and five years of parole. She was acquitted of being a member of a TN, self-indoctrination and attempt to move to foreign territory controlled by a TN.

HYPOTHESIZED LOCATION IN THE MODEL

Case 3 is again situated in the domain of violent radicalization and terrorist networks. The expected benefits from joining are located in the middle of the axis because the perpetrator was attempting to forge a new identity by adopting a lifestyle more meaningful than was her current life. The exit costs were rather low in this case, because the person did not join the terrorist network, but was only striving to do so. Based on the provided information, the indistinguishability to outsiders was also located at a low level, because the girl used her real name in regular social media channels and only switched to using fake names at a later stage.

The analysis and the facts-based interpretation regarding the location of the case on each of the three axes results in the visualized model in Figure 8.5.

Outlining further applications

While the allocation of particular cases in the TAKEDOWN model presented in the previous section represents a major step towards a better understanding of these phenomena by allocating them in a three-dimensional space, this section outlines future applications of the model, which are intended to trace the dynamics of the cases or the interconnections as well as the interdependencies of the OC and the TN domains.

Table 8.4 Allocation based on the case analysis

Model dimension	Hypothesized location and justification
Expected benefits from joining	medium (as they are mainly related with identity and belonging and not related to any financial or other benefits)
Exit costs	low (as the individual actually didn't join yet the IS but was mainly in contact through online networks and – if ever – through physical middlemen)
Indistinguishability to outsiders	low (the activities of the case where mainly online in social media and although by the end she was using fake names etc. she actually started by using her real name)

130 *Florian Huber* et al.

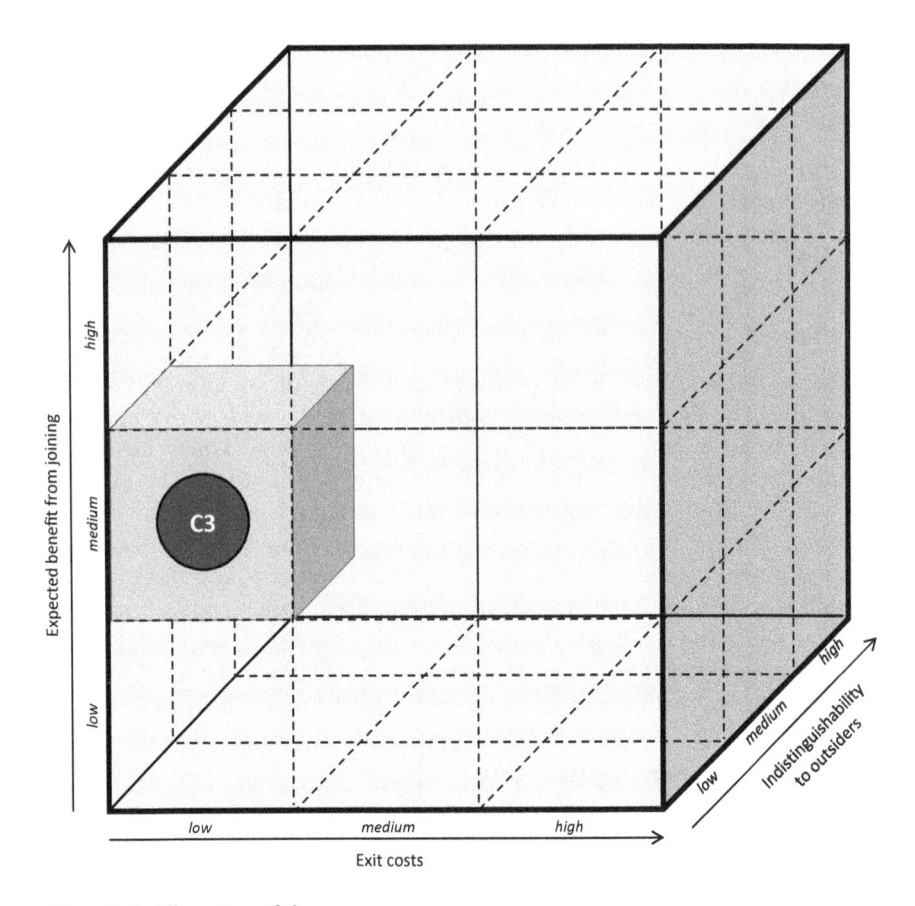

Figure 8.5 Allocation of the case.

Tracing the pathways of cases

One option to show the dynamics of a case is to use the TAKEDOWN model for visualizing how a case moves to different locations within the cube over time. Hence, the model can be used for tracing individual case histories or case 'careers'. For showing the potential of the model to highlight the careers of a criminal, Case 1, which is elaborated above in detail, is analysed in a second iteration and the major stages of the pathway are located in the three-dimensional space.

Changing locations (from L1 to L5) of Case 1 within the three-dimensional model

– From **L1** to **L2**: Coming from a non-religious background, Case 1 had a rather rapid radicalization process; the closer surrounding didn't really notice it; but when the individual was arrested for trying to travel to Syria, the case became recorded, but he was offered parole.

Understanding the crime-terrorism nexus 131

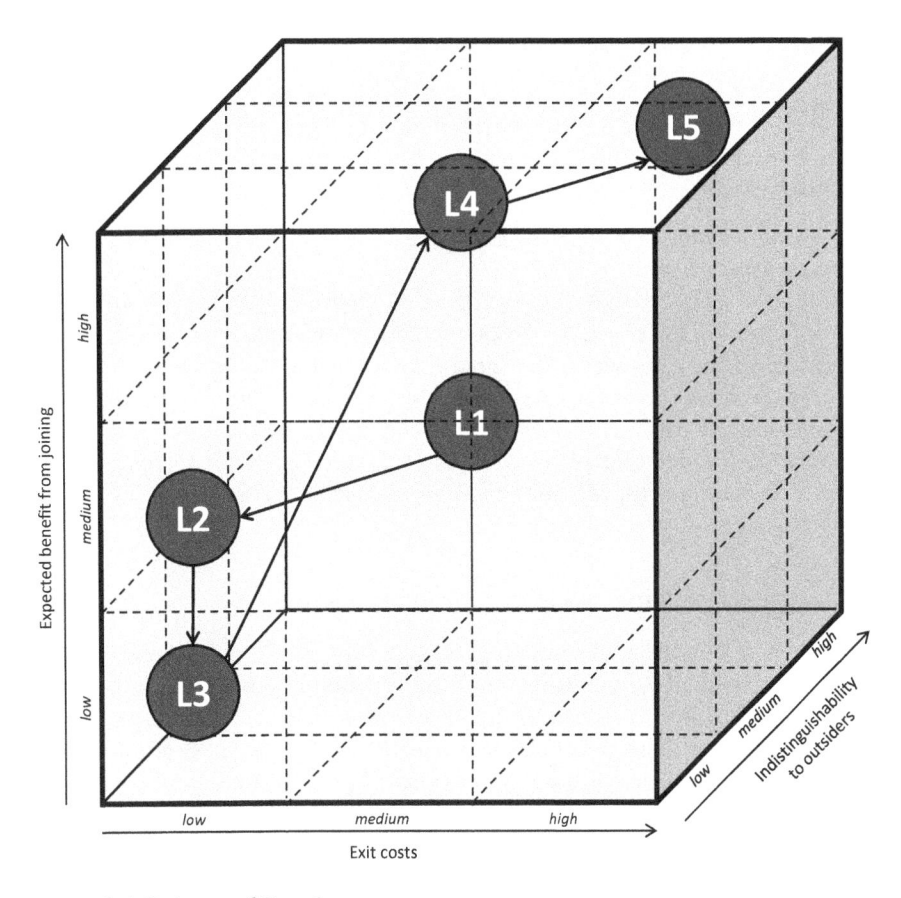

Figure 8.6 Pathway of Case 1.

→ *expected benefits from joining remaining medium; decreasing exit cost; decreasing indistinguishability to outsiders*

- From **L2** to **L3**: Case 1 tried to enter Syria again, but was caught and held in preventive custody for several months; he was approved for house arrest with an electronic tag and to go under 'supervision and support' of his close family and local social welfare institutions; everything was put in place for his de-radicalization and re-integration into society.

  → *decreasing expected benefits from joining; exit costs are low; indistinguishability to outsiders is low*

- From **L3** to **L4**: The perpetrator was sure that joining the IS or carrying out an attack would help him to overcome his depressions and his need for doing something significant; over several months he was more and more drawn into this idea.

→ *significantly increasing expected benefits from joining; increasing exit costs; increasing indistinguishability to outsiders*

- From **L4** to **L5**: The perpetrator was able to use a crypto-messenger service for finding a collaborator and for planning the attack; for unknown reasons the electronic tag was deactivated on the day of the attack; finally, the perpetrator carried out the attack.

→ *expected benefits from joining are high; exist costs are high; indistinguishability to outsiders is high*

The information on Case 1 allows the raw visualization of the dynamic movement of the case within the three-dimensional Cube Model. However, the more information on a case is available, the more precise the different locations and the pathways can be reproduced. This would furthermore allow a comparison of different pathways with each other in order to find similar patterns or common triggers for becoming radicalized, engaged in organized crime groups or in terrorist networks.

Integrating the OC/TN-Nexus

As regards the so-called 'nexus' of OC and TN, the Cube Model is also intended to be used for cases that are clearly situated in both domains or have changed these domains. Research has shown that there are several interconnections between these two fields, particularly when organized crime activities are used for financing terrorist networks.[5] Furthermore, research has also identified and elaborated on several individuals (cases) that were active in (small-scale) organized crime activities before becoming jihadists. When discussing the nexus, it is therefore crucial to differentiate between these aspects, which also lead to different representations within the model. The following two examples intend to discuss the 'nexus option' for applying the Cube Model and to provide hypothesized locations of these exemplary cases.

Example 1: ISIS carried out human trafficking, a form of organized crime, for financing its terrorist activities and was/is at the same time highly active as a terrorist network – using its resources for carrying out criminal activities. The following figure therefore shows a hypothesized double allocation of ISIS in the three-dimensional space, with both domains mutually dependent from each other (see Figure 8.7a).

The bottom-right dot shows the location of ISIS related to its organized crime activities in human trafficking. Here, the expected benefits from joining are on a medium level as they are mainly related to moderate financial benefit that are (compared to large-scale organized financial crime, for example) rather moderate. The exit costs are low as human trafficking can be stopped rather quickly and easily. Also the indistinguishability to outsiders is low, because it is a rather common organized crime activity, with clearly defined routes, practices and counter-measures.

Understanding the crime-terrorism nexus 133

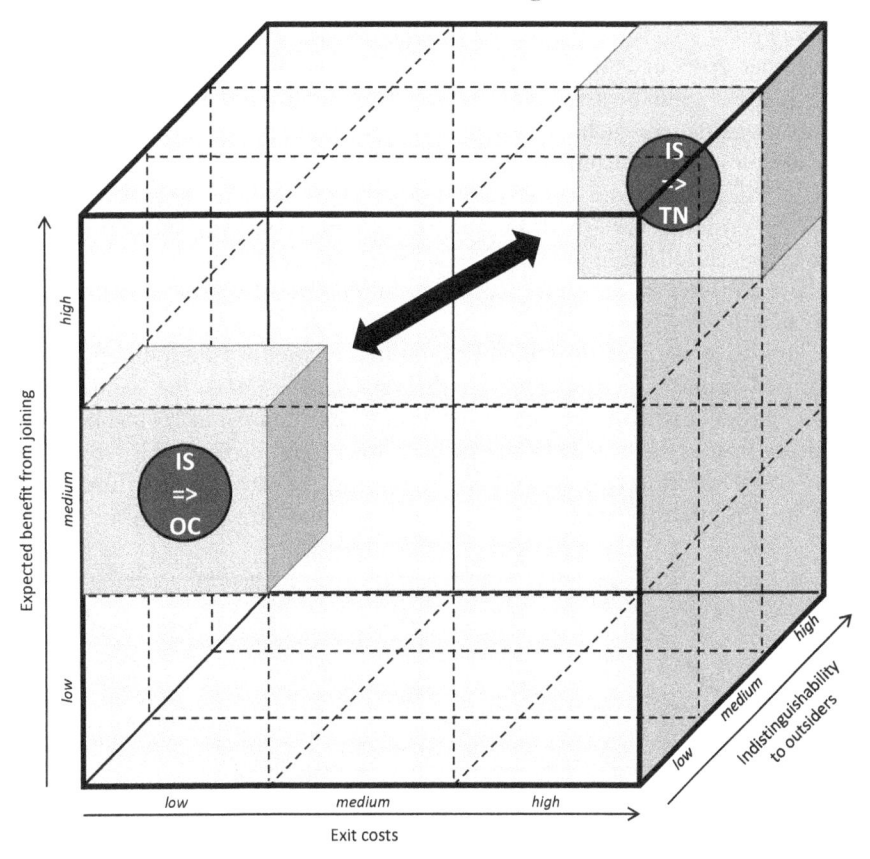

Figure 8.7a Example 1: IS active in different domains at the same time.

The top-right dot shows the location of terrorism activities by ISIS. In this domain, the expected benefits from joining are defined as high, because they are not only related with financial benefits through acquisition of territories. The expected benefits are mainly built on societal power and spiritual compliance. The exit costs are high, because fighters in Syria are killed, returning foreign fighters are put in prison and recruited terrorists are often killed during an attack. The indistinguishability is also high, because outsiders do not have many insights into the structures of the Caliphate. Furthermore, there are also many cases of recruited terrorists who were able to prepare an attack without being detected.

Example 1 intends to highlight the possibility of including both domains of activity into the same model in case an individual or group is active in OC and TN at the same time. The exercise aims to highlight how locations of the same case can vary depending on the domain, and how the different domains are mutually dependent on each other.

In contrast, the following example is closely related to the issue of pathways and careers, but is at the same time based on the concept of the nexus.

134 *Florian Huber* et al.

Example 2: Abdelhamid Abaaoud, who organized the terrorist attacks in November 2015 in Paris, had a criminal career before joining ISIS. Starting with petty crimes, he later dealt with stolen goods and was arrested for a number of offences such as violent disorder and robbery. He was arrested several times and spent time in prison.

The following figure shows a hypothesized changing allocation in the three-dimensional space, with the case moving from one domain to the other after being radicalized in prison and – after serving as a foreign fighter in Syria and as a recruiter in Belgium – finally becoming the mastermind behind the Paris attacks (see Figure 8.7b).

The box at the bottom-left shows the involvement of the perpetrator in organized crime activities. Due to the type and scale of the crimes, the expected benefits from joining were rather low (compared to the benefits of other crimes such as cyber-fraud or money laundering). Also the exit costs were low due to the types and the scope of the crimes committed. Finally, the indistinguishability to outsiders was low too, because the

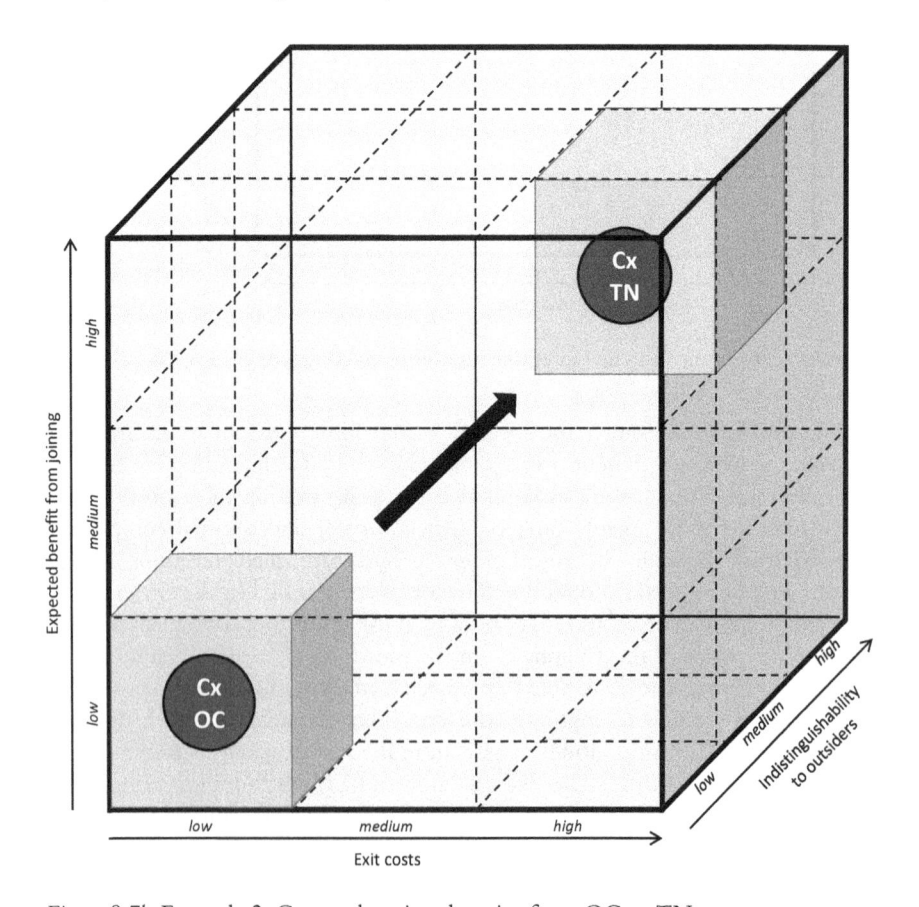

Figure 8.7b Example 2: Case x changing domains from OC to TN.

perpetrator had a criminal record, was previously arrested and spent time in prison.

During his time in prison, the perpetrator became radicalized. He travelled to Syria at least twice and finally acted as the mastermind of the attacks in Paris in November 2015. Hence, he changed the domain and moved to another location, which is represented by the top-right box in Figure 8.7. The expected benefits from joining increased as ISIS promised that its members would be part of an elite. At the same time, the exit costs increased, because the more an individual became involved with ISIS, the more difficult it became to enter mainstream society again. The indistinguishability to outsiders was of medium level, because although the perpetrator managed to travel back and forth between France or Belgium and Syria, the authorities as well as the public knew about his existence from an online video that showed him as an ISIS fighter, sharing his motivations with the public.

Example 2 intends to highlight the possibility of using the nexus-approach for highlighting the movement of a particular case from one domain to another, and for tracing at the same time its changing location in the three-dimensional model.

Understanding the (un)intended consequences of counter-measures

As already highlighted above, the potential scope and range for applying the model for practical use is very much dependent on the volume of information available for each case. When more information on counter-measures is included, the model may also be used for assessments of such activities.

Developing and analysing counter-scenarios

In addition to violent radicalization and terrorism, the model can be applied for tracing the pathways of particular cases against the counter-measures adopted. See for example, the EU Counter-Terrorism Strategy,[6] adopted by the European Council in 2005 and built on four major pillars. (1) *Prevent*: addresses the causes of radicalization and terrorist recruitment. (2) *Protect*: focuses on the protection of citizens and infrastructures and on the reduction of the vulnerability to attacks. (3) *Pursue*: aims to hinder the planning and organizational capacity of terrorists, and to bring terrorists to justice. (4) *Respond*: focuses on preparing, managing and minimizing the consequences of a terrorist attack.

By bringing in the factor 'time' as a fourth dimension and by using research and modelling methods such as scenario analysis,[7] a set of future scenarios along the main pillars of the EU Counter-Terrorism Strategy could be developed. The movement of the case based on the application of a particular measure can then be visualized by showing its changing location in the model.

The following figure shows a combination of possible scenarios for an exemplary case from the field of violent radicalization and terrorism. It

136 *Florian Huber* et al.

combines potential impacts on the location of the case within the model, when a particular pillar of the EU Counter-Terrorism Strategy is applied. Although it is not based on an actual scenario analysis, this example demonstrates the potential of the cube for evaluating counter-measures (see Figure 8.8).

Outlook

Previous research has shown that approaches to counter radicalization and terrorism need to be sensitive to the nature of the environment in which the specific problem lies. Against the background of situational crime prevention, this chapter tries to clarify the picture by demonstrating that the incidence of violent radicalization can be located within the three-dimensional model space (the Cube Model). Such a dynamic approach – especially when implemented as a case-based technological tool – can constitute a significant support for stakeholders such as first-line-practitioners and law enforcement agencies.

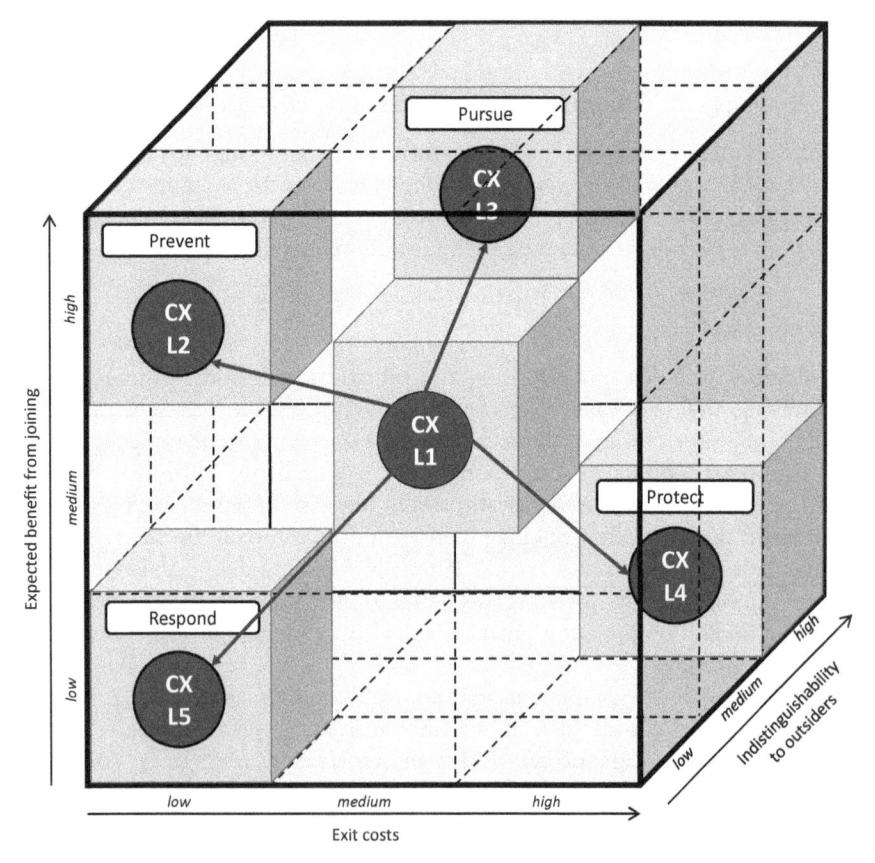

Figure 8.8 Hypothesized case location changes by different PPPR measures.

In addition to contributing to a better understanding of the phenomena and their dynamics (including the nexus of terrorism and organized crime), the model can provide additional intelligence for planning, implementing and evaluating counter-measures or strategies against individual engagement in extremist groups or terrorist networks.

For each case, the model considers a broad variety of drivers and variables, which feed into the allocation of a case in the cube. The more available information on a case, the more precise its location, but also the easier the comparative analysis of its trajectory with that of other cases. Therefore, detailed information on cases is crucial for supporting practical applications of the proposed Cube Model for first-line-practitioners and law enforcement agencies.

The concepts presented in this chapter could be transferred into a software tool and onto a case categorization matrix. Such a tool would rely on a database, where a large number of existing and accessible OC and TN cases are structured along the common situational-crime-prevention variables. The logic of the model, which allocates cases in the three-dimensional cube, could be used for performing semi-automated risk assessments of current cases by enabling comparisons with a large number of previous (closed) cases that show similar parameters. Such a tool would support first-line practitioners and law enforcement in making informed decisions on a current case by building on existing knowledge, information and data.

Acknowledgement

Funding has been received from the European Union's Horizon 2020 Research and Innovation Programme under Grant Agreement No. 700688. More information on the project: www.takedownproject.eu

Notes

1 www.takedownproject.eu.
2 TAKEDOWN Report D2.1 (Literature Exploration): https://takedownproject.eu/wp-content/uploads/2016/12/TAKEDOWN_700688_D2.1-Literature-exploration-and-open-access-bibliography....pdf.
3 TAKEDOWN Report D2.6 (European Baseline Report): https://takedownproject.eu/wp-content/uploads/2017/07/TAKEDOWN_700688_D2.6-European-Baseline-report-on-current-OCTN-specifics-....pdf.
4 The full case matrix is presented in a public TAKEDOWN-report: www.takedownproject.eu/wp-content/uploads/2018/04/TAKEDOWN_700688_D4.4-Initial-practitioners-toolkits-and-policy-recommendations.pdf.
5 https://icct.nl/wp-content/uploads/2017/04/OC-Terror-Nexus-Final.pdf.
6 https://register.consilium.europa.eu/doc/srv?l=EN&f=ST%2014469%202005%20REV%204.
7 www.oecd.org/site/schoolingfortomorrowknowledgebase/futuresthinking/scenarios/37246431.pdf.

Bibliography

Abrahms, M. (2008), 'What Terrorists Really Want: Terrorist Motives and Counter-terrorism Strategy', *International Security*, 32(4): 78–105.

Arango, T. (2014), 'A Boy in ISIS. A Suicide Vest. A Hope to Live', *New York Times*, www.nytimes.com/2014/12/27/world/middleeast/syria-isis-recruits-teenagers-as-suicide-bombers.html.

Barron, G. and Erev, I. (2003), 'Small Feedback-based Decisions and their Limited Correspondence to Description-based Decisions', *Journal of Behavioral Decision Making*, 16(3): 215–233.

Basra, R. and Neumann, P.R. (2016), 'Criminal Pasts, Terrorist Futures: European Jihadists and the New Crime-terror Nexus', *Perspectives on Terrorism*, 10(6): 25–40

BBC News (2015, September 21), 'More Islamic State Defectors Speaking Out – Report', www.bbc.com/news/world-middle-east-34313337.

Briggs, R. and Silverman, T. (2014), *Western Foreign Fighters: Innovations in Responding to the Threat*, London: Institute for Strategic Dialogue.

Canada – Attorney General v Ward (1993), 2 S.C.R. 689, www.asylumlawdatabase.eu/en/content/canada-attorney-general-v-ward-1993-2-scr-689-1993-dlr-4th-1.

Chesney, R.M. (2005), 'The Sleeper Scenario: Terrorism-support Laws and the Demands of Prevention', *Harvard Journal on Legislation*, 42(1): 1–89.

Chrisafis, A. (2015, February 16), 'Copenhagen Shooting Suspect Omar el-Hussein – A Past Full of Contradictions', *Guardian*, www.theguardian.com/world/2015/feb/16/copenhagen-shooting-suspect-omar-el-hussein-a-past-full-of-contradictions.

Cullen, C. (2014, August 29), 'Anti-radicalization Program being Developed by RCMP', *CBCNews*, www.derryjournal.com/news/death-of-informer-1-2143992.

Ducol, B., Bouchard, M., Davies, G., Ouellet, M. and Neudecker, C. (2016), 'Assessment of the State of Knowledge: Connections between Research on the Social Psychology of the Internet and Violent Extremism', www.tsas.ca/publications/assessment-of-the-state-of-knowledge/.

Federal Ministry for Europe, Integration and Foreign Affairs (BMeiA) (2016), 'EU Action in the Fight Against Terrorism', www.kommunalnet.at/fileadmin/Partner/BMeiA/EUGemeinderaeteinformation_Terrorismusbekaempfung_Newsletter_Juni_2016.pdf.

Frey, B.S. (2007), 'War on Terrorism and More Democratic Alternatives. Preconditions of Democracy', *Tampere Club Series*, 2: 187–201.

Frey, B.S. and Luechinger, S. (2002), 'Terrorism: Deterrence May Backfire', working paper series/Institute for Empirical Research in Economics No. 136, Zurich: University of Zurich.

Ganesh, L. (2015), 'Evaluating the Effectiveness of US Strikes as a Counterterrorism Policy in Yemen', Honors Thesis Collection, https://repository.wellesley.edu/thesiscollection/250.

Golan, G.D. (2016), *Countering Violent Extremism: A Whole Community Approach to Prevention and Intervention*, Long Beach: California State University.

Harrison, G. (2015), 'Austrian Girl Who Joined ISIS in Syria was Used as a Sexual Present for New Fighters before Being Beaten to Death', www.thesun.co.uk/archives/news/925373/austrian-girl-who-joined-isis-in-syria-was-used-as-a-sexual-present-for-new-fighters-before-being-beaten-to-death/.

Johnston, P.B. and Sarbahi, A.K. (2016), 'The Impact of US Drone Strikes on Terrorism in Pakistan', *International Studies Quarterly*, 60(2): 203–219.

Kronen Zeitung (2014), 'Mädchen ausgerissen, um im Dschihad zu kämpfen'. www.krone.at/wien/maedchen-ausgerissen-um-im-dschihad-zu-kaempfen-von-wien-nach-syrien-story-400570.

Kruglanski, A.W., Chen, X., Dechesne, M., Fishman, S. and Orehek, E. (2009), 'Fully Committed: Suicide Bombers' Motivation and the Quest for Personal Significance', *Political Psychology*, 30(3): 331–354.

Maccharles, T. (2015), '"Soft Security" Measures Also Needed to Battle Homegrown Radicalism, Experts Say', *The Star*, www.thestar.com/news/canada/2015/02/27/soft-security-measures-also-needed-to-battle-home-grown-radicalism-experts-say.html.

McDonald, H. and Holland, J. (2016), *INLA-deadly Divisions*, Dublin: Poolbeg Press Ltd.

McDonald, K. (2013), *Our Violent World. Terrorism in Society*, London: Palgrave Macmillan.

Mueller, J.E. (2013), *Terrorism Since 9/11: The American Cases*, Mershon Center, Ohio State University.

Musa, S. and Bendett, S. (2010), *Islamic Radicalization in the United States. New Trends and a Proposed Methodology for Disruption*, Washington: National Defense University Center for Technology and National Security Policy.

Neumann, P.R. (2015), *Victims, Perpetrators, Assets: The Narratives of Islamic State Defectors*, London: ICSR.

Rabasa, A., Pettyjohn, S.L., Ghez, J.J. and Boucek, C. (2010), *Deradicalizing Islamist Extremists*, Arlington: Rand Corporation.

Safi, M. (2015, 19 May), 'Australian Man Who Fled Syria Says He Never Joined "Vicious and Cruel" Isis', *Guardian*, www.theguardian.com/world/2015/may/20/australian-man-who-fled-syria-says-he-never-joined-vicious-and-cruel-isis.

Samra a-t-elle été battue à mort par Daech? (2015, November 25), 'Paris Match', www.parismatch.com/Actu/International/Samra-a-t-elle-ete-battue-a-mort-par-Daech-871069.

Sandeman, G. (2015, November 25), 'IS "Poster Girl" Beaten to Death after Trying to Escape Terror Group', *Sun*, www.thesun.co.uk/archives/news/785037/is-poster-girl-beaten-to-death-after-trying-to-escape-terror-group/.

Schmidt, M.S. (2014), 'Canadian Killed in Syria Lives on as Pitchman for Jihadis', *New York Times*, www.nytimes.com/2014/07/16/world/middleeast/isis-uses-andre-poulin-a-canadian-convert-to-islam-in-recruitment-video.html.

Smith, M.J. (2016), 'Situational Crime Prevention', in *Oxford Bibliography Online*, DOI: 10.1093/OBO/9780195396607-0040.

Smith-Spark, L. and Robertson, N. (2015), 'Who Was Copenhagen Gunman Omar Abdel Hamid El-hussein?', *CNN*, https://edition.cnn.com/2015/02/17/europe/denmark-copenhagen-gunman/index.html.

Spencer, A. (2006), 'The Problems of Evaluating Counter-terrorism', *UNISCI Discussion Papers*, (12): 179.

The Scotsman (2003, October 21), 'McGuinness is Named as Bomb Runner', www.scotsman.com/news/uk/mcguinness-is-named-as-bomb-runner-1-491632.

The Times of Israel (2014, October 11), 'Austrian Girls who Joined IS "Want to Come Home"', www.timesofisrael.com/austrian-girls-who-joined-is-want-to-come-home/

Ward, C. (2015, February 9), 'Former ISIS Member Explains Why He Left Terror Group', *CBSNews*, www.cbsnews.com/news/former-isis-member-explains-why-he-left-terror-group/?ftag=YHF4eb9d17.

Whiteside, C. (2016), 'New Masters of Revolutionary Warfare: The Islamic State Movement (2002–2016)', *Perspectives on Terrorism*, 10: 6–20.

Wilkinson, P. (2000), *The Strategic Implications of Terrorism. Terrorism and Political Violence: A Sourcebook*, New Delhi: Har-anand Publications.

9 Terrorism financing and the crime-terror relationships as challenges for security in Europe

Javier Ruipérez Canales

Introduction

Motivated by the huge financial capacity shown by terrorist groups like Al-Qaeda and later ISIS, as well as by the simplicity and the apparent cheapness of recent terrorist attacks against Europe, terrorism financing (TF) has received increasing attention in the last years. Most of the literature about TF mentions the crucial importance of money for terrorist activity (Keatinge, 2016; Normak and Ranstorp, 2015; Sánchez Medero, 2008; Giménez-Salinas, 2007; Marrero Rocha, 2017; European Commission, 2016). However, if financial resources are essential for such activity to be perpetuated, the constant need for money constitutes, at the same time, a weakness for terrorist organizations and, therefore, a source of opportunity for security. This is the idea that underlies the efforts of Counter Terrorism Financing (CTF), which aims at identifying and sanctioning the appropriation of funds by violent organizations and hampering their ability to move money around. Terrorism and counter-terrorism, in this sense, engage in a competitive game whereby, once one financing modality is detected, new ones are sought and adopted.

The issue of terrorism financing has also been at the core of the crime-terror nexus analysis, at least since the 1990s. The analysis has addressed the economic, political, ideological, tactical or operational dynamics underlying such nexus, exploring the connections, synergies, or even the symbiotic relationships between organized crime and terrorism (Martín Rodríguez, 2017). In fact, some observers would suggest that terrorists have always relied on conventional criminal organizations to satisfy their need for forged documents, weapons and finances (Napoleoni, 2004).

It is also since the 1990s that international efforts have contributed to the delineation of CFT strategies (Bantekas, 2003). Building on the previous Anti Money Laundering (AML) provisions, CTF has attempted to tackle, particularly, the trafficking in arms and the illicit use of the international financial system. Mainly conditioned by Al-Qaeda first and ISIS later, CTF measures and policies have been developed within the emergency climate caused by repeated large terror attacks (European Parliament, 2014). In response, terrorists have strived to identify other options in order to grant continuity to their action. Responses to the threatening evolution of terror, however, have not managed to hamper access to finances by organized violent groups, who keep raising money and hoarding resources (Wensink et al., 2017; Keatinge, Keen and Moiseienko, 2018). The modalities used are complex, at times making counter-measures relatively inadequate in terms of prevention and detection, and an analysis of such complexity may help understand the possible future development of FT as well as CTF (Keatinge, Keen and Moiseienko, 2018: 3).

Understanding terrorism financing

Terrorism adopts different organizational forms: networks, cells, lone actors or foreign fighters. Each poses a different threat, aims at different objectives and has different financial needs. Big international groups need large sums of money: Hezbollah's annual budget was estimated at between $100 and $400 million (Levitt, 2004). The Palestinian Liberation Organization (PLO) is said to have accumulated incomes between $8,000 million and $14,000 million in the mid-1990s (Napoleoni, 2015), while estimates of Al-Qaeda's annual budget are positioned between $16 million and $30 million (Shapiro and Siegel, 2007: 407). If attacks by lone terrorists carried out with knifes or vehicles require derisory amounts, the cost of bigger attacks requiring detailed planning, explosive and coordination of several actors may reach into the hundreds of thousands of dollars. If a cell is part of a larger organization, the expenses for its activity will be covered by that organization. In brief, costs depend on the size, type and activity being conducted (Acharya, 2009b: 24), and include not only operational costs, but also costs for the subsistence of members and their day-to-day reproduction (Oftedal, 2015: 14).

Terrorism financing, therefore, consists of a great diversity of continuously evolving methods and mechanisms. These have been identified by research addressed to big transnational organizations as well as to small cells or lone actors, leading to classifications and categorizations on which there is not always widespread agreement (Normak and Ranstorp, 2015; Bell, 2003; Acharya, 2009b). Legal, illegal and state-sponsored financing are the categories suggested by Krieger and Meierrieks (2011). Transfer mechanisms have also been examined, which explain the choice terrorist organizations face in acquiring and moving funds (Freeman and Ruehsen, 2013). Several types of fundraising methods are found in the work of Oftedal (2015), which also pinpoints 15 different financing sources and activities used by jihadist terrorist cells in Europe. Diversity and complexity tend to increase due to Information and Communication Technologies, speeding the financing process and conferring more power to organizations (FAFT, 2015a).

Some common patterns emerge from the examination of this literature, for instance, a broad distinction between self-sufficient financing and externally derived financing. The former includes all financial operations carried out by terrorists themselves while the latter is provided by donors, sponsors and other external sources. The two modalities, in fact, may or may not exclude each other, and money can also be obtained legally, for example through salaries, official businesses, savings or investments. Illegal activities, on the other hand, include arms trafficking, drug dealing, human beings smuggling, as well as many different forms of fraud, tax evasion, or dodgy financial operations. In most cases, a combination of all these methods is behind terrorism financing: that is, self-financing activities are accompanied by some external support, with money obtained through a combination of legal and illegal means.

All forms of terrorism, enacted by groups, cells, foreign fighters or lone individuals, can acquire funds legally or otherwise (FAFT, 2008, 2015a). Transnational terrorism, however, tends to use legal businesses and companies[1] to both raise and move funds around, to conceal operations and remove traces of dealings, just as conventional organized crime would do. Organizations take advantage of the opportunities offered by the financial arena, accessing mediators and agents who are normally available to all customers (Lin 2016; Ruggiero, 2017). Of course, financial operations require specific skills and competence, but these qualities are provided by new recruits and increasingly sophisticated leaders and accomplices, and it is therefore controversial whether financial markets are sufficiently protected from these types of customers (Napoleoni, 2015). Some studies have even pointed to the possibility that groups such as Al-Qaeda used their own 9/11 attacks to speculate on financial markets on the basis of the privileged information relating to events they themselves were creating (Buesa et al., 2007). In the case of small cells or lone actors, common legal methods include the use of salaries, wages, loans or even borrowing money from relatives or close friends (FAFT, 2008, 2015a; Giménez-Salinas, 2007; Oftedal, 2015). These have also been the preferred methods used by foreign fighters who travelled to Syria to join ISIS (Keatinge, 2015).

Illegal fund raising methods have been historically used by terrorists to obtain resources (Napoleoni, 2004). These include almost every kind of criminal activity we may think about[2] and can be used in different forms by smaller, bigger cells or international terrorist organizations.[3] Bigger terrorist organizations target fragile states and ineffective or absent governments and may engage in one or several of the following: trafficking in drugs or arms, different forms of counterfeit, illegal immigration and humans trafficking, extortion, kidnapping for ransom, smuggling of gold or other luxury articles, illegal trade in raw materials or energy sources (oil and gas), smuggling of antiques, tobacco, illicit trade in agricultural products, credit cards fraud, VAT fraud, environmental crime (the illegal disposal of waste) and cybercriminality (Passas, 2006; Giménez-Salinas, 2007; CAT, 2016; Martín Rodríguez, 2017).

In recent years, the spread of jihadist attacks within Europe suggests an increase in petty criminality associated with terrorism, thus adding new elements to the analysis of the crime-terror nexus (Basra, Neumann and

Brunner, 2016). Petty crime, such as drug dealing, street delinquency, robberies, theft, burglary and the sale of stolen goods are increasingly used to finance terrorist cells (Oftedal, 2015; Keatinge and Keen, 2017). VAT fraud, fraud against banks and other private firms, but also against social welfare agencies, have been common financing methods used by foreign terrorist fighters (FAFT, 2015a). Specific analyses of FTF financing methods[4] found that a combination of legal and illegal methods consists in the use of savings, individual or family resources, loans legitimately obtained, subsidies or government benefits and petty criminality: these were the resources used for travel and maintenance expenses by foreign fighters, who also brought some funds to the organization they joined (Keatinge, 2015).

The terrorism financing methods examined so far depict the trends and evolution of TF over the last decades. But a complete understanding on the phenomenon requires that the analytical effort be extended to a different aspect or phase of the terrorism financing process. Once the money is obtained, often it has to be moved, with the consequence that opportunities arise for security detection and disruption. Methods such as direct physical transportation and hand-out by terrorists, or the use of cash couriers, combine with different formal and non-formal systems. Money shipping services, money value transfer systems and remittance businesses, or even the formal banking system have been commonly used (FATF, 2008, 2015a). Among informal systems, the use of 'Hawala'[5] has been the most commonly explored in literature. In addition, mechanisms such as false trade invoicing of high-value commodities, traveller's cheques and pre-paid cards are among the possibilities that new technologies offer (Freeman, 2011; FAFT, 2015a; Normak and Randstorp, 2015: 18–22). In brief, a comprehensive set of methods is available and, again, possibilities tend to increase with the options offered by ICT developments. According to Freeman and Ruehsen (2013), the terrorists' choice of a transfer method will be given by a combination of factors that among other things include detection risk, reliability, simplicity, convenience and cost.

Counter terrorism financing and the common reactive evolution

The evolution of terrorism financing has been heavily influenced by the development of CTF measures, and vice-versa. During the Cold War period, terrorist funds derived from a mixture of criminal activities and external financing, while crime-terror relationships were mainly confined to the field of arms and drugs traffic (Napoleoni, 2004). State sponsorship and private donors were also common (Sánchez Medero, 2008; FAFT, 2015a). Things changed in the 1990s, when states drastically reduced their support to terrorist organizations as a consequence, on the one hand, of the fall of the Iron Curtain and, on the other, of the development of international counter-measures (Passas and Giménez-Salinas, 2007; Marrero Rocha, 2017; Krieger and Meierrieks, 2011). The original architecture of CTF, in a sense, can be traced back to the 1990s (Bantekas, 2003).

In the early 1990s, UN sanctions against countries providing economic support to terrorism were introduced and, later, extended to non-state entities and individuals (Wesseling, 2014). In 1989 the Financial Action Task Force (FATF) was created, entrusted with the drafting and enactment of an international framework for Anti Money Laundering (AML). Since then, FAFT has developed the main international tools adopted by CTF, including the Special Recommendations which are universally recognized as the international standard for combating money laundering, terrorist financing and arms proliferation. The Recommendations also postulate that terrorist financing be prosecuted as a distinct offence. Currently, no evidence exists indicating that European states finance terrorist organizations such as Al-Qaeda and ISIS (Oftedl, 2015; Passas and Giménez-Salinas, 2007; CAT, 2016).

After the creation of the Financial Action Task Force, some terrorist groups stopped their activity while others looked for new funding sources and financing strategies (Bantekas, 2003). The support to terrorism by non-state external sponsors and private donors increased (Passas and Giménez-Salinas 2007: 496), although new financial strategies were devised that took advantage of markets deregulation and economic globalization (Sánchez Medero, 2008; Marrero Rocha, 2017). This evolution meant, therefore, an increase in the use of donors and private supporters, on one hand, and the development financial skills for terrorists, on the other. Terrorists, in fact, allocated specialist human resources tasked with refining procedures and honing strategies of financial 'engineering' (FAFT, 2015a; Napoleoni, 2015).

In the following years, Al-Qaida expanded the spectrum of terrorist financing with new and complex financing techniques, including business and investments, though continuing to rely on external private donations and the proceeds of different illegal activities (drugs and arms) (Passas and Giménez-Salinas, 2017). The attacks against the US embassies in Kenya and Tanzania led the UN to launch the Security Council Resolution 1267, focused on Taliban involvement in crime and in the financial arena. The Convention for the Suppression of Terrorism Finances was launched by the UN and FAFT in 1999, and contained an extended revision of previous recommendations pertaining to the criminal sphere (FAFT, 2012). In Europe, the development and implementation of measures in line with international UN and FAFT efforts followed the bomb attacks by the Algerian GIA network in 1995 and the aborted plot against the Christmas market in Strasbourg in 2000.

The attacks against the US in 2001 marked a dramatic turning point not only in the fight against terrorism, with the official launch of the 'War on Terror', but also in development of counter-measures in the realm of terrorist financing. The 9/11 attacks reshaped the international scene and terrorism financing became an urgent priority and core component in international and European agendas (Giménez-Salinas, 2007). Since the movement and transfer of big amounts of money were achieved through the formal banking system,

(Keating, Keen and Moiseienko, 2018), the role of financial institutions was placed in the spotlight and strategies were devised that might increase public–private cooperation in the field. In December 2001, EU governments agreed, in the Common Position 2001/931/CFSP, to create a list of individuals, groups and entities involved in terrorism whose funds and financial assets had to be frozen. The strategy was reinforced by Council Regulations (EC) No 2580/2001 and (EC) 881/2002.

The extensive monitoring of data from financing institutions became acceptable and possible due to technical smart software possibilities (Wesseling, 2014). This served to launch the Terrorist Finance Tracking Program (TFTP) set up by the US Treasury Department. The Program ensured that the Society for Worldwide Interbank Financial Telecommunications (SWIFT) gave access to its database, and in 2010 EU member states were also granted access thanks to the EU–US TFTP Agreement (European Commission 2017a).[6] These changes placed financial institutions at the frontline of CTF (Lin 2016) and pushed towards further developments in the area of financial intelligence (FININT). Collaboration is also offered by EUROPOL's FIU.net, a decentralized computer network connecting the national member states Financial Intelligence Units (FIUs), while the informal Egmont Group provides FIUs around the world with a confidential information exchange forum.

The attacks perpetrated in Europe by home-grown terrorists in the first part of the twenty-first century determined yet a new turning point. The bombings in Madrid in 2004 and in London in 2005 modified the general perception of terrorism and made its better understanding urgent. The study of radicalization grew, revealing that terrorists were not foreigners crossing the borders of Europe with the intent to attack its territories, but European residents and citizens bombing their own countries after embracing fundamentalist ideas and radical narratives. The Madrid attack was carried out by individuals engaged in petty crime and drug trafficking, who got hold of bombs through a drugs-explosives exchange deal (Passas and Giménez-Salinas, 2007). Estimates of the total cost of the operations vary by up to 90 per cent: while FAFT reports the figure of $10,000, other commentators indicate $60,000 or $100,000. The cost of the London bombings in July 2005 is estimated at between $8,000 and $15,000 (FAFT, 2008; Oftedal, 2015; Passas and Giménez-Salinas, 2007).

Emergency reactions translated into a new set of measures being developed at international level as well as in Europe. The Counter-Terrorism Implementation Task Force (CTITF) was established in 2005 to coordinate efforts, and a specific Working Group on Tackling the Financing of Terrorism was created to assist States in implementing counter-measures. The European Union's Strategy on combating the financing of terrorism was presented in December 2004.[7] The 2005 Third Anti-Money Laundering Directive (2005/60/EC)[8] extended the scope of AML to terrorist financing, moving from a rule-based to a risk-based approach, and enhancing the 'know your customer' principle to push financial institutions into increasing vigilance on transactions. The cash control Regulation[9] (EC) No 1889/2005 and the Regulation (EC) No 1781/2006 stipulated the gathering of information on customers transferring funds, while the Payments Services Directive 2007/64/EC addressed alternative remittance systems, reinforcing public–private cooperation (Wesseling, 2014; Wensink et al., 2017).

Terrorism financing trends and the 'new' crime-terror relations

During the second decade of this century, ISIS widely modified, again, the global terrorism scene. In 2014, the organization reached an annual income between $1,890 million (Heißner et al., 2017) and $2,900 million (CAT, 2016).[10] The money helped ISIS to continue the war, maintain a vast territory under its control and invest large sums in marketing and propaganda. It quickly became one of the richest ever terrorist organizations, managed with efficiency as a perfect financial machine and promoting a totally new model of terrorist organization (FAFT 2015b; Sánchez 2008; Napoleoni 2015). The new threat forced once more CTF to react and adapt responses to the emerging financing methods and trends (FAFT, 2015a; Wensink et al., 2017). Directive 2014/42/EU set minimum security standards, reinforced cross-border cooperation and established common practices in the freezing and confiscation of assets. The Payment Services Directive 2015/2366/EU amended previous Directives, while Regulation (EU) 2015/847 relating to information on payers and beneficiaries of money transfers expanded the scope of surveillance by financial institutions. Later, specific efforts included the Council Decision 1693/2016 and Council Regulation 1686/2016 to adopt restrictive measures independently from the UN (European Commission, 2017b).

In February 2016 the European Union's Strategy on combating the financing of terrorism gave way to the European Commission's action plan, which is expected to inform EU policies and act as the main European instrument to be utilized by CTF. The Action Plan, which in fact has not yet been adopted or fully implemented, contains legislative and non-legislative propositions as well as the suggestion of strategic practices in full respect of the different EU Treaties. The Plan identifies the main objectives as: to disrupt terrorism revenue sources, prevent and detect fund transfers, and trace terrorists through their financial operations (European Commission, 2017b). As part of the Action Plan, in July 2016 the Commission presented a proposal of revision of the Fourth Anti-Money Laundering Directive to further strengthen EU rules on anti-money laundering and better counter-terrorist financing. The proposal set out a series of measures to ensure increased transparency of financial transactions, the use of virtual currencies or pre-paid cards and enhancing the access of Financial Intelligence Units to information. To reinforce cooperation and coordination, the European Counter Terrorism

Centre (ECTC) launched in 2016 by Europol included within its mandate the sharing of information, intelligence and expertise on terrorism financing (European Commission, 2017b).

ISIS produced an impact not only on international terrorism, but also on the modus operandi of terrorism in Europe (Europol, 2016). With the decline of the 'Caliphate', (Heißner et al., 2017) Europe has to face the novel threats to security posed by new terrorist groups. As is well known, ISIS attempted to mobilize Muslims in the West not only through direct recruitment, but also by persuading them to enact Jihad in their home country. It incited independent attacks to be perpetrated in the Western world without these being coordinated by the central organization, producing explicative manuals, tactical guidelines and a plethora of other military material (Europol, 2016). As different scholars have argued, the new strategy resulted in a reinforcement of operational procedures adopted by terrorists within Europe which are relevant for financing and, at the same time, bring the crime-terror nexus to a different level. Changes can be noted in the ways in which terror attacks are committed as well as in the choice of radicalization and recruitment pathways. Large and carefully planned terrorist attacks, like the one launched in Paris in January and November 2015, have coexisted with more rudimentary but equally effective attacks. The relative simplicity and costless character of the latter have contributed to a dramatic increase in social anxiety and feelings of insecurity among Europeans (Nitsch and Ronert, 2017). High impact attacks committed with the mere use of knives or rented vehicles (like those in Nice and Berlin in 2016, followed in 2017 by more in Stockholm, London, Manchester and Barcelona), though described as 'low-cost' or 'low-tech' terrorism, cause as much fear as large-scale operations (Levitt, 2017; Acharya, 2009a; Witherspoon, 2017; Zoli, 2017).

Moreover, the spread of low-tech terrorism goes hand in hand with the legitimation of conventional crime victimizing the 'infidels', thereby adding a further source of funds for terrorist activity. In brief, stealing or robbing is permitted if the final goal of the Caliphate is simultaneously pursued (Neumann and Salinas de Frías, 2017). In this respect, the relationships between terrorism and petty crime have been duly highlighted, unveiling new aspects of radicalization, recruitment and the financial issues accompanying them (FATF, 2018). Simcox (2015) found that 22 per cent of the 58 individuals associated with terrorist activity in the West, between July 2014 and August 2015, had a criminal record or were known to law enforcement, while other authors found similar or higher percentages among individuals engaged in terrorist financing: 33 per cent in Germany, 50 per cent in France and Belgium, up to 60 per cent in Norway and The Netherlands (Neumann and Salinas de Frías, 2017). Surely, larger property offences are still important, but the fact that many terrorists have a conventional criminal background deserves proper attention, as it could prove that conventional organizations and terrorist organizations, at least partly, recruit from the same pool of individuals (Normak and Ranstorp, 2015; FAFT, 2018; Basra,

Neuman and Brunner, 2016). This circumstance appears to provide terrorist groups with the advantage of recruiting people who are already trained in criminal activities and are, therefore, malleable when training aimed at refining other illegal, operational skills is offered. In addition, and contrary to what we might think, the use of individuals with a criminal record does not increase the risk of detection, since evidence has shown that terrorist cells involved in crime to finance their activity, between 1994 and 2013, were not more often detected than others (Oftedal, 2015).

Financially self-sufficient organizations possess more operational independence in that they are not obliged to abide by rules and procedures established by external donors. Such organizations are not subordinated to control by peripheral agents, nor do they risk compromising their activities in case of donors' withdrawal (as was the case in the 1990s, when state sponsorship of terrorism came to an end). In Europe, as we have seen, large, costly operations coexist with low-cost ones, both having a huge impact thanks to the successful recruitment and radicalization of home-grown fighters. Both disseminate insecurity and fear, thus making terror all the more effective. Besides, the autonomy given to cells and lone actors helps to dodge CTF controls, allowing the preparation of attacks to merely depend on small amounts of money in what we can term practices of microfinancing. Paradoxically, sophisticated financial operations conducted by large terror groups are easier to detect as they offer a variety of options to law enforcers and other public or private agents. On the contrary, given that European terrorists act, move and spend money in ways that are 'remarkably ordinary' (Oftedal, 2015), their behaviour in the financial sphere is difficult to distinguish from that of their law-abiding counterparts. Leaving fewer footprints, they can easily escape institutional control.

Autonomy gives some groups the possibility of recruiting their own members, conducting criminal activity aimed at acquiring funds, and concealing themselves better in European societies. 'Cells' and 'lone actors' can easily mingle in urban contexts and become indistinguishable, also because they are in no need to keep contacts or establish communication with the larger organizations. Moreover, cells and lone actors have detailed knowledge of the context in which they operate, being able to identify targets and weigh risks in areas familiar to them. In the case of individuals with a previous criminal background, training needs and costs will be substantially reduced, while their capacity to access illegal networks turns out to be an added value. We can therefore hypothesize that international terrorist groups will, in the future, inspire and support attacks in Europe without directly funding them, and will limit their tasks to general indoctrination, emotional communication, marketing operations, and the production of manuals, propaganda and ideological guidelines. If home-grown terrorist attacks in Madrid 2004 and London 2005 made Europeans realize that terrorists did not necessarily come from abroad, the recent evolution shows that European terrorism, day after day, becomes increasingly context specific.

Neither new nor unknown: looking at the future of CTF

While evading law enforcement, terrorism in Europe is changing in a way that facilitates financing procedures and simplifies the planning, preparation and enactment of attacks. The reduction of costs is simultaneous with the ideological rationalization encouraging the resort to conventional crime as a way of securing funds. All these aspects, however, are not new and have also characterized previous terrorist activities in Europe.

Since the middle 1990s, the use of petty crime to fund European jihadist cells has been the second most used method: the financing of 28 per cent of the terrorist acts perpetrated between 1994 and 2013 included illegal activities like drugs trafficking or illicit trade in cars, weapons or forged documents (Oftedal, 2015). The GIA members were described as a group of 'gangster terrorists' in French newspapers due to the fact that many of them had been involved in local criminal groups and gangs (Lia and Kjøk, 2001). The group was able to carry out a bombing attack in 1995 whose total cost, around $20,000, was financed by criminal activities and through the support of its own network located in the UK (Oftedal, 2015). The Madrid attacks constitute a relevant precedent in terms of the current relationships between criminality and terrorism. Already engaged in petty crime and drug trafficking, the attackers obtained the required resources by accumulating criminal proceeds and exchanging quantities of drugs for explosives (Passas and Giménez-Salinas, 2007). A similar strategy was later used in The Netherlands in 2004, but also in the Stockholm bombing of 2010 and in Toulouse in 2012 (Reitano, Clarke and Adan, 2018).

Further studies have also focused on these aspects. For instance, research conducted in 2006 into jihadi terrorism found that many of the sampled individuals involved had been previously active in different forms of crime, with 25 per cent having a criminal record (Bakker, 2006). Finally, the role of prison in fostering radicalization, recruitment and networking has also been examined, showing the strong effect custodial institutions may have on radicalization processes (Reitano, Clarke and Adan, 2018; Neumann and Salinas de Frías, 2017; Basra, Neumann and Brunner, 2016).

On the declining costs of terrorist attacks carried out in Europe, discussions were lively even prior to 9/11 (Wesseling, 2014). An empirical study led by the Norwegian Defence Research Establishment (Oftedal, 2015) analysed the financing of 40 jihadi cells involved in attacks on European soil in the 1994–2013 period. One of the main findings of the study was that those attacks were generally cheap, with 75 per cent costing under $10.000 and only 8 per cent over $20,000. In brief, low-cost terrorism is hardly something new, as by no means new is the circumstance whereby low-cost terror mixes up with larger, thoroughly planned and costly terror operations.

Recent developments are the result of CFT action, to which some concluding remarks must be devoted. CFT strategies and measures have mainly addressed the international dynamics and the financing of big terrorist groups, thus failing to respond to the new developments described above. As terrorism financing is conditioned by CTF initiatives, future institutional responses should predict their own possible effects and foresee the potential counter-responses by terrorist organizations. Midterm strategies, for example, should proceed with detailed evaluations of the outcomes each component of such strategies is likely to produce. Currently, CTF does boost control by creating barriers to external funding sources. However, specific measures that address self-financing through legal or illegal activities need to be strengthened. In addition, public–private cooperation and the role of financing institutions need to be reviewed. This is because the plethora of new modes of terrorist financing remain untouched by public–private concerns. The new response strategies will probably require intelligence-led approaches fostering collaboration among the diverse law enforcement agencies. Ultimately, changes in CTF measures will have to bear in mind the counter-measures that can be potentially adopted by terrorist organizations.

Notes

1 These can be real or ghost companies which usually have a key role in moving funds, buying and shipping materials and other resources.
2 Those are extensive to different illicit fraud and related mechanisms, credit card fraud, insurance fraud and tax evasion to the use of forms of petty or mass criminality and even violence.
3 As an example, while fraud may be used for FTF, other methods as robbery can be used by cells or massive drug or arms traffic will relate to big criminal or terrorist organizations.
4 Interesting and relevant are Keatinge (2015) which specifically analyses the complete FTF joining process including many study cases and communications, and the specific section of FAFT (2015a: 13–23) on the FTF financing methods and techniques.
5 Hawala means transfer in Arabic, but has different denominations as Fei-Chi'I (China), Padala (Philipines), Hundi (India), HuiKuan (Hong Kong) or Pei Kwan (Thailand). A good description can be found in a specific FATF's report (2013).
6 The agreement took effect after EU requirements for providing the appropriate safeguards to accommodate legitimate concerns about security, privacy and respect of fundamental rights.
7 The strategy would be later revised in 2008 and 2011.
8 The Directive is result of previous AML Directives 91/308/EEC and 02001/97/EC.
9 This regulation requires the disclosure of cash or equivalent in excess of €10,000 when entering or leaving the EU.
10 Its incomes and capital widely vary among different analysis (Heißner et al., 2017) but in 2014 roughly rounded $2 billion in 2014 (Stergiou, 2016: 191), much more even than some countries gross profit.

References

Acharya, A. (2009a), 'Small Amounts for Big Bangs? Rethinking Responses to "Low Cost" Terrorism', *Journal of Money Laundering Control*, 12(3): 285–298, doi: https://doi.org/10.1108/13685200910973655.

Acharya, A. (2009b), *Targeting Terrorist Financing: International Cooperation & New Regimes*, London: Routledge.

Bakker, E. (2006), 'Jihadi Terrorists in Europe: Their Characteristics and the Circumstances in Which They Joined the Jihad, An Exploratory Study'. Netherlands Institute of International Relations, Clingendael.

Bantekas, I. (2003), 'The International Law of Terrorist Financing', *The American Journal of International Law*, 97(2): 315–333.

Basra, R., Neumann, P.R. and Brunner, C. (2016), 'Criminal Pasts, Terrorist Futures: European Jihadists and the New Crime-Terror Nexus', *Perspectives on Terrorism*, 10(6). Terrorism Research Initiative and the Center for Terrorism and Security Studies, www.terrorismanalysts.com/pt/index.php/pot/article/view/554.

Bell, R. (2003), 'The Confiscation, Forfeiture and Disruption of Terrorist Finances', *Journal of Money Laundering Control*, 7(2): 105–125.

Buesa, M., Baumert, T., Valiño, A., Heijs, J. and González Gómez, J. (2007), '¿Pueden servir los atentados como fuente de financiación del terrorismo?', La Ilustración Liberal, No 31, www.clublibertaddigital.com/ilustracion-liberal/31/pueden-servir-los-atentados-como-fuente-de-financiacion-del-terrorismo-mikel-buesa-thomas-baume.html.

CAT – Centre for the Analysis of Terrorism (2016), 'ISIS Financing 2015', France, http://cat-int.org/wp-content/uploads/2016/06/ISIS-Financing-2015-Report.pdf.

European Commission (2016), Communication From the Commission to the European Parliament and the Council on an Action Plan for Strengthening the Fight against Terrorist Financing COM (2016)50/F1. European Commission, Estrasburg, http://ec.europa.eu/transparency/regdoc/?fuseaction=list&coteId=1&year=2016&number=50&version=ALL&language=en.

European Commission (2017a), Joint Review Report of the implementation of the Agreement between the European Union and the United States of America on the Processing and Transfer of Financial Messaging Data from the European Union to the United States for the Purposes of the Terrorist Finance Tracking Program, European Commission, Brussels, Belgium, http://eur-lex.europa.eu/legal-content/EN/TXT/?uri=COM:2017:031:FIN.

European Commission (2017b), Comprehensive Assessment of EU Security Policy. Accompanying the document: Communication from the Commission to the European Parliament, the European Council and the Council. Ninth progress report towards an effective and genuine Security Union. European Commission, Brussels, www.europarl.europa.eu/cmsdata/125861/comprehensive%20security%20assessment%20part%201.pdf.

European Parliament (2014), 'Evaluation of EU Measures to Combat Terrorism Financing. In Depth Analysis for the LIBE Committee', Directorate-General for Internal Policies, Policy Department C: Citizens' Rights and Constitutional Affairs (2014), Brussels, Belgium, www.europarl.europa.eu/RegData/etudes/note/join/2014/509978/IPOL-LIBE_NT(2014)509978_EN.pdf.

Europol (2016), 'Changes in Modus Operandi of Islamic State Terrorist Attacks.' Review held by experts from Member States and Europol on 29 November and 1

December 2015, The Hague, Netherlands. www.europol.europa.eu/publications-documents/changes-in-modus-operandi-of-islamic-state-terrorist-attacks.
FATF (2008), 'FATF Terrorist Financing Typologies Report', Financial Action Task Force Paris, France, www.fatf-gafi.org/publications/methodsandtrends/documents/fatfterroristfinancingtypologiesreport.html.
FAFT (2012; Updated October 2016), International Standards on Combating Money Laundering and the Financing of Terrorism and Proliferation. The FATF Recommendations, www.fatf-gafi.org/media/fatf/documents/recommendations/pdfs/FATF_Recommendations.pdf.
FATF (2013), 'The Role of Hawala and Other Similar Service Providers in Money Laundering and Terrorist Financing', Hawala report, Financial Action Task Force Paris, France, www.fatf-gafi.org/publications/methodsandtrends/documents/role-hawalas-in-ml-tf.html.
FATF (2015a), 'Emerging Terrorist Financing Risks, FATF, Financial Action Task Force', Paris, France, www.fatf-gafi.org/publications/methodsandtrends/documents/emerging-terrorist-financing-risks.html.
FATF (2015b), 'Financing of the Terrorist Organisation of the Islamic State and the Levant (ISIL)', (the 'FATF ISIL report'), Financial Action Task Force Paris, France, www.fatf-gafi.org/publications/methodsandtrends/documents/financing-of-terrorist-organisation-isil.html.
FATF (2018), FATF Report: Financing of Recruitment for Terrorist Purposes January 2018, Financial Action Task Force Paris, France, www.fatf-gafi.org/media/fatf/documents/reports/Financing-Recruitment-for-Terrorism.pdf.
Freeman, M. (2011), 'The Sources of Terrorist Financing: Theory and Typology', *Studies in Conflict and Terrorism*, 34(6): 461–475.
Freeman, M. and Ruehsen, M. (2013), 'Terrorism Financing Methods: An Overview', *Perspectives on Terrorism*, 7(4), www.terrorismanalysts.com/pt/index.php/pot/article/view/279/html.
Giménez-Salinas, F.A. (2007), 'Las finanzas del terrorismo de al-Qaida: una lucha desenfocada', *Athena Intelligence Journal*, 2(22), www.files.ethz.ch/isn/47322/Vol. 2%20No%204%20Art%209.pdf.
Heißner, S., Neumann, R.P., Holland-McCowan, J., Basra, R. (2017), 'Caliphate in Decline: An Estimate of Islamic State's Financial Fortunes', *The International Centre for the Study of Radicalisation (ICSR)*, London, http://icsr.info/wp-content/uploads/2017/02/ICSR-Report-Caliphate-in-Decline-An-Estimate-of-Islamic-States-Financial-Fortunes.pdf.
Keatinge, T. (2015), 'Identifying Foreign Terrorist Fighters: The Role of Public-Private Partnership, Information Sharing and Financial Intelligence', *The International Centre for Counter-Terrorism and RUSI* 6(6), Netherlands: The Hague, https://icct.nl/publication/identifying-foreign-terrorist-fighters-the-role-of-public-private-partnership-information-sharing-and-financial-intelligence/.
Keatinge, T. (2016), 'Rethinking CTF Strategy: Using Finance to Stop Terrorists', RUSI Newsbrief, Vol. 36 'Tackling Terrorist Financing', https://rusi.org/publication/newsbrief/rethinking-ctf-strategy-stopping-terrorist-financing-using-finance-stop.
Keatinge, T. and Keen, F. (2017), 'Lone-Actor and Small Cell Terrorist Attacks. A New Front in Counter-Terrorist Finance?', RUSI Occasional Paper, January.
Keatinge, T., Keen, F. and Moiseienko, A. (2018), 'From Lone Actors to Daesh: Rethinking the Response to the Diverse Threats of Terrorist Financing', RUSI

Newsbrief, Vol. 38, https://rusi.org/sites/default/files/20180123_terrorist_financing_proof1.pdf.

Krieger, T. and Meierrieks, D. (2011), *Terrorist Financing and Money Laundering*, http://papers.ssrn.com/sol3/papers.cfm?abstract_id=1860069.

Levitt, M. (2004), 'Going to the Source: Why Al Qaeda's Financial Network Is Likely to Withstand the Current War on Terrorist Financing', *Studies in Conflict and Terrorism*, 27(3): 169–185.

Levitt, M. (2017), 'Low Cost, High Impact: Combating the Financing of Lone-Wolf and Small-Scale Terrorist Attacks'. Testimony submitted to the Terrorism and Illicit Finance Subcommittee, House Financial Services Committee. 6 September, www.washingtoninstitute.org/uploads/Documents/testimony/LevittTestimony20170906.pdf.

Lia, B. and Kjøk, A. (2001), 'Islamist Insurgencies, Diasporic Support Networks, and Their Host States'. Norwegian Defence Research Establishment (FFI) RAPPORT-2001/03789. FFI, Norway.

Lin, T.C.W. (2016), 'Financial Weapons of War', *Minnesota Law Review*, 100. Temple University Legal Studies Research Paper No. 2016-25 pp. 1377–1441. Minnesota, US.

Marrero Rocha, I. (2017), 'Nuevas dinámicas en las relaciones entre crimen organizado y grupos teroristas', Revista Española de Derecho Internacional REDI Vol 69/2, julio-diciembre, pp. 145–169 Asociación de Profesores de Derecho Internacional y Relaciones Internacionales, Madrid – Spain.

Martín Rodríguez, Pablo (2017), European Baseline Report on Organised Crime and Terrorist Network Specifics and Collection of Sources (Deliverable No. 2.6). TAKEDOWN H2020 EU-Project, www.takedownproject.eu.

Napoleoni, L. (2004), *Yihad: Como se financia el terrorismo en la nueva economía*. Ediciones Urano, Barcelona, Spain.

Napoleoni, L. (2015), 'El fénix islamista. El estado islámico y el rediseño de oriente próximo', Espasa Libros S.L.U, Barcelona, Spain.

Neuman, P. and Salinas de Frías, A. (2017), 'Report on the Links between Terrorism and Transnational Organised Crime'. Committee of Experts on Terrorism CODEXTER 4. Council of Europe Secretariat of the Counter-Terrorism Division. Strasbourg, www.coe.int/terrorism.

Nitsch, H. and Ronert, S. (2017), 'Community Policing and Radicalization: Evaluation and European Examples', in Bayerl, P., Karlović, R., Akhgar, B. and Markarian, G. (eds) *Community Policing – A European Perspective. Advanced Sciences and Technologies for Security Applications*. Springer, Cham, pp. 67–82.

Normark, M. and Ranstorp, M. (2015), *Understanding Terrorist Finance. Modus Operandi and National CTF Regimes*, Swedish Defence University, Stockholm, Sweden, www.fi.se/contentassets/1944bde9037c4fba89d1f48f9bba6dd7/understanding_terrorist_finance_160315.pdf.

Oftedal, E. (2015), *The Financing of Jihadi Terrorist Cells in Europe, Norwegian Defence Research Establishment (FFI)*, Norway, www.ffi.no/no/Rapporter/14-02234.pdf.

Passas, N. and Giménez-Salinas, F.A. (2007), 'La financiación del terrorismo de Al Qaida: Mitos y realidades', Revista de Derecho Penal y Criminología, No 19, http://e-spacio.uned.es/fez/eserv.php?pid=bibliuned:DerechoPenalyCriminologia2007-15&dsID=financiacion_terrorismo.pdf.

Reitano, T., Clarke, C. and Adan, L. (2018), 'Examining the Nexus between Organised Crime and Terrorism and Its Implications for EU Programming'. Report result of the CT-MORSE EU funded project CT-MORSE, www.ct-morse.eu/.

Ruggiero, V. (2017), *Dirty Money: On Financial Delinquency*, Oxford: Oxford University Press.

Sánchez, Medero G. (2008), 'La fuentes de financiación legales e ilegales de los grupos terroristas', Revista Política y Estrategia, No 112 https://es.scribd.com/document/148069008/LAS-FUENTES-DE-FINANCIACION-LEGALES-E-ILEGALES-DE-LOS-GRUPOS-TERRORISTAS.

Shapiro, J. and Siegel, D. (2007), 'Underfunding in Terrorist Organizations', *International Studies Quarterly*, 51(2): 405–429.

Simcox, R. (2015), '"We Will Conquer Your Rome": A Study of Islamic State Terror Plots in the West', The Henry Jackson Society, Centre for the Response to Radicalisation and Terrorism.

Wesseling, M. (2014), 'Evaluation of EU Measures to Combat Terrorist Financing. In-Depth Analysis for the LIBE Committee. Policy Department Citizens' Rights and Constitutional Affairs', European Parliament, Brussels, www.europarl.europa.eu/. RegData/etudes/note/join/2014/509978/IPOL-LIBE_NT(2014)509978_EN.pdf

Wensink, W., Warmenhoven, B., Haasnoot, R., Wesselink, M., Van Ginkel, B., Wittendorp, S., Paulussen, C. *et al.* (2017), The European Union's Policies on Counter-Terrorism: Relevance, Coherence and Effectiveness. Study for the LIBE Committee. European Parliament, Policy Department C: Citizens' Rights and Constitutional Affairs, Brussels: European Union, www.europarl.europa.eu/RegData/etudes/STUD/2017/583124/IPOL_STU(2017)583124_EN.pdf

Witherspoon, J.A. (2017), 'Analysis of Low-Tech Terrorism in Western Democracies: Attacks with Vehicles, Blades and Incendiary Devices', Canadian Network for Research on Terrorism, Security, and Society (TSAS), Waterloo, ON, Canada, http://tsas.ca/wp-content/uploads/2017/11/2017-05_witherspoonWP.pdf.

Zoli, C. (2017), 'Is There Any Defense Against Low-Tech Terror?', Foreign Policy, Lawfare, http://foreignpolicy.com/2017/10/02/terror-has-gone-low-tech/.

10 Tackling the nexus at the supranational level

Matteo E. Bonfanti and Lukas Meyer-Daetsch

Introduction

Terrorism, on one side, and organized crime, on the other, are menaces to the stability, security, integrity, and cohesion of several communities across the world. Not least, the development in recent years of terror groups using everyday criminal skills in their pursuit of terror, which is often referred to as the crime-terror nexus, or the 'the nexus' in this chapter (Makarenko, 2004; Makarenko and Mesquita, 2014; Ruggiero, 2019; also Musotto and Wall in this collection (Chapter 4) for different interpretations). Countering these menaces tops the policy agendas of many national governments, drives the adoption of specific measures by domestic institutions, and is the object of different transnational cooperation initiatives promoted at both the global and regional level. With regard to Europe, supranational organizations like the European Union (EU), the Organization for Security and Co-operation in Europe (OSCE) and the Council of Europe (CoE) have been extensively engaged in fighting terrorism and organized crime for many years. Within the scope of their remits and capabilities as well as by employing multiple perspectives, programmes and tools, they favour coordinated interventions and actions aimed at preventing and responding to the threats posed by these phenomena. They adopt policies and legal instruments, as well as establish ad hoc mechanisms, which are progressively implemented by the states that are members of these organizations. Overall, they promote a holistic and integrated approach towards terrorism, on one side, and organized crime, on the other; an approach that covers different aspects of these issues – from their inherent causes to the manifestations – and mobilizes several actors (public institutions, private organizations, and the civil society) for its implementation.

As far as the EU cooperation framework is concerned, different institutions, bodies and agencies are dealing with organized crime and terrorism. Their initiatives and actions are multi-level and multi-sector. Overall, they address terrorism and organized crime from a social, economic, law enforcement (judicial and policing), and security perspective. Interventions range from the adoption of legislation criminalizing these phenomena (as a whole, or with regard to their specific elements) or sustaining operational cooperation among national authorities (e.g. through the setting up of information sharing platforms and systems), to the funding of research and development projects aimed at enhancing stakeholders' prevention and response capabilities. Given the complexity, diversity, and articulation of terrorism and organized crime, the EU tends to address them separately. Some of the initiatives and programmes introduced to tackle organized crime eventually came to cover more explicitly terrorist activities as well. This is the case, for example, with measures aimed at identifying proceedings from illicit activities that can be also used for financing terrorism. Other measures include enhanced border and travel control to identify both criminals and terrorists. The overlap between interventions depends also on the fact that terrorism itself, like organized crime, is a serious crime.

During the last few years, however, the EU seems also interested in understanding and tackling the possible intersections between terrorism and crime. Not always deliberately and explicitly, the EU seems to orient its actions also towards the contrast and disruption of the so-called 'nexus' between the two phenomena. From a conceptual point of view, the word 'nexus' refers to the interplay between terrorism and crime. It refers to the (evolving) relationships and links between terrorist and criminal activities (and groups). In Europe, links between crime and terrorism have recently been reported in different countries. For example, there is enough evidence of cross-fertilization between criminal and terrorist milieus within prisons in Italy, the Netherlands, France, Austria, Germany, Belgium and Luxembourg, the UK and Ireland (Rekawek *et al.*, 2018). In these countries, jihadists with criminal records have leveraged criminal skills and connections for the purposes of terrorism, and actively encouraged crime for the sake of jihad. In some of these countries, there are also criminal organizations, which have not intentionally or formally collaborated with terrorist groups, but – especially through their involvement in human smuggling, arms or other illicit good trafficking – may unwittingly facilitate terrorist organizations.

From a law enforcement perspective, tackling the nexus involves identifying, investigating, and disrupting the interactions between criminal groups and terrorists. It requires an understanding of the existing or potential connections and areas of 'adherence' or 'continuity' between these groups or individuals to intervene adequately. Understanding involves the collection and analysis of information on actors (individual or groups), their capabilities, modus operandi, intentions, relationships, activities and other risk indicators. It involves the sharing of actionable knowledge among anti-crime and anti-terrorism agencies. To happen and be effective, the sharing of information at both the domestic and supranational level should be based on trust and on established relationships among the involved parties. It should occur through defined frameworks, channels and mechanisms that support the flow of information. These frameworks and mechanisms do exist in Europe (Bonfanti, 2016).

In light of the above, this chapter examines the EU approach towards the nexus and presents the array of tools and measures the Organization can deploy to counter the phenomenon from a law enforcement and, to a lesser extent, intelligence perspective. First, it looks at the EU's view on the nexus by analysing relevant documentation issued by its institutions and agencies. Then, it reviews the mechanisms that are relevant for tackling the nexus between organized crime and terrorist networks from a law enforcement and security perspective. It focuses on the instruments that favour the collection and sharing of criminal or security information/intelligence and discusses their main advantages and limits. It also reviews the initiatives covering specific areas of convergence or cooperation between terrorist and organized criminal groups, i.e. (i) the generation of funds; (ii) access to weapons, forged documents and other services; (iii) and the recruitment of terrorists from the criminal milieu. Drawing on the results from a qualitative survey which questioned the main issues European and national decision makers face when confronted with organized crime and terrorism, the chapter concludes by providing recommendations for improving the EU response to the nexus.

The EU' view on the nexus: convergence and cooperation across three areas of activities

The EU's interest in the crime-terror nexus can be traced back to 2012 when the European Parliament commissioned a study on the topic. The study addressed the academic scepticism regarding the existence of established and long-term cooperation between criminals and terrorists in the EU at the time. The scepticism pointed towards it being counterintuitive for organized criminal groups to cooperate with terrorists. These latter not only strive to disrupt the political environment in which organized criminal groups become embedded; they also presumably make organized criminal groups more vulnerable to authorities. The study, however, also indicates the existence of various organizational and operational linkages between terrorist and organized criminal groups (European Parliament, 2012: 8).

It did not take long for the EU to take an official position on the matter. In 2015, the European Agenda on Security mentioned there are interlinked areas among terrorism and organized crime (European Commission, 2015: 13). A few years later, the Directive 2017/541 on Combating Terrorism acknowledged that '[…] the increasing links between organised crime and terrorist groups constitute a growing security threat to the Union and should therefore be taken into account by the authorities of the Member States involved in criminal proceedings' (European Union, 2017a, No. 13). Recently, the Council of the European Union and its working groups have been even more explicit. In a note, the Presidency of the Council called for further analysis of the possible links between crime and terrorism and asked relevant authorities to increase their cooperation in identifying these links (Council of the European Union, 2018a: 5). Rather than speaking of hybrid

Tackling the nexus at the supranational level 159

groups, the Council emphasizes the need to investigate the macro areas of activities in which convergence or cooperation between terrorist and organized criminal groups may occur, i.e. (i) the generation of funds; (ii) access to weapons, forged documents and other services; (iii) and the recruitment of terrorists from the criminal milieu. The Council's reference to these macro areas does not seem random. It is indeed in line with the forms of cooperation or convergence that member states' authorities and EU agencies have suggested, identified and monitored so far. In particular, it acknowledges EU INTCEN and Europol analytical assessments, which have been delivered recently. Overall, this suggests that the EU interpretation of, and approach to, the nexus tends to be pragmatic and evidence-based. It seems grounded on data and intelligence provided by agencies having counter-terrorism and/or anti-crime remits. Data and intelligence which seems to demonstrate that – as far as the EU is concerned – the nexus takes the forms of convergence/confluence, cooperation and collaboration across three specific areas of activities.

The first activity is recruitment. Analytical assessments provided by Europol reveal a trend towards terrorist suspects having an extensive criminal background (Europol, 2017a). In other words, there is a significant number of individuals reported to Europol for both terrorism-related offences and involvement in serious and/or organized crime, including migrant smuggling, drug and firearms trafficking, financial crimes and organized property crime. Almost all of these individuals were first reported for serious/organized criminal, and only later, for terrorism-related offences (Europol, 2016a).

The second is funding. Available information and assessments show that terrorist groups acquire money through: the smuggling of drugs (Salinas de Frías, 2017; Europol, 2011); tobacco (Europol, 2017a); oil; stolen cultural goods, antiquities and artefacts (European Parliament, 2018; Europol, 2017b); and trafficking in human beings/migrant smuggling (Europol, 2016b; European Parliament, 2016, No. 9). Furthermore, organized offences groups might help with financial crime services, including money laundering, tax evasion and large-scale VAT fraud (European Parliament, 2018: lit. G; Europol, 2017b; Europol, 2016c: 12). Finally, terrorists might be able to cooperate with organized criminal groups or engage themselves in acquiring funds in cyberspace, especially in connection with cryptocurrencies, which might increasingly be used to launder money, and money-making malware such as ransomware (Europol, 2016d, 2018).

The third activity is collaboration. There are concerns about the provision of services, particularly the procurement of weapons and forged documents. Terrorist groups are known to not only have acquired automatic firearms, but also hand grenades, rocket launchers and high-grade plastic explosives and detonators (Europol, 2016a, 2016c, 2017a, 2017c, 2018). Terrorists with a criminal background might already know relevant personal sources from their past, but they are also readily available online. Of concern in this regard is the role of the Darknet in facilitating the sale of firearms. Other services that terrorists might outsource is the forging of documents, including documents used for money laundering activities, travel or identification documents and work permits (Europol, 2013, 2014, 2016d, 2017b; Frontex, 2017a). Forged documents can also help terrorist groups in entering Europe by posing as refugees. Migration-affected countries expect European foreign fighters to use organized crime groups engaged in illegal migration to facilitate their return to Europe (Europol, 2017a, 2018; Frontex, 2016a). Finally, there is evidence that terrorists learn from cyber-criminals in the online environment, which leads to growing cyber capabilities among terrorist groups as their cyber expertise expands (Europol, 2016d).

The linkages between terrorism and criminal activities described above are believed to be pragmatic, ad hoc and short-term. There is evidence, however, that terrorists with extensive criminal backgrounds manage to sustain cooperation with criminal groups in the longer term. For instance, some of the terrorists involved in the November 2015 attacks in Paris are believed to have been active participants in criminal networks rather than their clients. Moreover, the relative incidence of existing connections appears to have increased (Europol, 2016a). It is worth noting that, according to Europol, while cooperation between terrorist groups and organized criminal groups constitute an increased security threat to the EU, they also make both entities more vulnerable to detection (Europol, 2015). Mutual support between agencies working on counter-terrorism and on fighting organized crime should be further extended, given the existing linkages and areas of adherence between the two phenomena for improved detection, cooperation, and information/intelligence exchange.

This is not only true for the domestic dynamics in many European countries, with anti-crime and counter-terrorism being treated as different 'silos', but has also impacted the activities on the EU level. There needs to be a stronger ability and willingness of counter-terrorism and anti-crime agencies on both national and international levels to share intelligence, cooperate on an operational level and identify and monitor existing and potential links between organized criminal groups and terrorist networks (European Parliament, 2012). The EU should explore its existing capabilities to the full, improve the tools in place and connect the different stakeholders, rather than adopt policies and measures in the wake of terrorist incidents that are outdated the moment they are implemented (Wensink *et al.*, 2017). This means to improve effective information collection and sharing through the already established channels and platforms.

The EU capabilities to tackle the nexus from a law enforcement perspective

There are different EU agencies and instruments that can contribute to the tackling of the nexus and enhance the law enforcement-based response to the phenomenon. Although not always and specifically tasked or designed for that, these agencies and instruments can be useful in pursuing and disrupting the nexus. On the one hand, they support the collection and, above all, sharing of information and intelligence between national authorities having counter-terrorism and/or anti-crime remits. Therefore, they can in principle generate the multi-stakeholders' understanding of the linkages and areas of continuity between terrorism and organized crime and allow for more effective law enforcement interventions. On the other hand, they tackle the three areas of concern identified by the EU.

Understanding and tracking the nexus: agencies, information systems, and cooperation frameworks

A significant contribution in pursuing the nexus can be provided by the EU's Justice and Home Affairs (JHA) agencies, in particular Eurojust, Europol, and Frontex, which represent the central hubs for police and judicial cooperation across Europe. Eurojust coordinates judicial investigations and prosecutions across two or more member states (European Union, 2002). When member states share their information with Eurojust, it is stored in Eurojust's Case Management System. Moreover, the agency maintains the so-called Terrorism Convictions Monitor (TCM), which is a non-public overview and analysis of trials and court proceedings linked to terrorism (Wensink et al., 2017). Europol fosters coordination of investigation in criminal cases with transnational implications (European Union, 2016a). Over the years, Europol has started to incorporate new tasks in its mandate depending on threat developments, including terrorism. The agency collects, stores, analyses and exchanges information and intelligence on serious crime and terrorism with the member states and other EU institutions. The gathering and sharing is boosted by technological systems like the Europol Information System (EIS; see below) and the SIENA network. The latter is a secure electronic communication infrastructure shared by Europol, member states' designated authorities, including customs, asset recovery offices, as well as third parties that have a cooperation agreement with Europol. Finally, Frontex is in charge of the monitoring of external borders and promotes information and intelligence gathering and sharing in matters relevant for the fight against transnational crime and terrorism at the EU external borders (European Union, 2016b). The agency now carries out risk analyses with regard to all aspects of integrated border management, conducts multi-purpose operations, and has deepened its cooperation with Eurojust and Europol (Frontex, 2016a, 2016b, 2017a, 2017b; Eurojust, 2017).

These agencies play an important role in the EU's fight against terrorist networks and organized crime. First, as shown, they are mandated to work on both phenomena. Second, they implement their mandates into specific activities regarding both phenomena. For example, while not established for counter-terrorist purposes, the counter-terrorism drive that followed 9/11 gave Eurojust a boost. Coolsaet (2010) highlights Eurojust's proactive approach that is making it possible to disrupt criminal activities, including terrorism, while achieving good results at trials. Europol pools expertise and shares best practices on both phenomena, it outlines trends and assesses threat developments in its Terrorism Situation and Trend (Te-Sat) and Serious and Organised Crime Threat Assessment (SOCTA) reports. Frontex processes personal data related to suspects of both terrorism and organized crime, for example by transmitting 'information packages' on suspects to Europol for further investigation (Council of the European Union, 2018b). Third, these agencies have access to vast amounts of information related to both phenomena in their databases. These factors make the agencies the predestined actors in the EU to see links, identify parallels and connect the dots in the nexus area.

The EU hosts information systems and databases used for border management and law enforcement purposes that can be useful for the agencies to get an even clearer picture on the nexus (European Commission, 2017a; Dumbrava, 2017). The main ones are: the Schengen Information System (SIS) which contains information on wanted or missing EU and third-country nationals or wanted and stolen objects (firearms, vehicles, identity documents, industrial equipment, etc.) as well as information related to the refusal of entry for individuals (European Commission, 2016a). EURODAC gathers the fingerprint data of asylum applicants and third-country nationals who have crossed the external borders irregularly; the Visa Information System (VIS) collects data on short-stay visas; the Europol Information System (EIS) is a centralized criminal database which includes information on persons, identity documents, cars, firearms, telephone numbers, e-mails, fingerprints, DNA and cybercrime-related information (European Commission, 2016a); the Entry/Exit System (EES) reports information on individuals entering or leaving the EU (Aden, 2018), and the Advance Passenger Information (API) system gathers information about passengers' identity (name, date of birth, nationality, number and type of travel document, etc.) before they board an inbound flight to the EU. Furthermore, there are other decentralized tools and frameworks favouring law enforcement information exchange in the EU. The Council Decision 2008/615/JHA (so-called 'Prüm' Decision) is one of them. It enables the exchange of DNA, fingerprints and Vehicle Registration Data and is based on the interconnection of a national system to all other participating national systems to enable remote cross-searching (European Union, 2008). The European Criminal Records Information System (ECRIS) is an electronic system that enables the exchange of information on previous convictions handed down against an individual by criminal courts in the EU (European Union, 2009a; European Union, 2009b). Additionally, the Passenger Name Records (PNR) exchange mechanism provides for the collection and sharing of information on passenger's travel requirements held in carriers' reservation and departure control systems (European Union, 2016c). Criminal intelligence can also be shared within the cooperation framework established by the Council Framework Decision (CFD) 2006/960/JHA. The Decision establishes the process by which competent law enforcement agencies in each EU member state exchange existing information and intelligence on serious crime to conduct a criminal investigations or intelligence operations (European Union, 2006). It allows law enforcement agencies across the EU to exchange information and intelligence internationally in the same way they would domestically.

Similar to the EU JHA agencies discussed, these information systems and databases provide data that can be useful in identifying the nexus both at European and national levels. They cover data ranging from criminal records and convictions, wanted or missing EU and third-country nationals to travel and migration data, which are all relevant for the areas of concern and should enable the EU and member states to prevent, detect and investigate organized crime and terrorism. The EU thus has both the actors and the systems that are useful in storing and sharing data among all involved stakeholders on the two phenomena. Member states, with proper interoperability of domestic and supranational systems, the right technological tools and staff expertise, should be able to leverage the sources that cover different phenomena to bring out a clearer picture on the nexus. This better understanding of the nexus, enabled by the actors and databases in place, will lead to more effective counteractions.

Specific measures against areas of concern

As mentioned above, there are policies and measures adopted by the EU that can prove to be particularly relevant and useful for tackling the nexus. Reference is made to policies, regulations and other instruments that address the three areas of concern for the EU.

Recruitment of terrorists with criminal backgrounds

The EU Strategy for Combating Radicalisation and Recruitment to Terrorism, revised in 2014, guides the EU's approach to terrorist radicalization and recruitment (Council of the European Union, 2014a), a domain that lies primarily with the member states. The Strategy does not specifically address the nexus, however, because according to its 2017 revised strategy version, the radicalization of prison inmates is a matter of concern (Council of the European Union, 2017a). This is interesting from a nexus perspective, as inmates who radicalize will have per se a criminal background.

In the case of radicalization in general, but also with regard to radicalization in prison, the Radicalisation Awareness Network (RAN) constitutes one of the most important transnational networks. It runs the Working Group on Prison and Probation (P&P) that brings together European practitioners ranging from probation and prison officers, justice department and intelligence services representatives to civil society organizations, to discuss risk factors and develop best practices and recommendations. The group contends that classified information constitutes the overarching issue around multi-agency cooperation on prison radicalization, especially in the relationship between intelligence services and prison officers as well as social workers (RAN, 2016a, 2016b, 2018). The fact, however, that it involves representatives from all stakeholder groups has to be welcomed, as it is reasonable to assume that the interactions might establish relationships of trust and understanding.

Radicalization in prison has gained more attention by the EU in recent years, and the Commission has supported various projects, including the risk assessment toolsets of the Radicalisation Risk Assessment in Prisons (RRAP) and Violent Extremist Risk Assessment 2 Revised (VERA-2R). These tools help practitioners assess the risk of radicalization and extremism in the offender population. For example, VERA-2R works with analysis factors related to criminal and personal history and mental disorders and is used in interventions and programs supporting rehabilitation of individuals (RAN, 2018).

Terrorist use of crime to acquire funding

In terrorist financing, the EU's adopted measures follow two main strands of action (see Chapter 9). First, they are supposed to disrupt the terrorists' capacity to raise funds. Second, they are supposed to detect and prevent terrorist groups from moving funds and other assets as well as ensure that financial movements help law enforcement to trace terrorists (European Commission, 2016b). With regard to the latter strand, some EU member states and the European Commission are part of the Financial Action Task Force (FATF), which is an intergovernmental organization that set international standards for the fight against money laundering and terrorist financing (FATF, 2012). The EU is then partnering with the US in the Terrorist Finance Tracking Programme (TFTP) aimed at tracking terrorist money flows as well as identifying and locating terrorist operatives and their financiers. While the TFTP is based on queries linked to terrorist financing, the generated information has at times also led to the identification of new lines of inquiry (that were initially not related to terrorism) (Europol, 2017a: 33). Europol is also fully engaged in countering terrorism financing. The agency hosts: the FIU.net system that facilitates the exchange of information between the Member States' Financial Intelligence Units (FIUs); the Anti-Money Laundering Operational Network (AMON); and the Camden Asset Recovery Inter-Agency Network (CARIN). Europol also has an Analysis Project called Sustrans and the Criminal Assets Bureau, which help member states analyse suspicious transaction reports and assist in tracing criminal proceeds (Council of the European Union, 2018b). In December 2017, Europol launched a program that incorporates private entities more directly.

The so-called Public Private Partnership in Financial Intelligence (EFIPPP) includes not only police, customs and regulatory authorities as well as national FIUs, but also major European banking institutions. It attempts to enhance the detection of suspicious financial operations and the exchange of strategic information and operational data (Council of the European Union, 2018b). The above initiatives are complemented by other measures like the fourth Anti-Money Laundering Directive (Council of the European Union, 2017b, 2018c; Krais, 2018). In addition, the EU strives to increase the powers on freezing and confiscating assets of terrorist groups. On 20 June 2018, the European Parliament and the Council agreed on a new regulation regarding the mutual recognition of freezing and confiscation orders among member countries. This measure complements the 2014 Directive on the Freezing and Confiscation of Instrumentalities and Proceeds of Crime (European Union, 2014). While the latter facilitates the seizing and confiscating of assets at national levels, the new regulation improves the cross-border enforcement of freezing and confiscation orders (Council of the European Union, 2018d).

Many of these measures make it harder for organized criminals and terrorists to move funds and finance themselves. As responses adapt, however, so do terrorist networks. As seen, terrorist plots involving lone actors and small cells are not only low-cost attacks (Oftedal, 2015), but are increasingly self-funded through legitimate means such as personal and business income (FATF, 2015). Even when criminal means of funding are involved, the international banking sector remains an attractive way to move funds, in spite of the discussed measures. Its sheer size and scope make it difficult to distinguish illegitimate from legitimate financial transactions undertaken each day. Moreover, terrorist groups started to explore virtual currencies and internet-based payment services (FATF, 2015) to move funds, again making it harder for existing measures to keep up.

As demonstrated above, the ways terrorist networks fund themselves can be varied, but include criminal activities, such as drug trafficking, cybercrime, illicit trade in cultural objects, and human smuggling. The EU's JHA agencies play a particular role in the fight against such means of funding with their coordination platforms and databases. Generally speaking, the EU is approaching these issues internally with a mix of legal measures, intelligence and policing, and financial tools, and externally by participating in international initiatives and direct support in third countries.

The way the EU has adopted legislative tools to disrupt drug smuggling activities is a good example of this approach. Internally, it has been characterized by the elements of risk assessment and trend reports (e.g. Council Decision 2005/387/JHA of 10 May 2005 on the information exchange, risk assessment and control of new psychoactive substances), forensic analysis and criminal investigation (e.g. Council Recommendation of 30 March 2004 regarding guidelines for taking samples of seized drugs (2004/C 86/04)), information exchange (e.g. with the Prüm decision – Council Decision 2008/615/JHA), and judicial and police cooperation (e.g. Council Framework Decision 2004/757/JHA of 25 October 2004 laying down minimum provisions on the constituent elements of criminal acts and penalties in the field of illicit drug trafficking). Externally, with more than 70 per cent of the EU's external borders being maritime, the EU has developed a European

Maritime Security Strategy that includes the fight against drug trafficking (Council of the European Union, 2014b). Furthermore, the EU participates in several initiatives fighting the illicit drug trade, including the UNODC/World Customs Organization Cargo Container Programme or the Heroin and Cocaine Route Programmes (EMCDDA, 2017).

Still, the Commission identified the need for a stronger judicial cooperation in drug-related cases at the EU level, especially with regard to Europol, Eurojust and the European Monitoring Centre for Drugs and Drug Addiction (EMCDDA). In the Evaluation of the implementation of the EU Drugs Strategy 2013–2020, the Commission also had to encourage the gathering of evidence of potential connections between drug trafficking and the financing of terrorist cells in the EU (European Commission, 2017b). Similar to the way terrorist groups are adaptable to find new means of moving funds acquired by criminal activity, perpetrators keep finding new ways to produce and traffic in drugs as responses to new measures (EMCDDA, 2017, 2018).

There is evidence that terrorist groups use the illicit trafficking of cultural goods (such as antiques) as a source of income (European Commission, 2016b; Howard, Prohov and Elliott, 2016; Pineda 2018; Pringle 2014). Two Regulations impose trade restrictions on cultural goods illicitly removed from Iraq and Syria and provide a legal basis for import controls. Since their effectiveness is limited, however, the European Parliament called for a traceability certificate for artworks and antiques entering the EU market and for member states to establish police units specializing in the trafficking of cultural goods. Moreover, according to the Parliament, companies in the art dealing industry should be obliged to report suspicious transactions and even be subjected to penalties for the financing of terrorism through negligence when they fail to report (European Parliament, 2018; European Union, 2003, 2012).

Exchange of illicit goods and services

Fraudulent or fraudulently obtained travel and identity documents are an important part of the smuggling package and are generally a crucial illicit service for terrorist groups. There is a booming market for fake documents, and terrorists sometimes do not even have to acquire fake documents, but can buy or come to possess genuine documents either from dead soldiers or civilians in conflict areas, or from the growing set of lost and stolen documents in the EU. As presented above, there are several initiatives in place to verify travel information and manage borders, including the cited information systems (PNR, EES, SIS and EURODAC). The EU is working on a regulation to establish a framework for boosting their interoperability (European Commission, 2017c; Council of the European Union, 2018e).

JHA agencies are active in the fight against document forging too. Frontex is creating training activities in relation to the detection of fraudulent documents at the EU's external borders as well as a number of tools to support member states in the fight against document fraud. Europol's Counter-Terrorism Centre

(ECTC) is working on the link between fraudulent documents and terrorism, while its Migrant Smuggling Centre is working on efforts to boost document security. There are also initiatives that incorporate private entities (Council of the European Union, 2016a, 2018b; Europol, 2017b). Of particular importance is Interpol's Stolen and Lost Travel Documents database (STLD), which enables the EU agencies and member states to conduct searches on 55 million travel documents (Paravicini, 2016). The database, however, is underutilized and suffers from inconsistent reporting on lost or stolen travel documents (Schmitt, 2014), thus making it still possible to illegally use legitimate passports.

Beyond forged documents, terrorists also engage with criminals in order to acquire firearms. The main tool regulating firearms in the European Union is the European Firearms Directive, which is presently undergoing an amendment procedure (European Union, 2017b). The Directive is market and governance-oriented and fails to sufficiently integrate the counter-terrorism paradigm. Since it remains a regulation of the legal market, it is questionable that the rules are able to curb the illicit trade in and trafficking of firearms (Wensink *et al.*, 2017). While the Firearms Directive is not regulating international external cooperation, the EU also cooperates with third countries on these issues, for instance with its joint EU–Western Balkans Action Plan on illicit trafficking in firearms (Council of the European Union, 2017c: No. 11).

Finally, the EU is active in the fight against the proliferation of chemical, biological, radiological and nuclear (CBRN) agents and explosives. For instance, Europol's ECTC has a CBRN and Explosives Team assisting member states operationally in terrorism and organized crime investigations. It also facilitates the cooperation between CBRN and explosives specialists through the European Explosive Ordnance Disposal Network (EEODN). The EU Bomb Data System (EBDS), meanwhile, is an expert platform for the timely sharing of relevant information and intelligence on incidents involving explosives and CBRN materials (Europol, 2017a, 2018). Similar to the points raised above, however, legal ways of obtaining chemical substances that can be used for explosives continue to be a concern. The EU has taken action to combat explosives precursors. Its Regulation No. 98/2013 on the marketing and use of explosives precursors restricts the public's access to and use of certain chemical substances, which member states can only grant access to through a system of licences and registration. Similar to the financial regulations in the fight against terrorist financing, operators must also report any suspicious transactions. Its implementation is being monitored by an expert group called the Standing Committee on Precursors (SCP). Again, there are familiar challenges to the control regime: not all member states have fully implemented the regulation (as of February 2017), the size of the market (large number of economic operators) makes it difficult to control, and the regime is undermined by internet sales. Moreover, the criteria for licences and registration have been somewhat unspecific and uneven across member states (European Commission, 2017d). And although the Commission has proposed a revision of the regulation, recent terrorist attacks (e.g. Manchester and Parsons Green in the UK in 2017) that have featured such explosives precursors (European Commission, 2018) revealed how it is still possible to circumvent the regulation. With regard to the nexus, the same criticism put forward against the Firearms Directive applies to Regulation No. 98/2013: it is questionable that the rules are able to curb the illicit acquisition of explosives precursors.

The same old limits to improved action against the nexus

In light of our discussion above, the EU and its member states are provided with instruments that can prove useful in tackling the nexus between terrorism and organized crime. These instruments contribute to the generation of more knowledge on the nexus, enable the sharing of this knowledge among relevant stakeholders, and encourage the tailoring of better law enforcement intervention. They also directly affect the areas of cooperation and convergence between terrorism and organized crime by exploiting and disrupting the identified linkages. The full employment of such instruments, however, seems limited by some (already known) issues that generally affect the EU supranational policing and counter-terrorism cooperation. The hubs, systems, channels for collecting and sharing relevant information, as well as the measures impacting the three areas of adherence, lack overall consistency and coherence (Aden, 2018). Moreover, there is lack of willingness from relevant member states' authorities to fully cooperate. These old problems can undermine the effective use of the EU capabilities to tackle the nexus. For example, although member states are obliged to share information with EU agencies, this is not always done in a timely and systematic manner. In fact, in 2016, the Council of the European Union lamented that there is

> little justification why information about all prosecutions, convictions, links with other relevant cases, as well as requests for judicial assistance, including 'rogatory letters' and European Arrest Warrants, along with the relevant responses are not being transmitted to Eurojust in a timely and systematic manner, as legally required by Council Decision 2005/671/JHA.
>
> (Council of the European Union, 2016b)

Although information sharing within Eurojust on counter-terrorism prosecution and convictions has improved since then, the EU Counter-Terrorism Coordinator is still calling for a consistent sharing of information that should enable Eurojust to provide more efficient support to the member states' authorities and to identify links with organized crime cases ('of growing importance'), which in turn may trigger national authorities to launch new investigations or extend ongoing ones (Council of the European Union, 2018b: 9).

Different studies specifically found that there were gaps in member states sharing data with Europol (Deloitte and European Commission Directorate-General Migration and Home Affairs, 2015; Disley *et al.*, 2012; Wills *et al.*, 2011; Fägersten, 2010). They found that some police officers are hesitant to upload information on Europol databases in order to avoid compromising ongoing operations. Others meanwhile were not aware that there even is an obligation to share certain information with Europol (Deloitte and European Commission Directorate-General Migration and Home Affairs, 2015). In 2016, SIENA was still struggling due to a lack of implementation in member states and – where implemented – it was not used in a significant manner (Council of the European Union, 2016c; Deloitte and European Commission Directorate-General Migration and Home Affairs, 2015). At the same time, the Paris November 2015 attacks also seemed to have had a lasting impact on data sharing with Europol. In fact, Europol's most extensive involvement has been through Task Force Fraternité dealing with the investigation of the attacks. In January 2017, Europol released a statement saying that information sharing on counter-terrorism, across European countries as well as through and with Europol, had reached an all-time high by the end of 2016 (Europol, 2017d). The statement mentions how member states and third parties increasingly use the ECTC as a hub to exchange information, conduct analysis and coordinate operational support, and how Europol supported 127 counter-terrorism operations in 2016, signifying an increase of almost 50 per cent in comparison with 2015 (Europol, 2017d).

The terrorist attacks in Paris in November 2015 were seen as a 'wake-up call' with regard to SIS (Schengen Information System). While all the perpetrators were subjects of an SIS alert, there was not enough information in the alert, so that the system did not reveal that the person was wanted for terrorism. A further problem was that the perpetrators were travelling under false identity documents and SIS was not able to capture them on the basis of an alphanumeric search. In a more general vein, although having had more information on foreign terrorist fighters than Europol at the time, member states did not systematically enter them into SIS or did not provide full information. To tackle these shortcomings, the EU therefore called for the member states to remove national obstacles for their security services to enter complete information into SIS, the introduction of common criteria to define whether a person is involved in terrorism or terrorism-related activity, as well as the introduction of the SIS Automated Fingerprint Identification System (AFIS), which enables the identification of a person from their fingerprints alone and which was launched by eu-LISA in the beginning of 2018 (Council of the European Union, 2016b).

With regard to VIS and EURODAC data, member states have reported practical problems (in the case of VIS) and implementation limitations (in the case of EURODAC) for law enforcement to access the two databases. With regard to API and PNR, the Commission felt there was a need to revise the legal basis for the processing of API data and to extend the linkages of the two to improve data sharing in the fight against terrorism and organized crime (European Commission, 2016a). Also, Prüm (Council Decision 2008/615/JHA), initially established outside of the EU Treaties, had issues with member states not being politically willing or able to coordinate their policing and intelligence forces more closely (Tekin, 2015). Even when an increasing number of countries joined, many countries continued to refrain from the in-depth exchange Prüm is based on. Niemeier explains the difficulties with the extensive technical, financial and administrative efforts that are required for states to implement reciprocal access to national-level DNA, fingerprint and vehicle registration databases on a hit/no-hit base. Once the comparison system has actually been implemented and the system has produced a hit, there is still a long and complex process until the asking country receives the necessary information from its partner (Niemeier, 2015).

So, although it looks like there are developments pointing towards more efficient cooperation and data sharing, as long as there is a lack of implementation in member states and limited use of databases and cross-searches, the pure existence of EU actors and databases will not lead to a more holistic and better picture of the nexus. There are overarching elements in the identified problems. Gerspacher and Dupont (2007: 353) generally speak of 'an inherent paradox'. The databases and information platforms were deliberately created by governments to facilitate cooperation, but 'many of the legal, logistical, and technical limitations that these international actors encounter are due to restrictions designed by States in order to maintain state supremacy in matters related to law and order'. The Council of the European Union more specifically identifies five main problems. First, the human factor, meaning that information will only be effectively exchanged if there is trust among the agents involved, and that errors in the interaction might be caused by the complexity of available tools and procedures, by different law enforcement traditions, as well as different expertise levels. Second, the legal requirements, such as criminal procedural law, data protections, purpose limitations, etc. that limit what information can be shared, when, and with what actors or databases. Third, limited resources at the national and European level might make it very challenging for the agencies involved to address all needs they have. Fourth, there are technical requirements which lead to shortcomings in the functionalities of existing systems. This is also related to the existing systems often being created for specific areas rather than based on a systematic approach. Finally, existing legislation, policies and procedures on EU information management in the JHA area have not been implemented fully and the capabilities of JHA agencies have not been used to their full extent to support member states (Council of the European Union, 2016c). Thus, the problems associated with making full use of the actors and databases are not only stemming from a lacking willingness from member states but are also connected to broader systemic elements.

Various member states insist that intelligence matters should remain outside of the realm of the integration process. Most of the cooperation between secret services takes place outside the institutional framework of the EU (Coolsaet, 2010; Bonfanti 2016). The most important information sharing platform remains the informal non-EU Club of Berne with its Counter Terrorist Group (CTG) (Aden, 2018; Cross, 2013; Wensink et al., 2017). While the EU runs the EU Intelligence Analysis Centre INTCEN, which coordinates secret information sharing and provides meta-evaluation of intelligence provided by the member states' services (European Union Intelligence Analysis Centre, 2015), bi- and multilateral cooperation still prevails (Aden, 2018). The same seems to be true for cooperation between secret services and law enforcement agencies (Wensink et al., 2017). Although there is a certain level of cooperation between secret services and law enforcement agencies, it is often limited due to organizational or legal reasons. For instance, while Europol and EU INTCEN both have the task of analysing terrorist threats from their perspectives, they often share analyses but not the operational data that these are based on (Aden, 2018; Mogherini, 2016).

Related to this last point is the observation that cooperation between agencies fighting organized crime and agencies focusing on counter-terrorism continues to be a challenging task. Although there has been a great deal of cooperation between terrorist groups and their organized crime counterparts, the bureaucratic reality in most member states is that national anti-crime and counter-terrorism agencies still work independently of each other with limited intelligence sharing and operational collaboration. This also translates to the transnational and supranational level. Some of the problems raised above also apply here. Trust between and desire of different agencies to cooperate with each other are relevant factors. There are also institutional and organizational factors relevant in the cooperation between anti-crime and counter-terrorism agencies. Wensink et al. (2017) discuss how certain member states combine security and intelligence capabilities in one organization (e.g. the Netherlands, Belgium, and Slovakia) while others have separate organizations (e.g. France, Germany, Bulgaria and Spain); some security services are police organizations (e.g. Denmark) while others are not (e.g. in the Netherlands and Germany). Moreover, limited resources in many member states may hinder the development of better linkages (Wensink et al., 2017). Consequently, lacking multilateral cooperation between secret services and a continuing silo-ization of anti-crime and counter-terrorism agencies further undermine a holistic approach to the nexus.

Conclusion

In light of what has been described so far, it seems the EU has different capabilities that can be deployed to tackle the nexus between terrorism and organized crime. The EU JHA agencies and information systems provide platforms to coordinate activities, share best practices and store and analyse data. They deal with both phenomena and already support member states in the areas of concern identified by the EU. A more consistent and coordinated approach that brings together information, intelligence and data, both on counter-terrorism and anti-crime, could help in getting a more holistic picture of the nexus and feeding back into more efficient law enforcement policies and actions. The above means that the wheel should not be reinvented. The capabilities that are already in place should be made more effective rather than new ones to be adopted, thereby creating – or adding to – a cacophony of tools and approaches. Generally speaking, however, in order to do so, some overarching issues have to be addressed. Member states should fully implement the existing tools. As discussed, different national legislation and questions of sovereignty make it harder for member states to implement the established instruments. However difficult this may be, some level of harmonization might be necessary for various member states to even be allowed to share some information. Furthermore, there are technical issues at hand with some of the information systems. A better interoperability among them is crucial for a functioning information sharing process. This often requires not only investments in IT systems, but also the appropriate expertise and training of staff. This inevitably is connected to resources spending, which not all member states might find feasible in these times. Finally, with existing systems often being created for specific areas rather than by a systematic approach, it should be ensured that agents understand the different databases. Equally, there should be no more overlaps or gaps across the different databases. For instance, criminals that are aligned with terrorist groups should lead to hits in the databases (SIS) not only for their criminal records, but for some kind of terrorism-related category. The Commission's discussion of how interoperability could be increased has to be welcomed and further developed (European Commission, 2016a). Furthermore, there are bureaucratic cultures that hinder efficient cooperation and information sharing. The EU could establish a working group on the nexus that regularly meets to discuss trends and share best practices on nexus dynamics. This would lead to more familiarity between anti-crime and counter-terrorism experts and practitioners across Europe. As for the measures adopted at the EU level to tackle specific areas of contact between terrorism and organized crime, they are not perfect. It is worth mentioning, however, that they keep being refined. The Firearms Directive, the Regulation on explosives precursors and the AMLD are examples of this. Gaps and new trends were identified and revisions to the existing measures proposed. However, the effectiveness of the amendments has still to be assessed.

To conclude, the EU can be the forum that provides member states with a clearer picture of the nexus and the tools to tackle it. However hard it is, there are some technological, logistical, cultural and legal issues to overcome. A smoother cooperation of judiciaries, law enforcement and intelligence agencies is needed, which means that anti-crime and counter-terrorism agencies should better work together within member states, across member states and within forums available at the supranational level.

Bibliography

Aden, Hartmut (2018), 'Information Sharing, Secrecy and Trust Among Law Enforcement and Secret Service Institutions in the European Union', *West European Politics*, 41(4): 981–1002.

Bonfanti, Matteo E. (2016), 'Collecting and Sharing Intelligence on Foreign Fighters in the EU and its Member States: Existing Tools, Limitations and Opportunities', in de Guttry, Andrea; Paulussen, Christophe; Capone, Francesca (eds) *Foreign Fighters under International Law and Beyond*. The Hague: Springer, pp. 333–353.

Coolsaet, Rik (2010), 'EU Counterterrorism Strategy: Value Added or Chimera?', *International Affairs*, 86(4): 857–873.

Council of the European Union (2014a), 'Note from the Presidency to COREPER/Council'. Revised EU Strategy for Combating Radicalisation and Recruitment to Terrorism. 9956/14.

Council of the European Union (2014b), 'Note from the General Secretariat of the Council to Delegations'. European Union Maritime Security Strategy. 11205/14.

Council of the European Union (2016a), Communication from the Commission. Enhancing Security in a World of Mobility: Improved Information Exchange in the Fight Against Terrorism and Stronger External Borders. 12307/16.

Council of the European Union (2016b), Note from the EU Counter-Terrorism Coordinator to the Council. Systematic Feeding and Consistent Use of European and International Databases – Information Sharing in the Counter-terrorism Context. 7726/16.

Council of the European Union (2016c), Note from Presidency to Council. Roadmap to Enhance Information Exchange and Information Management Including Interoperability Solutions in the Justice and Home Affairs Area. 9368/1/16 REV 1.

Council of the European Union (2017a), Note from the Presidency to Delegations. Review of the Guidelines for the EU Strategy for Combating Radicalisation and Recruitment to Terrorism. 6700/17.

Council of the European Union (2017b), 'Money Laundering and Terrorist Financing: Presidency and Parliament Reach Agreement'. Press Release 794/17, 20/12/2017. www.consilium.europa.eu/en/press/press-releases/2017/12/20/money-laundering-and-terrorist-financing-presidency-and-parliament-reach-agreement/pdf (accessed 25 September 2018).

Council of the European Union (2017c), Council Conclusions on EU External Action on Counter-terrorism (19 June 2017). 10384/17.

Council of the European Union (2018a), Note from Presidency to Delegations. EU Threat Assessment in the Field of Counter-terrorism. 7879/1/18 REV 1.

Council of the European Union (2018b), Note from EU Counter-Terrorism Coordinator to Permanent Representatives Committee/Council. JHA agencies' role in counter-terrorism. 6146/18 ADD 1 EXT 1.

Council of the European Union (2018c), 'Money Laundering and Terrorist Financing: New Rules Adopted'. Press Release 242/18, 14/05/2018. www.consilium.europa.eu/en/press/press-releases/2018/05/14/money-laundering-and-terrorist-financing-new-rules-adopted/pdf (accessed 25 September 2018).

Council of the European Union (2018d). 'Crime Will No Longer Pay: Council Agrees New Rules on Mutual Recognition of Freezing and Confiscation Orders'.

Press Release 358/18, 20 June 2018, www.consilium.europa.eu/en/press-press-releases/2018/06/20/crime-will-no-longer-pay-eu-agree-new-rules-on-mutual-recognition-of-freezing-and-confiscation-orders/pdf (accessed 25 September 2018).

Council of the European Union (2018e), Note from Presidency/outgoing Presidency to Delegations. Renewed European Union Internal Security Strategy and Counter-Terrorism Implementation Paper: report of the second half of 2017 and programme for the first half of 2018. 5670/18.

Cross, Mai'a K. Davis (2013), 'A European Transgovernmental Intelligence Network and the Role of IntCen', *Perspectives on European Politics and Society*, 14(3): 388–402.

Deloitte and European Commission Directorate-General Migration and Home Affairs (2015), 'Study on the Implementation of the European Information Exchange Model (EIXM) for Strengthening Law Enforcement Cooperation', https://ec.europa.eu/home-affairs/sites/homeaffairs/files/e-library/documents/policies/police-cooperation/general/docs/eixm_study_-_final_report_en.pdf (accessed 25 September 2018).

Disley, Emma, Irving, Barrie, Hughes, William and Patruni, Bhanu (2012) 'Evaluation of the Implementation of the Europol Council Decision and of Europol's Activities', Technical Report. Rand Corporation. www.europol.europa.eu/sites/default/files/documents/rand_evaluation_report.pdf (accessed 11 December 2018).

Dumbrava, Costica (2017), 'European Information Systems in the Area of Justice and Home Affairs: An Overview', European Parliamentary Research Service Publication, www.europarl.europa.eu/RegData/etudes/IDAN/2017/603923/EPRS_IDA%282017%29603923_EN.pdf (accessed 25 September 2018).

EMCDDA (2017), 'Drug Supply Reduction: An Overview of EU Policies and Measures', EMCDDA Papers. www.emcdda.europa.eu/system/files/publications/3633/TDAU16002ENN_web_file.pdf (accessed 25 September 2018).

EMCDDA (2018), 'European Drug Report 2018: Trends and Developments', www.emcdda.europa.eu/system/files/publications/8585/20181816_TDAT18001ENN_PDF.pdf (accessed 25 September 2018).

Eurojust (2017), 'Meeting on Illegal Immigrant Smuggling', The Hague, 15 June 2017. Outcome Report, www.eurojust.europa.eu/doclibrary/Eurojust-framework/ejstrategicmeetings/Outcome%20report%20of%20Eurojust%20meeting%20on%20illegal%20immigrant%20smuggling%20(June%202017)/2017-06_Outcome-Report_Eurojust-Meeting-on-IIS_EN.pdf (accessed 25 September 2018).

European Commission (2012), Communication from the Commission to the European Parliament and the Council on Strengthening Law Enforcement Cooperation in the EU: The European Information Exchange Model (EIXM). COM(2012)735 final.

European Commission (2015), Communication from the Commission to the European Parliament, the Council, the European Council and Social Committee and the Committee of the Regions. The European Agenda on Security. COM(2015)185 final.

European Commission (2016a), Communication from the Commission to the European Parliament and the Council. Stronger and Smarter Information Systems for Borders and Security. COM(2016)205 final.

European Commission (2016b), Communication from the Commission to the European Parliament and the Council on an Action Plan for Strengthening the Fight against Terrorist Financing. COM(2016)50 final.

European Commission (2017a), 'EU Information Systems: Security and Borders', https://ec.europa.eu/home-affairs/sites/homeaffairs/files/what-we-do/policies/

european-agenda-security/20171212_eu_information_systems_security_and_borders_en.pdf (accessed 25 September 2018).

European Commission (2017b), Communication from the Commission to the European Parliament and the Council. Evaluation of the Implementation of the EU Drugs Strategy 2013–2020 and of the EU Action Plan on Drugs 2013–2016: A Continuous Need for an EU Action Plan on Drugs 2017–2020. COM(2017)195 final.

European Commission (2017c), Proposal for a Regulation of the European Parliament and of the Council on Establishing a Framework for Interoperability between EU Information Systems (Police and Judicial Cooperation, Asylum and Migration). COM(2017)794 final.

European Commission (2017d), Report from the Commission to the European Parliament and the Council on the Application of, and Delegation of Power under, Regulation (EU) 98/2013 of the European Parliament and of the Council on the Marketing and use of Explosives Precursors. COM(2017)103 final.

European Commission (2018), Proposal for a Regulation of the European Parliament and of the Council on the Marketing and Use of Explosives Precursors, Amending Annex XVII to Regulation (EC) No 1907/2006 and Repealing Regulation (EU) No 98/2013 on the Marketing and use of Explosives Precursors. COM(2018)209 final.

European Parliament (2012), Directorate-General for Internal Policies, Policy Department C, Citizens' Rights and Constitutional Affairs. Europe's Crime-Terror Nexus: Links between Terrorist and Organised Crime Groups in the European Union. Study for the LIBE Committee, www.europarl.europa.eu/document/activities/cont/201211/20121127ATT56707/20121127ATT56707EN.pdf (accessed 25 September 2018).

European Parliament (2016), Report on the Fight Against Trafficking in Human Beings in the EU's External Relations (2015/2340(INI)). A8–0205/2016. www.europarl.europa.eu/sides/getDoc.do?pubRef=-//EP//NONSGML+REPORT+A8-2016-0205+0+DOC+PDF+V0//EN (accessed September 25 2018).

European Parliament (2018), Report on a European Parliament Recommendation to the Council, the Commission and the Vice-President of the Commission/High Representative of the Union for Foreign Affairs and Security Policy on Cutting the Sources of Income for Jihadists – Targeting the Financing of Terrorism (2017/2203(INI)). A8–0035/2018, www.europarl.europa.eu/sides/getDoc.do?pubRef=-//EP//NONSGML+REPORT+A8-2018-0035+0+DOC+PDF+V0//EN (accessed 25 September 2018).

European Union (2002), 'Council Decision of 28 February 2002 Setting up Eurojust with a View to Reinforcing the Fight against Serious Crime (2002/187/JHA)', *Official Journal of the European Union*, L 63: 1–13.

European Union (2003), 'Council Regulation (EC) No 1210/2003 of 7 July 2003 Concerning Specific Restrictions on Economic and Financial Relations with Iraq and Repealing Regulation (EC) No 2465/96', *Official Journal of the European Union*, L 169: 6–23.

European Union (2004a), 'Council Recommendation of 30 March 2004 Regarding Guidelines for Taking Samples of Seized Drugs (2004/C 86/04)', *Official Journal of the European Union*, C 86, 10–11.

European Union (2004b), 'Council Framework Decision 2004/757/JHA of 25 October 2004 Laying Down Minimum Provisions on the Constituent Elements of

Criminal Acts and Penalties in the Field of Illicit Drug Trafficking', *Official Journal of the European Union*, L 335: 8–11.

European Union (2005), 'Council Decision 2005/387/JHA of 10 May 2005 on the Information Exchange, Risk-assessment and Control of New Psychoactive Substances', *Official Journal of the European Union*, L 127: 32–37.

European Union (2006), 'Council Framework Decision 2006/960/JHA of 18 December 2006 On Simplifying the Exchange of Information and Intelligence between Law Enforcement Authorities of the Member States of the European Union', *Official Journal of the European Union*, L 386: 89–100.

European Union (2008), 'Council Decision 2008/615/JHA of 23 June 2008 on the Stepping up of Cross-border Cooperation, Particularly in Combating Terrorism and Cross-border Crime', *Official Journal of the European Union*, L 210: 1–11.

European Union (2009a), 'Council Framework Decision 2009/315/JHA of 26 February 2009 On the Organisation and Content of the Exchange of Information Extracted from the Criminal Record between Member States', *Official Journal of the European Union*, L 93: 23–32.

European Union (2009b), 'Council Decision 2009/316/JHA of 6 April 2009 On the Establishment of the European Criminal Records Information System (ECRIS) in Application of Article 11 of Framework Decision 2009/315/JHA', *Official Journal of the European Union*, L 93: 33–48.

European Union (2012), 'Council Regulation (EU) No 36/2012 of 18 January 2012 Concerning Restrictive Measures in View of the Situation in Syria and Repealing Regulation (EU) No 442/2011', *Official Journal of the European Union*, L 16: 1–32.

European Union (2013), 'Regulation (EU) No 98/2013 of the European Parliament and of the Council of 15 January 2013 on the Marketing and Use of Explosives Precursors', *Official Journal of the European Union*, L 39, 1–11.

European Union (2014), 'Directive 2014/42/EU of the European Parliament and of the Council of 3 April 2014 on the Freezing and Confiscation of Instrumentalities and Proceeds of Crime in the European Union', *Official Journal of the European Union*, L 127: 39–50.

European Union (2016a), 'Regulation (EU) 2016/794 of the European Parliament and of the Council of 11 May 2016 on the European Union Agency for Law Enforcement Cooperation (Europol) and Replacing and Repealing Council Decisions 2009/371/JHA, 2009/934/JHA, 2009/935/JHA, 2009/936/JHA and 2009/968/JHA', *Official Journal of the European Union*, L 135: 53–114.

European Union (2016b), 'Regulation (EU) 2016/1624 of the European Parliament and of the Council of 14 September 2016 on the European Border and Coast Guard and Amending Regulation (EU) 2016/399 of the European Parliament and of the Council and Repealing Regulation (EC) No 863/2007 of the European Parliament and of the Council, Council Regulation (EC) No 2007/2004 and Council Decision 2005/267/EC', *Official Journal of the European Union*, L 251: 1–76.

European Union (2016c). 'Directive (EU) 2016/681 of the European Parliament and of the Council of 27 April 2016 on the Use of Passenger Name Record (PNR) Data for the Prevention, Detection, Investigation and Prosecution of Terrorist Offences and Serious Crime', *Official Journal of the European Union*, L 119: 132–149.

European Union (2017a), 'Directive (EU) 2017/541 of the European Parliament and of the Council of 15 March 2017 on Combating Terrorism and Replacing Council Framework Decision 2002/475/JHA and Amending Council Decision 2005/671/JHA', *Official Journal of the European Union*, L 88: 6–21.

European Union (2017b), 'Directive (EU) 2017/853 of the European Parliament and of the Council of 17 May 2017 Amending Council Directive 91/477/EEC on Control of the Acquisition and Possession of Weapons', *Official Journal of the European Union*, L 137: 22–39.

European Union Intelligence Analysis Centre (EU INTCEN) (2015), Fact Sheet. http://statewatch.org/news/2016/may/eu-intcen-factsheet.pdf (accessed 25 September 2018).

Europol (2011), 'EU Organised Crime Threat Assessment (OCTA) 2011', www.europol.europa.eu/sites/default/files/documents/octa2011.pdf (accessed 25 September 2018).

Europol (2013), 'EU Serious and Organised Crime Threat Assessment 2013', www.europol.europa.eu/sites/default/files/documents/socta2013.pdf (accessed 25 September 2018).

Europol (2014), 'European Union Terrorism Situation and Trend Report (TE-SAT) 2014', www.europol.europa.eu/sites/default/files/documents/europol_tsat14_web_1%20%281%29.pdf (accessed 25 September 2018).

Europol (2015), 'European Union Terrorism Situation and Trend Report (TE-SAT) 2015', www.europol.europa.eu/sites/default/files/documents/p_europol_tsat15_09jun15_low-rev.pdf (accessed 25 September 2018).

Europol (2016a), 'Changes in Modus Operandi of Islamic State (IS) revisited', www.europol.europa.eu/sites/default/files/documents/modus_operandi_is_revisited.pdf (accessed 25 September 2018).

Europol (2016b), 'Migrant Smuggling in the EU', www.europol.europa.eu/sites/default/files/documents/migrant_smuggling__europol_report_2016.pdf (accessed 25 September 2018).

Europol (2016c), 'European Union Terrorism Situation and Trend Report (TE-SAT) 2016', www.europol.europa.eu/sites/default/files/documents/europol_tesat_2016.pdf (accessed 25 September 2018).

Europol (2016d), 'Internet Organised Crime Threat Assessment (IOCTA) 2016', www.europol.europa.eu/sites/default/files/documents/europol_iocta_web_2016.pdf (accessed 25 September 2018).

Europol (2017a), 'Europol Review 2016–2017', www.europol.europa.eu/sites/default/files/documents/europol-review-2016.pdf (accessed 25 September 2018).

Europol (2017b), 'European Union Serious and Organised Crime Threat Assessment. Crime in the Age of Technology', www.europol.europa.eu/sites/default/files/documents/report_socta2017_1.pdf (accessed 25 September 2018).

Europol (2017c), 'Internet Organised Crime Threat Assessment (IOCTA) 2017', www.europol.europa.eu/sites/default/files/documents/iocta2017.pdf (accessed 25 September 2018).

Europol (2017d), 'Information Sharing on Counter Terrorism in the EU Has Reached an All-Time High'. Press Release, 30 January 2017, www.europol.europa.eu/newsroom/news/information-sharing-counter-terrorism-in-eu-has-reached-all-time-high (accessed 25 September 2018).

Europol (2018), 'European Union Terrorism Situation and Trend Report (TE-SAT) 2018', www.europol.europa.eu/sites/default/files/documents/tesat_2018_1.pdf (accessed 25 September 2018).

Fägersten, Björn (2010), 'Bureaucratic Resistance to International IntelligenceCooperation – The Case of Europol', *Intelligence and National Security*, 25(4): 500–520.

FATF (2012), 'International Standards on Combating Money Laundering and the Financing of Terrorism & Proliferation: The FATF Recommendations', www.fatf-gafi.org/media/fatf/documents/recommendations/pdfs/FATF_Recommendations.pdf (accessed 25 September 2018).
FATF (2015), 'Emerging Terrorist Financing Risks'. FATF Report, www.fatf-gafi.org/media/fatf/documents/reports/Emerging-Terrorist-Financing-Risks.pdf (accessed 25 September 2018).
Frontex (2016a), 'Annual Activity Report 2015', https://frontex.europa.eu/assets/Key_Documents/Annual_report/2015/General_Report_2015.pdf (accessed 25 September 2018).
Frontex (2016b), 'Programming Document 2017–2019', https://frontex.europa.eu/assets/Key_Documents/Programming_Document/2017/Programme_of_work_2017.pdf (accessed 25 September 2018).
Frontex (2017a), 'Annual Activity Report 2016', https://frontex.europa.eu/assets/Key_Documents/Annual_report/2016/Annual_Activity_Report_2016.pdf (accessed 25 September 2018).
Frontex (2017b), 'Programming Document 2018–2020', https://frontex.europa.eu/assets/Key_Documents/Programming_Document/2018/Programming_Document_2018-2020.pdf (accessed 25 September 2018).
Gerspacher, Nadia and Dupont, Benoit (2007), 'The Nodal Structure of International Police Cooperation: An Exploration of Transnational Security Networks', *Global Governance*, 13(3): 347–364.
Howard, Russell D., Prohov, Jonathan and Elliott, Marc D. (2016), 'IS and Cultural Genocide: Antiquities Trafficking in the Terrorist State', *JSOU Report* 16(11).
Krais, Juergen (2018). 'EU: 5th EU Anti-Money Laundering Directive Published'. Global Compliance News 16 July 2018, https://globalcompliancenews.com/eu-5th-anti-money-laundering-directive-published-20180716/ (accessed 25 September 2018).
Makarenko, Tamara (2004), 'The Crime-terror Continuum: Tracing the Interplay between Transnational Organised Crime and Terrorism', *Global Crime*, 6(1): 129–145.
Makarenko, Tamara and Mesquita, Michael (2014), 'Categorising the Crime–terror Nexus in the European Union', *Global Crime*, 15(3–4): 259–274.
Mogherini, Federica (2016), 'Role of the EU Intelligence Analysis Centre in Improving the Exchange of Intelligence. Answer on Behalf of the Commission to a Written Question' (Question E-002849-16). www.europarl.europa.eu/sides/getAllAnswers.do?reference=E-2016-002849&language=EN (accessed 25 September 2018).
Niemeier, Michael (2015), 'The Exchange of Information between Police Organisations in the EU Under the Treaty of Lisbon – Routine and Difficulties from a Practical Perspective', in Hartmut Aden (ed.) *Police Cooperation in the European Union under the Treaty of Lisbon – Opportunities and Limitations*, Baden-Baden: Nomos, pp. 235–244.
Oftedal, Emilie (2015), 'The Financing of Jihadi Terrorist Cells in Europe. Norwegian Defence Research Establishment (FFI)', www.ffi.no/no/Rapporter/14-02234.pdf (accessed 25 September 2018).
Paravicini, Giulia (2016), 'EU's Passport Fraud "Epidemic"'. Politico, www.politico.eu/article/europes-fake-forged-stolen-passport-epidemic-visa-free-travel-rights/ (accessed 25 September 2018).

Pineda, Sam (2018), 'Tackling Illicit Trafficking of Antiquities and its Ties to Terrorist Financing'. U.S. Department of State DipNote. https://blogs.state.gov/stories/2018/06/20/en/tackling-illicit-trafficking-antiquities-and-its-ties-terrorist-financing (accessed 10 December 2018).

Pringle, Heather (2014), 'ISIS Cashing in on Looted Antiquities to Fuel Iraq Insurgency', *National Geographic*. https://news.nationalgeographic.com/news/2014/06/140626-isis-insurgents-syria-iraq-looting-antiquities-archaeology/ (accessed 10 December 2018).

RAN (2016a), 'Dealing with Radicalisation in a Prison and Probation Context', RAN P&P Practitioners working paper, https://ec.europa.eu/home-affairs/sites/homeaffairs/files/what-we-do/networks/radicalisation_awareness_network/ran-news/docs/ran_p_and_p_practitioners_working_paper_en.pdf (accessed 25 September 2018).

RAN (2016b), 'Approaches to Violent Extremist Offenders and Countering Radicalisation in Prisons and Probation', RAN P&P Practitioners working paper. https://ec.europa.eu/home-affairs/sites/homeaffairs/files/what-we-do/networks/radicalisation_awareness_network/about-ran/ran-p-and-p/docs/ran_pp_approaches_to_violent_extremist_en.pdf (accessed 25 September 2018).

RAN (2018), 'Developing, Implementing and using Risk Assessment for Violent Extremist and Terrorist Offenders', RAN Ex Post Paper. https://ec.europa.eu/home-affairs/sites/homeaffairs/files/what-we-do/networks/radicalisation_awareness_network/about-ran/ran-p-and-p/docs/ran_pp_developing_implementing_using_risk_assessment_brussels_09-10_07_2018_en.pdf (accessed 25 September 2018).

Rekawek, Kacper, Matějka, Stanislav, Szucs, Viktor, Beňuška, Tomáš, Kajzarová, Karin and Rafay, Jakub (2018), 'Who Are the European Jihadis? From Criminal to Terrorists and Back?', Project Midterm Report. Bratislava: GLOBSEC, Defence and Security Programme.

Ruggiero, V. (2019), 'Hybrids: On the Crime-Terror-Nexus', *International Journal of Comparative and Applied Criminal Justice*, 43(1): 49–60.

Salinas de Frías, Ana (2017), 'Part II: Legal Instruments Combating TOC and Terrorism: Overlapping, Lacunae or Opportunities?', in Council of Europe, Committee of Experts on Terrorism (CODEXTER): Report on the Links between Terrorism and Transnational Organised Crime. 4, 8–26, https://rm.coe.int/report-on-the-links-between-terrorism-and-transnational-organised-crim/1680711352 (accessed 25 September 2018).

Schmitt, Eric (2014), 'Use of Stolen Passports on Missing Jet Highlights Security Flaw', *New York Times*, www.nytimes.com/2014/03/11/world/asia/missing-malaysian-airliner-said-to-highlight-a-security-gap.html (accessed 25 September 2018).

Tekin, Funda (2015), 'Differentiated Integration: Ever More Relevant for Police Cooperation after the Treaty of Lisbon?', in Hartmut Aden (ed.) *Police Cooperation in the European Union under the Treaty of Lisbon – Opportunities and Limitations*, Baden-Baden: Nomos, pp. 81–98.

Wensink, Wim, Warmenhoven, Baas, Haasnoot, Roos, Wesselink, Rob, Van Ginkel, Bibi, Wittendorp, Stef, Paulussen, Christophe, Douma, Wybe, Boutin, Bérénice, Güven, Onur and Rijken, Thomas (2017), Directorate-General for Internal Policies, Policy Department C, Citizens' Rights and Constitutional Affairs. The European Union's Policies on Counter-Terrorism: Relevance, Coherence and Effectiveness. Study for the LIBE Committee. www.europarl.europa.eu/RegData/

etudes/STUD/2017/583124/IPOL_STU(2017)583124_EN.pdf (accessed 25 September 2018).

Wills, Aidan, Vermeulen, Mathias, Born, Hans, Scheinin, Martin and Wiebusch, Micha (2011), Directorate-General for Internal Policies, Policy Department C, Citizens' Rights and Constitutional Affairs. Parliamentary Oversight of Security and Intelligence Agencies in the European Union. Study for the LIBE Committee. www.europarl.europa.eu/document/activities/cont/201109/20110927ATT27674/20110927ATT27674EN.pdf (accessed 11 December 2018).

11 Identity crime in the UK

Aida Fazely

Introduction

This chapter deals with the definition, measurement, detection and prosecution of offences that appear to defy the categories to which criminology has made us accustomed. Identity crime is characterized by a degree of hybridity, in that it can be perpetrated by offenders from diverse backgrounds and affiliations. It presents itself with the hazy traits perceptively identified in the introduction to this collective volume. In brief, it prompts questions around the possible evolution of crime, the professional skills this requires and the type of subculture in which offenders are embedded. The chapter begins by looking at definitions of identity crime provided by the Home Office and the various types of identities that are of value to criminals. The different stages of committing this crime are explained next which include 'identity theft' (via offline and online methods) and 'committing fraud on stolen identities'. In order to clarify further the methods being used by fraudsters, some real-life examples have been examined and explained. The chapter then moves on to review how ID crime has come to prominence, been recognized as a threat and early attempts to tackle it in the UK, examining the formation of the National Fraud Authority (NFA) and the victim support service provided by the credit reference agencies.

There are a number of major organizations that play an important role in tackling this crime such as NFA, CIFAS, credit reference agencies and law enforcement. NFA was established by the government with identity crime as one of its major projects/focus but unfortunately was dissolved in 2014 and its responsibilities were passed on to various other organizations. CIFAS and credit reference agencies provide support for victims, a fraud database and a number of solutions to help businesses protect themselves against this crime. And finally, there are the law enforcement agencies which run a number of projects to tackle various aspects of this crime. The scope and activities of these organizations will be discussed in more detail in this chapter.

Cybersecurity (of which identity theft is part) has attracted the attention of the authorities in the last few years. The latest strategies employed to tackle this element of identity crimes will be examined along with national and international efforts focusing on the EU and UNODC.

And to conclude, the extent of the problem and the way that it is measured is examined, which includes data provided by the financial sector, CIFAS and the reports that have been published by the NFA.

Identity crimes and its definition

According to Yang, Manoharan and Barber (2014) ID crime has become the defining crime of the information age, with an estimated nine million incidents per year. Academia, governments and the private sector all work to get this ever increasing crime under the control. Helser (2015) points out that not only is this crime on the rise but that it affects individuals, businesses and industry worldwide, compromising the integrity of the systems that are fundamental components of our society.

The damage that this crime causes its victims is significant to the point that what is stolen is almost never returned, and criminals keep on selling and trading stolen identities to other criminals for further misuse via illicit criminal marketplaces within the dark net (Lacey, Zaiss and Barber, 2016).

Camp (2007) takes the argument further by stating that we have lost control of our identities and that all the data about them is publicly available. The technological achievements and the new ways that we conduct our lives such as increased mobility of individuals, and the new payment infrastructures and methods are to be blamed for this crime becoming so widespread and ubiquitous. The concerns about this crime have been reflected in media, academic discourse, government and private sector rhetorics.

One of the issues that have been challenging the industry for the last few years is defining this crime. The Home Office Identity Fraud Steering Group (2009) in order to bring some clarity and unity provided a set of definitions on their website for everyone to use. They state that:

> Identity fraud and identity theft are often used very loosely to describe any situation in which personal details are misappropriated for gain.

It then moves on to provide definitions on the following:

> Identity Crime: a generic term for identity theft, creating a false identity or committing identity fraud.

> False identity: a fictitious (i.e. invented identity) or an existing identity (i.e. genuine identity) that has been altered to create a fictitious identity.

> Identity theft: occurs when sufficient information about an identity is obtained to facilitate identity fraud, irrespective of whether, in the case of an individual, the victim is alive or dead.

Identity fraud: occurs when a false identity or someone else's identity details are used to support unlawful activity, or when someone avoids obligation/ liability by falsely claiming that he/she was the victim of identity theft.

There are three types of identities that can be stolen: personal individual identity, identity of directors of companies and corporate identity. Personal individual identity is when the identity of a person is stolen and used to access services or acquire goods. Identity of directors is when the identity of a director of a company is stolen and used to access company data in order to obtain assets, goods or services. This can be very damaging for small businesses as they rely on cash flow to help them continue trading. Companies House, in order to tackle this issue, introduced PROOF (PROtected Online Filing) which enables companies to protect themselves from unauthorized changes to their company's record as it prevents the filing of certain paper forms. These include documents for an appointment/termination/change of particulars of company officers and the change of the registered office (Companies House Website).

Corporate identity crime is when the identity of a corporation is stolen and used to obtain data or other goods and services. Mass marketing fraud also falls into this category as fraudsters use this method to pretend to be banks or other institutions, by way of e-mails or by calling people in order to acquire their personal identifying details.

As it was seen from the definition provided by Home Office there are two major elements to identity crime: identity theft and identity fraud. There are many ways that each of these can be committed. Although the identity fraud steering website provided definitions, in practice there are still issues around this area. The latest attempts to introduce definitions that can be used have not only done nothing to solve the problem but rather they have created further confusion both for the public and for the market.

The identity information that fraudsters seek to steal in order to carry out the 'cashing out' stage are: (Cendrowski, Petro and Martin, 2007) name, address, National Insurance number, date of birth, phone number, ATM, debit and credit card numbers, Credit card security codes and Personal Identification Numbers (PIN) for bank and credit cards, bank account numbers and balances, income and credit history, driver's license number, passwords, e-mail address.

Committing different stages of identity crime

Committing identity theft

Allison, Schuck and Lersch (2005) categorize identity theft into two types: low-technology and high-technology or offline and online methods.

Offline methods

- Burglaries: previously it was valuable items that thieves were after but now it is people's cards or card numbers that they seek to steal. One card's data has a street value between £250 and £500. In some instances, fraudsters work with subcontracted burglars.
- Insider thieves: fraudsters are on the lookout for people who work inside businesses where cards or card data are used to conduct transactions. The nature of such businesses usually means that employees are on low incomes so the lucrative nature of the fraudsters' offer proves to be too good to miss. In some cases, fraudsters even lurk around the offices of such businesses very openly to recruit their staff to their ID crime objectives. In some instances, they even seek jobs in such businesses themselves. These include bars, call centres and retail stores. Often, the criminal gangs use threats to coerce the employees to comply.
- Stealing the deceased's data from the obituary part of the local newspapers is another method that fraudsters use to obtain identity data.
- Intercepting mail.
- Sophisticated methods to capture card data at ATM cash points. These attacks consist of using devices inside the cash machine to capture card data and hidden cameras to record the PIN.

Online methods

- Usage of chat rooms and social media sites such as Facebook and Twitter to acquire data.
- There are also sites where fraudsters can buy fake identity documents. These fake documents can be obtained relatively cheaply and easily.
- Cloning the sites of well-known companies and institutions.
- Phishing attacks which happen when fraudsters send random e-mails to consumers, pretending to be from major companies such as banks, in order to deceive them and obtain their identifying information.
- Tapping into wireless networks of retailers is another method used by fraudsters. They achieve this by simply positioning themselves close to the stores. Often these are open networks (such as Starbucks) which have no protection/encryption hence data can be easily stolen.
- Hacking: the hackers break into the systems of companies which have less secure databases or websites. The data is then sold in specific chat rooms that fraudsters use. Just like the fraud prevention community, fraudsters have forums where they can share information and maximize their illegitimate business. The data that are sold on such sites are mainly card data which are then used to commit Card Not Present fraud.

Committing fraud on stolen identities or 'Cashing Out'

Obtaining services

Once the criminals obtain personal data, they use it to acquire services such as State Benefit and/or hospital care. In one of the recent cases, for example, a national of Zimbabwe, having changed his name on arrival to the UK, claimed benefit on his true name and pocketed three years of Government education grants on top of the State and housing benefits he had been claiming (Double identity immigrant benefit thief jailed, 2011).

Acquiring goods and products

Once fraudsters acquire the necessary data, they then conduct some research in order to find out which website is less secure so they can attack and misuse the data. It is believed that fraudsters target these sites when they believe that the chances of getting caught are lower, at times such as at night or Friday afternoons.

There are a number of methods that fraudsters use in order to make sure that their efforts bring them the result that they desire such as: testing the cards or the card data to make sure that it is working by purchasing low value goods before going for the major buy, not making very big purchases for fear of being detected, buying goods for under £500 mostly and only sometimes spending over this value but making sure that they make the most of the short window of opportunity.

When receiving delivery, fraudsters use a number of methods to make sure that they receive their goods. The methods include: waiting outside for the delivery van to show up and pretend that they are the friendly neighbour, using empty houses by breaking in, collaborating with estate agents or finding recently deceased individual's homes through the obituary section of local papers. In some instances, fraudsters use multiple addresses to conduct their operations. In addition, some fraudsters use rental properties to conduct their businesses and once they make the most off that address they move on. Others go as far as purchasing properties in some cases dividing them to flats with different numbers, renting them out and then getting goods delivered there claiming that they belong to the previous tenant and need to be redirected.

Once fraudsters have safely acquired their goods, they then employ a number of methods to turn them into cash. They are sold on auction websites, which provide an anonymous place for selling goods in addition to having the advantage of providing the fraudster with enough identifying information of the person who makes the purchase to start the identity fraud loop again

Additionally, the creation of bogus identities is another way of committing identity fraud. This is perhaps the most challenging aspect of this crime as it is extremely difficult to detect and quantify the losses. In most cases, they are simply treated as bad debt.

Finally, some criminals use stolen or created identities to avoid arrest or use them to travel to other countries without being noticed by Police or the border agencies. This has been more prevalent in the US, to the extent the Attorney General's Office provides a service where victims of identity theft can present their passports to law enforcement agencies to help prevent arrest for offences committed by someone using stolen information.

A brief look at Action Fraud UK, in the News and Alerts section, reveals a list of recent fraudulent methods and what the public need to look out for. By looking at this list it could truly be said that this crime is out of control. Some of the recent attempts are:

- Fraudsters target university staff in pay rise scam along with police and government employees.
- NHS members targeted by tax rebate scam.
- ID Fraud victims from internet dating websites are being reported at the rate of one every three hours.
- Medical practices targeted by CEO fraud.
- HMRC and Apple gift card fraud.
- Social media used to harvest fake charity donations.
- 'Migrant helpline' phishing e-mails lead to Ramnit malware.

What is constant is the misuse of identity information, but the ways that fraudsters abuse this data to acquire goods and services changes significantly. They are very good at using world events (such as the migrant crisis and other disasters) and special events (Such as Valentine's Day or Christmas) to deceive people and persuade them to part with their personal data.

In order to illustrate ID crime more clearly, two real-life examples of identity crimes are included below:

> Theophillus Madekurozwe stole letters from unlocked mailboxes at blocks of flats and the identities inside enabled him to obtain a series of credit cards for the amount of £113,000. He then used the bank cards to buy high value gift cards which funded a massive spending spree on designer goods including iPad tablets iMac laptops and high-end tech goods. He almost managed to escape because he spent the gift cards in stores where he hadn't obtained them. He was apprehended and jailed.
> (The fraudster who lived the high life thanks to identity theft, 2014)

In what was deemed UK's worst-case of identity crime, a British man's passport was stolen and then used with a different photograph to set up a communications company in the Isle of Man. The company was fined for breaching codes of practice and as the company was in the victim's name he was facing a £34,000 court order and unpaid VAT totalling more than £110,000. The battle against tax authorities to clear his name took him three years (Our £130,000 bill from identity theft, 2013).

Identity crime in UK

Although identity crime has been committed for years in one form or another it was not until 19 years ago that the first attempt was made by banks to collectively start measuring this fraud. It was then the constant presence of identity crime in the media, people's increasing concerns and the soaring figures of this crime that raised its profile and placed it prominently on the agenda of Government agencies and other major organizations. A number of forums and working groups were developed and information started being disseminated on what identity crime is and what people can do to protect themselves.

In 2002 the Cabinet Office published a report examining the identity fraud problem in the UK and estimated that identity fraud was costing £1.2 billion. The report recommended a multi-task force of public and private sector collaboration to be set up in order to tackle the harm caused by this crime to the UK economy. This work was sent to the Home Office in 2003 and the Identity Fraud Steering Committee was set up to work with public and private sectors to 'identify *and implement cost effective measures to counter identity fraud*' (New Estimate of Cost of Identity Fraud to the UK Economy, 2006–2007).

In 2005, a number of MPs and Peers from both sides of Parliament, concerned with the prevalence of identity crime, established the All Party Parliamentary Group (APPG on Identity Fraud). In 2006 the APPG was asked by Andy Burnham MP, the then Home Office Minister, to conduct an 'investigation into identity fraud with a view to making recommendations to government of the immediate steps which can be taken to tackle this issue' (All Party Parliamentary Group Report into Identity Fraud, 2007). Fifty-three recommendations were made by the report but three key issues, to address identity crime more effectively, were highlighted: better public awareness, a more accurate understanding of the scale of the problem, and the provision of more resources for law enforcement and the authorities to tackle identity crime. In 2007 a total of £29m was allocated to implement the recommendations of this report, and finally in 2008 the National Fraud Authority was established to fight against identify fraud and fraud in general which was a major step forward in addressing this issue (National Fraud Authority Business Plan, 2010/11).

In addition to the formation of NFA, and following on from discussions between the UK Card Payments industry and the National Consumer Group, a specialized service called the Victims of Fraud Service was developed in 2008. The service is run by the three credit referencing agencies (Callcredit, Experian and Equifax) with the objective of assisting victims with the following support:

- Providing advice to victims on how to protect themselves from further identity compromise i.e. signing up to CIFAS Protective Registration.
- Handling credit report related issues on an individual case management basis on behalf of the victim where the victim has the option to contact any of the three credit reference agencies by telephone, e-mail or in writing.
- Contacting lenders on the victim's behalf, in order to restore the victim's credit history to its former state.
- Provision of regular updates and advice to victims on the progress of amendments to the victims' credit report.

This was the first and a major step on behalf of the industry to acknowledge the pain caused by identity fraudsters to their victims and a very positive move towards helping the victims to rectify the damage caused to their lives by this crime. Previously it would have been the victim's responsibility to contact all the major banks or financial service providers which was a very stressful and time consuming task and in some cases the victims were completely oblivious as to what was happening to them and how their identifying information had been stolen and used.

In addition to the above efforts, the following actions were taken to assist in tackling identity crime:

- Provisions were made in the Serious Crime Act 2007 to allow for the 'targeted exchange of data between the public and private sector through an anti-fraud organisation to highlight potentially fraudulent applications for goods and services'.
- Provisions in the Police and Justice Act 2006 allowing for the release of information on the recently deceased to the private sector to help prevent those identities from being used by criminals.
- Identity and Passport service deploying a number of measures to increase the security of UK passports and to prevent fraudulent passport applications by conducting face-to-face interviews for first time adult passport applications.
- Establishment of the Get Safe Online website to help provide awareness and guidance for the public and small businesses to keep their computers safe and conduct online business and transactions safely.

Major organizations

There are a number of public and private organizations that make significant contributions to tackling identity-related crimes in the UK. Some of them also represent the UK in international forums. These organizations are the NFA, CIFAS, credit reference agencies and a number of law enforcement agencies.

Formation of the National Fraud Authority

The NFA was legally established as an executive agency of the Attorney General's Office with four main strategic priorities and 15 key projects, one of which was focused on identity crime. Although the four strategic priorities were not identity-crime specific, they would have had a significant impact on this crime. It is acknowledged that not only is the fraud landscape complex and the response to it fragmented but also that fraud in general is misunderstood and not always taken seriously (National Fraud Authority Business Plan, 2010/11).Therefore, it was the NFA's responsibility not only to raise the profile of fraud among the public but also to bring unison in tackling fraud and to draw the efforts of industry together.

There were some general and some identity crime specific actions. The latter fell under strategy number six which included the following approaches (National Fraud Authority Business Plan, 2010/11):

- Continue to lead multi-agency work to crack down on identity crime.
- Deliver a strategic threat assessment of the harms caused by ID crime, how ID fraud is perpetrated and the vulnerabilities of ID credentials.
- Conduct an evaluation of ID authentication, establish best practice and make recommendations to improve ID fraud prevention and detection.
- Disseminate best practice and ensure vulnerabilities exploited by criminals are shared with the counter-fraud community.
- Work with public and private sectors to improve public awareness of ID crime.
- Improve and roll out the ID victims toolkit to all Victim Care units and partner agencies.

There were two major developments in 2009. The formation of the National Fraud Reporting Centre (called Action Fraud) by the City of London Police and the National Fraud Authority and the launch of the National Fraud Intelligence Bureau (National Fraud Authority Business Plan, 2010/11). Action Fraud, which started operating on 26 October 2009, is providing a 'simple and central point for individuals and small and medium sized businesses to report fraud' (National Fraud Authority Business Plan, 2010/11). The NFA believed that more than half of all fraud victims do not report the crime because of embarrassment. This service is focused not only on recording the reported fraud but also providing victims with support (Fraud Focus, February 2010). The National Fraud Intelligence Bureau's role is analysing the collected and collated reports alongside data inputs from the public sector and industry as a whole (National Fraud Authority Business Plan, 2010/11).

The last news release from NFA indicated that in the first year of Action Fraud 150,000 people contacted them to report fraud totalling £78m and although this total is not identity fraud specific, online shopping and application fraud (which are classed as identity fraud) are among the five most commonly reported frauds (Fraud Focus, October 2010). At the moment Action Fraud is not recording and reporting identity crime separately but there is some indication that this could change in the future. The NFA however believes that the correct recording of identity-related crime will be influenced by the public's perception of the crime in that it is important enough to be reported. For example, when somebody calls the service to log in a fraud on their credit card, if they call it card fraud it will be recorded as card fraud if they call it identity fraud it will be reported as identity fraud. Additionally, there is so much overlap between identity fraud and other types of fraud, such as mass marketing and phishing, that sometimes it seems almost impossible to have a clear-cut distinction.

In dealing with identity fraud the NFA has set up a task force which oversees a programme of work delivered by the three subsidiary groups. There were also a number of activities that the NFA was undertaking which have not been carried out previously. The first one was the provision of a tool kit for victims of identity fraud. The support will target those that make phone calls or send e-mails to Action Fraud and report their victimization. Once a report is made the person contacting the centre will be asked whether they require further support and if the reply is affirmative they will be visited by a community representative to hand them the tool kit and answer their questions and concerns.

The second activity concerns the identity-related materials confiscated by law enforcement agencies. When police interrupts an identity factory or a website selling false identities, they will end up with a lot of material, so they will possibly prosecute the people involved but as part of the operation they will have thousands of false identities. NFA produced guidance to police and banks and others on what they should do when they get this material, they have also established a way that this material could be shared with other fraud partners.

The NFA's third role was to represent the UK in the international forums dealing with identity fraud. In addition, they were tasked with coordinating the UK approach to international engagement. And finally, the fourth area was to produce a UK strategic threat assessment. There is a lot of information and knowledge on identity fraud but there has never been a coordinated approach to drawing all this data together in order to form a more coherent understanding of the issue. The NFA was to clearly fill this gap.

One of the other key issues that the NFA addressed was to measure the monetary losses due to fraud. A measurement unit has been set up that has been producing an elaborate report on the fraud losses to the UK economy on an annual basis. Identity fraud is part of this exercise. For their first exercise the NFA used the £1.2 billion figure calculated in 2006 but going forward, this figure was to be revisited on an annual basis. In order to complete such an exercise the measurement unit has been relying on data from various organizations which have all been collaborative in providing information and assistance.

The NFA's role was to focus the numerous amount of activity that is currently being carried out by other organizations. In order to accomplish this objective a taskforce was set up with a specific time limit. The task force was run by its board which comprised of chairs of ACPO (Association of Chief Police Officers) Working Group on identity fraud and SOCA (Serious Organised Group Crime Agency) programme 17 and the IFCAG (Identity Fraud Consumer Awareness Group) plus HMRC and the City of London Police. The taskforce board oversees a program of work which is delivered by the three subsidiary groups.

Unfortunately, the NFA's existence was short-lived and it was dissolved in March 2014. Action Fraud was transferred to the City of London Police and Strategic development of threat analysis transferred to the National Crime Agency. The e-confidence campaign went to the Home Office and responsibility for the development of the counter-fraud checking service was taken on by the Cabinet Office. The responsibility for managing the Annual Fraud Indicator was passed to non-Governmental organizations (Experian, PKF Littlejohn and the University of Portsmouth's Centre for Counter Fraud Studies).

CIFAS (UK's fraud prevention service)

One of the other major players in the identity fraud and fraud in general arena is CIFAS which was established in 1988 by the major lenders in the UK consumer credit industry. CIFAS is a not-for-profit membership association representing the private and public sectors dedicated to the prevention of fraud, including staff fraud, and the identification of financial crime. It has over 260 members spread across banking, credit cards, asset finance, retail credit, mail order, insurance, savings, telecommunications, factoring, share dealing and the public sector. Although at present CIFAS Members are predominantly private sector organizations, public sector bodies may also share fraud data reciprocally through CIFAS to prevent fraud. CIFAS's role is to facilitate the sharing of information provided by its members in order to prevent further fraud (CIFAS website).

In addition to information sharing, CIFAS provides a service called the Protective Registration service which is a tool to assist individuals and organizations to combat identity crime. The service is run both for individuals and for organizations. CIFAS Protective Registration for individuals enables them to seek protection against possible impersonation attempts when they have good reason to believe that their details might be used by a fraudster. For example, there may have been a burglary or a violent crime where personal documents have been stolen. CIFAS Member organizations dealing with requests for credit or other services from someone who has taken out CIFAS Protective Registration will be alerted to the need for caution. During their routine checks, they will see a CIFAS warning flag marked 'Protective Registration' against the individual's name and personal details which indicates that he or she has been recorded on the CIFAS database for their protection. As a result of the entry, CIFAS Members will undertake additional checks to make sure that the applicant is genuine and not a fraudster trying to commit identity theft. This offers reassurance that the identity of an individual (who has taken out Protective Registration because they are at heightened risk of identity theft) is protected against further fraudulent applications.

CIFAS Protective Registration for organizations on the other hand is devised to help them in protecting their consumers and employees from identity fraud in the event that there has been a data security breach. When a laptop bearing customer details is stolen, or payroll or other information is intercepted, for example, a straightforward solution is available from CIFAS. The service is known as the CIFAS Bulk Protective Registration Service. It enables organizations to coordinate and to submit to the CIFAS database, as a batch, the details of all those individuals who require protection. The service allows those who are at risk of identity theft to have a special CIFAS warning 'flag' placed on their credit reference agency file. Then when, for example, an application for credit or insurance is received by a CIFAS member (such as a bank, building society or insurance company), the member is alerted by the warning 'flag' of the need to undertake additional verification checks to ascertain that the applicant is genuine, and not a fraudster trying to commit identity theft.

In addition to the above, CIFAS also publishes data on the extent of the issue on a regular basis and proactively participates in the Identity Fraud Consumer Awareness Group.

Credit reference agencies

The credit reference agencies play a prominent role in the identity crime arena. This role has traditionally been as the credit risk and information providers to credit risk decisions and decision makers. These fraud solutions have been perceived as a major business development opportunity for credit reference agencies and are provided to consumers, businesses and government agencies as well as law enforcement bodies. The products are risk based and involve identity verification and authentication. These solutions not only assist in tackling identity fraud but also help in combating money laundering. These services and products can be listed as:

- Solution on authentication to prevent id fraud.
- Product to detect any discrepancies in applications. Comparing the data with information provided on previous applications and highlighting if they do not match. Also, looking for matches against other applications to highlight possible fraud.
- Product recording where fraud has happened, whether an application has been declined or accepted, looking at mortgage brokers and whether they have been involved in fraudulent mortgage applications, basically building intelligence.

- Providing credit reports and credit report monitoring to consumers.
- Victim of fraud service.
- Solution for companies that have suffered a data breach. The credit reference agencies would offer a discounted version of their credit expert service to such companies to be offered to their customers. They also advise companies on ways they can help their affected customers to protect themselves.
- Provide credit reports on business to business so that when businesses want to trade with other businesses they may identify where there may be fraud in trade-credit relationships. This service also helps companies to prevent, for example, trading with fictitious companies.

In addition to the above, the data that credit reference agencies generate enables other organizations that primarily verify data for businesses and government agencies to exchange information. The source of the data for the credit reference agencies comes from public sources (such as electoral roll, court judgments, bankruptcies and so on) and the data from lenders (such as accounts).

Law enforcement

There are a number of law enforcement agencies taking an active role in fighting identity crime. These are the City of London Police, the Association of Chief Police Officers (ACPO), NCA (National Crime Agency) and DCPCU (Dedicated Cheque and Plastic Crime Unit). Currently there is no single legislative definition of identity crime and thus no single law designed to address it. This is unhelpful to law enforcement agencies. There are, however, a range of other criminal offences which together provide appropriate tools to combat this crime. The following two Acts have criminalized the methodologies that identity fraudsters use to commit these offences.

- The Fraud Act of 2006 which created a new offence of fraud which can be committed in three ways: by making a false representation (dishonestly, with intent to make a gain, cause loss or risk of loss to another), by failing to disclose information, and by abuse of position.
- It also established, in section 6, the crime of being in possession or in control of 'articles for use in or in connection with any fraud'.
- Sections 25 and 26 of the Identity Cards Act 2006, since repealed, created new criminal offences of being in possession or control of false identity documents, or apparatus or material for making false identity documents.

Cyber security strategies

In November 2011, the Government published the UK Cyber Security Strategy which focuses on all risks relating to internet use. By 2015, the

Government's aspiration was that the measures outlined in the strategy would mean the UK is in a position where Law Enforcement is tackling cyber-criminals, citizens know what to do to protect themselves, effective Cyber security is seen as a positive for UK businesses, a thriving cyber security sector has been established, public services online are secure and resilient, and the threats to national infrastructure and national security have been confronted.

Cyberspace plays a very important role in facilitating identity crimes. As mentioned above, criminals easily harvest personal identifications using the World Wide Web. Cyber security is finally having the attention that it needs.

The opening paragraph of the UK cyber security report reads:

> The future of the UK's security and prosperity rests on digital foundations. The challenge of our generation is to build a flourishing digital society that is both resilient to cyber threats and equipped with the knowledge and capabilities required to maximise opportunities and manage risks.
> (The UK Cyber Security Strategy, 2011–2016)

The national response is about Defend, Deter and Develop along with international action.

In the report, it is acknowledged that cyber security is an area of relative immaturity when it comes to the measurement of outcomes and impacts (normally referred to as metrics). Absence of data is also acknowledged.

> We will ensure that this strategy is founded upon a rigorous and comprehensive set of metrics against which we measure progress towards the outcomes we need to achieve.
> (The UK Cyber Security Strategy, 2011–2016)

Additionally, a National Cyber Security Centre which is part of the intelligence agency GCHQ was established and started to work in October 2016 as part of a £1.9 billion five-year strategy. One-hundred private sector employees were seconded to the centre to help identify threats. Chancellor Philip Hammond was quoted saying

> Government cannot protect business and the general public from the risks of cyber-attack on its own. It has to be a team effort. It is only in this way that we can stay one step ahead of the scale and pace of the threat that we face.
> (Hammond, 2017)

The centre will be working on a voluntary basis with political parties and giving advice to high profile individuals – including MPs on how to protect their sensitive data.

Extent of the problem and how it is measured

In dealing with any kind of crime or fraud it is imperative to discover the extent of the problem under examination. A brief study of recent media indicates identity crime to be one of the most modern and fastest-growing types of crime in the UK. However, the question is: how accurate is this assertion?

There are a number of organizations that publish data on losses due to identity-related crimes. One of the responsibilities of NFA was to provide an accurate figure of how much was lost to fraud in general and identity crimes but after NFA's abolition this responsibility was transferred to the University of Portsmouth. There are certain organizations that also produce statistics related to identity crimes such as UK Payments who provides services to the banks and financial service providers. UK Payments, in its publication 'Fraud the Facts' (2018), refers to identity crime as card ID theft and explains that these are incidences where 'a criminal uses a fraudulently obtained card or card details, along with stolen personal information to open or take over a card account held in someone else's name'. It then categorizes this fraud into two main types, 'application fraud' and 'account take over'. 'Application fraud happens when fraudsters use stolen or fake documents to open an account in someone else's name' while account takeover

> involves a criminal fraudulently using another person's credit or debit card account, first by gathering information about the intended victim, then contacting their bank or credit issuer whilst masquerading as the genuine cardholder. The criminal will then arrange for funds to be transferred out of the account, or will change the address on the account and ask for new or replacement cards to be sent to the new address.
>
> (ibid: 3)

UK Payments however does not regard other types of fraud as identity crime but recognizes them as, fraud types in their own right. The discrepancies in using an agreed set of definitions are further evidenced by the following assertion

> There are two different types … transaction fraud and identity fraud. Transaction is an id fraud to enable a transaction, it is a card id, and someone's credit card is a part of their id. It is a bigger id fraud when somebody takes your whole demographic, represents you completely as your age, job and the rest of it, that is a different level and that is why victims vary.
>
> (ibid: 5)

It is due to these differences of opinion that there are different data and measures of identity fraud.

The different fraud types and their definitions that UK Payments do not recognize as identity fraud are:

196   *Aida Fazely*

- **Card-not-present:** This crime most commonly involves the theft of genuine card details that are then used to make a purchase over the internet, by phone, or by mail order.
- **Counterfeit card fraud:** occurs when a fake card is created by fraudsters using compromised details, from the magnetic strips of a genuine card.
- **Lost and stolen fraud:** this occurs when a customer's card is lost or stolen and fraudulent purchases are made on it either in shops that do not have chip and PIN or online/ mail order or telephone.
- **Mail non-receipt fraud:** this type of fraud happens when the cards involved are stolen while being sent to the customer. This can happen either when the card is posted to the customer or in some cases where communal letterboxes or halls are used. It can also happen to people who do not redirect their mail when they move.

However, these definitions are not shared by all of the identity crime prevention practitioners and academics and therefore, for the purposes of this study, all identity-related crimes (card or non-card) will be included.

The graph below depicts the losses to the banking industry through the different types of fraud. All the different typologies have been included. Although the total fraud losses are decreasing, card-identity theft seems to have increased gradually and then plateaued out in the last three years.

These figures are only representative of identity crime in the financial sector, but other sectors have also been impacted heavily by this crime. While these figures are only a small portion of identity-fraud losses, they are the most robust figures in terms of the transparency and methodology used to collect them. UK Payments has a dedicated team that, on a monthly basis, collects and collates data from member banks and financial institutions and uses these data to prepare and publish monthly, quarterly and yearly reports which are then disseminated to all their members and are published for the general public on their website. There is no other sector that publishes data on identity crimes in such a scientific manner. The appetite of different

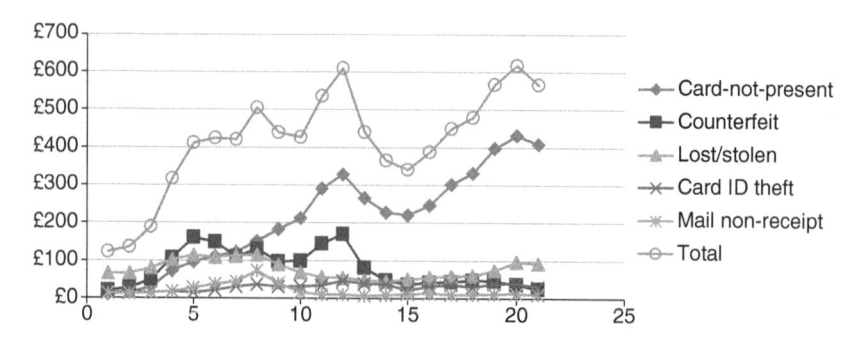

Figure 11.1 UK Payments identity-related fraud figures in millions of pounds.

Identity crime in the UK 197

organizations for implementing the processes to monitor and accurately record identity crime is important. Apart from the banking industry which is transparent with the amount of money that is lost to this type of crime, no other organization (either public or private) seems to be publishing their figures independently. It is only after the exercise carried out by the IFSC that the losses of other organizations have come to light.

CIFAS, the UK's Fraud Prevention Service, is the second source of information on the scale of identity fraud and (very similar to the UK Payments) regards identity fraud as account takeover and application fraud. CIFAS, in collaboration with a number of private and public sector bodies, publishes a report that combines research, statistics, maps, prevention tips, case studies and opinion pieces on this issue. The methodology that is used to examine identity fraud is based on the number of reported fraudulent cases. This data is based on the data provided by CIFAS members and therefore may present a significant bias as it will only capture the data presented by CIFAS members and will not reflect all the identity-crime incidences.

The trend shows a sharp increase in 2009, 2010 and 2011 and even though the figures decline in 2012 they continue to rise year by year. Although there is hardly any data available on the identity theft part of this crime, an important assertion states that the decreases in identity theft may not necessarily mean that identity fraud or crime is decreasing. It could simply be that the criminals are getting more money out of old identities rather than looking for new ones.

Although the data and sources captured above are valid and reliable, they do not provide a holistic picture of identity crime in the UK. To address this issue, the Identity Fraud Steering Group in 2006 made an estimation of the losses suffered by the UK economy to this type of fraud. The estimated figure was £1.72 billion which was then reduced to £1.2 billion when the study was revised in 2007. This figure includes losses suffered by a large number of public and private organizations.

The methodology used to collect this data takes into account three different costs associated with identity crime. These are: anticipation costs

Table 11.1 Number of identity-related fraud cases per year

Year	ID Fraud cases identified
2007	77,500
2008	77,600
2009	102,300
2010	217,385
2011	236,516
2012	123,58
2013	108,554
2014	114,000
2015	169,592
2016	173,000
2017	174,523

(costs associated with risk assessment, deterrence, prevention and identification/detection), reaction costs (investigation, recovery and restoration) and finally financial loses (net cost of detected identity fraud and estimated cost of undetected identity fraud).

Since 2007 there has not been any consistency in providing figures for this crime. NFA used the figure from 2007 for their reports in 2010, 2011 and 2012. In the 2013 Annual Fraud Indicator a new estimate was published by NFA putting identity crime losses at an all-time high of £3.3 billion but following their demise in 2014 no report was produced for 2014. Once the responsibility of the Annual Fraud Indicator report was transferred to Centre for Counter Fraud Studies, they produced a figure of £5.4 million for 2015 and used the same figure for 2016. A new estimate was reported in the 2017 report for 1.3 million (Annual Fraud Indicators, 2010, 2011, 2012, 2013, 2015, 2016 and 2017).

Conclusion

Identity criminals do not discriminate, they victimize people, young and old even dead and then move on to governments and private companies small and large. The impact on individual victims in some cases has been so severe that the only option left for the victim has been to take their own life. Dealing with this crime is challenging to everyone involved, individuals and organizations and the impact of this crime on society is severe as it can call into question the integrity of the systems that we have in place.

Regulatory pressure has been seen to be effective in this area. But there is a conflict between what government perceives and what it is prepared to do to address this issue. Even though government acknowledges this as a priority they have failed, to address it adequately and their efforts are patchy and inconsistent. This attitude was evident from the formation and subsequent dissolution of the NFA and the political climb-down surrounding the aborted attempt to introduce ID cards.

One of the major issues in this area is that no one body or organization has an overall measure of the amount of identity crime being committed. The issues of definition and measurement are still present and despite such patchy work by government they still have not been resolved. Home Office's definition was to bring some unity in this area but they are viewed as too broad by some practitioners and in fact the challenge is in defining 'identity' itself.

Action Fraud which is the overall body in collecting data on fraud does not actually record and report identity crimes as a standalone category therefore this crime type does not have the visibility that it needs.

There are lots of pockets of activities when it comes to tackling this issue. One of the responsibilities of NFA was to bring all these activities together and provide a focus for industry to go forward by way of an identity fraud threat assessment. After NFA's depletion that responsibility has gone to City of London Police, but little is known about the effectiveness of that.

There is a need for one national body to champion the fight against identity crimes. A lot of organizations (both public and private) have an interest in this crime type but this is no one's number one priority. The government needs to show commitment to a long-term strategy and resources and create a central department to win and champion the fight against ID crime. The NFA was to provide this role but it was dissolved therefore there is a need for a government body to provide such leadership and direction but also a body with regulatory powers. Additionally only 3 per cent of detected ID crimes are investigated and prosecuted. This crime needs to be higher up on law enforcement's agenda both on a local and national level. It must feature in the high-level national strategic plan in order to receive the attention and support it needs at local level.

Identity crime challenges traditional criminological typologies: is it a form of white-collar crime? What degree of organization does it require? Is it, rather, a 'lone' variety of patrimonial offence? Are we witnessing, as Ruggiero suggests in the Introduction to this book, the opening of novel illicit opportunities made available to all? This type of crime seems to grant 'equal opportunities' to very different actors who, after acquiring the necessary technological skills, will then act and, perhaps, even mobilize the specific techniques of neutralization more consistent with their social group and subculture. Further research should assess whether and how organized crime and terrorist networks engage in this type of crime and whether, by doing so, they indeed shape new distinctive 'hybrids' that supersede those discussed in this book.

Bibliography

All Party Parliamentary Group Report into Identity Fraud (Saturday 6 October, 2007), www.fhcreative.co.uk/idfraud/downloads/APPG_Identity_Fraud_Report (accessed 27 March 2008).

Allison, S.F.H., Schuck, A.M. and Lersch, K.M. (2005), 'Exploring the Crime of Identity Theft: Prevalence, Clearance Rates and Victim/Offender Characteristics, *Journal of Criminal Justice*, 33: 19–29.

Annual Fraud Indicator (2010), https://assets.publishing.service.gov.uk/government/uploads/system/uploads/attachment_data/file/118536/afi-2010.pdf (accessed November 2018).

Annual Fraud Indicator (2011), https://assets.publishing.service.gov.uk/government/uploads/system/uploads/attachment_data/file/118532/annual-fraud-indicator-2011.pdf (accessed November 2018).

Annual Fraud Indicator (2012), https://assets.publishing.service.gov.uk/government/uploads/system/uploads/attachment_data/file/118530/annual-fraud-indicator-2012.pdf (accessed November 2018).

Annual Fraud Indicator (2013), https://assets.publishing.service.gov.uk/government/uploads/system/uploads/attachment_data/file/206552/nfa-annual-fraud-indicator-2013.pdf (accessed November 2018).

Annual Fraud Indicator (2015), www.pkf.com/media/31640/PKF-The-financial-cost-of-fraud-2015.pdf (accessed November 2018).

Annual Fraud Indicator (2016), www2.port.ac.uk/media/contacts-and-departments/icjs/ccfs/Annual-Fraud-Indicator-2016.pdf (accessed November 2018).

Annual Fraud Indicator (2017), www.experian.co.uk/assets/identity-and-fraud/annual-fraud-indicator-report-2017.pdf (accessed November 2018).

Camp, L.J. (2007), *Economics of Identity Theft: Avoidance, Causes and Possible Cures*, New York: Springer.

Cendrowski, H., Petro, L.W. and Martin, J.P. (2007), *The Handbook of Fraud Deterrence*, Oxford: John Wiley & Sons.

CIFAS (nd), www.cifas.org.uk/ (accessed 24 February 2014).

Companies House (nd), www.companieshouse.gov.uk/infoAndGuide/proofFaqsWebFiling.shtml (accessed 1 August 2011).

Double Identity Immigrant Benefit Thief Jailed (2011), http://benefitfraud.blogspot.co.uk/2011/02/double-identity-immigrant-benefit-thief.html (accessed 1 December 2011).

Fraud the Facts (2018), www.financialfraudaction.org.uk/fraudfacts16/ (accessed 4 September 2018).

Fraud Focus (October 2010), www.homeoffice.gov.uk/publications/agencies-public-bodies/nfa/fraud-focus-newsletter/fraud-focus-oct10?view=Binary (accessed 12 April 2010).

Fraud Review (2007), www.attorneygeneral.gov.uk/Fraud%20Review/Terms%20of%20NFSA.pdf (accessed 30 March 2017)

Hammond, P. (2017), 'Chancellor's Speech at the National Cyber Security Centre Opening', www.gov.uk/government/speeches/chancellors-speech-at-the-national-cyber-security-centre-opening (accessed 12 June 2018).

Helser, S. (2015), 'FIT: Identity Theft Education', IEEE International Symposium on Technology in Society (ISTAS) Proceedings.

Home Office Identity Fraud Steering Group (2009), 'Identity Crime Definitions', www.identity-theft.org.uk/definition.html (accessed 17 March 2008).

Identity Cards Are to Be Scrapped (nd), www.homeoffice.gove.uk/media-centre/news/identity-cards-scrapped (accessed 5 September 2017).

Identity Fraud Steering Group (nd), www.identity-fraud.org.uk (accessed 9 June 2009).

Lacey, D., Zaiss, J. and Barber, K.S. (2016), 'Understanding Victim-enabled Identity Theft: Perpetrator and Victim Perspectives, Privacy, Security and Trust (PST)', 14th Annual Conference.

National Fraud Authority Business Plan (2009), https://assets.publishing.service.gov.uk/government/uploads/system/uploads/attachment_data/file/118514/business-plan-2010-11.pdf (accessed 26 January 2011).

National Fraud Authority (2010/11, 26 October), www.attorneygeneral.gov.uk/nfa/WhatAreWeSaying/NewsRelease/Pages/78million-fraud-loss-reported-to-Action-Fraud.aspx (accessed January 2011).

New Estimate of Cost of Identity Fraud to the UK Economy (2006–2007), www.identitytheft.org.uk/cms/assets/cost_of_identity_fraud_to_the_uk_economy_2006-07.pdf

Our £130,000 Bill from Identity Theft (2013), www.telegraph.co.uk/finance/personalfinance/money-saving-tips/10388791/Our-130000-bill-from-identity-theft.html (accessed June 2017).

The Fraudster Who Lived the High Life Thanks to Identity Theft (2014), www.manchestereveningnews.co.uk/news/greater-manchester-news/jailed-fraudster-who-lived-high-8114301 (accessed 11 January 2017).

The UK Cyber Security Strategy (2011–2016), www.gov.uk/government/uploads/system/uploads/attachment_data/file/516331/UK_Cyber_Security_Strategy_Annual_Report_2016.pdf (accessed 4 February 2017).

Yang, Y., Manoharan, M. and Barber, S. (2014), 'Modelling and Analysis of Identity Threat Behaviours Though Text Mining of Identity Theft Stories', IEEE Joint Intelligence and Security Informatics Conference.

Index

Page numbers in **bold** denote tables, those in *italics* denote figures.

9/11; counter-terrorism responses 84, 85, 145–6

Abedi, Salman 83
Abouyaaqoub, Younes 91–2
Action Fraud 189–90, 199
advanced fee fraud 64–5
Advance Passenger Information (API) system 162, 169–70
Agenfor Media 20
Albanese, Jay 43
Albanian Mafia 101
Allison, Stuart 183–4
Al-Mourabitun 110
Al-Nusra 110–11
Al-Qaeda 79, 80, 104, 142, 143, 145
Al-Qaeda in the Arabic Peninsula (AQAP) 81–2, 86, 89
Al-Qaeda in the Islamic Maghreb (AQIM) 35, 110
Amri, Anis 90–1
Anarchist Cookbook (Powell) 81
Ansar-al Sharia 109
Ansar-Eddine 109
anti-money laundering measures: credit reference agencies 192–3; crime-terror activities 159; EU legislation/regulations 15, 141, 146–7, 164, 165; international frameworks 145, 164
arms trafficking: EU counter measures 167; organized crime/terrorist links 101, 159; terrorism financing 141, 143, 145; Trans-Saharan activities 109–10
asset freezing and confiscation 165
auction and trade fraud 63–4

Bakhshi, Taimur 61

Beccaria, Cesare 26, 28
Belgium bomb attacks 80
Belmokhtar, Mokhtar 110
Bentham, Jeremy 26, 28
Bibes, Patricia 34
BigBotPein 49
Blackholing 62
Boko Haram 109
Borsellino, Paolo 15, 101
Breivik, Anders Behring 79
Burgess, Ernest 84, 86
Butt, Khuram 91

call ID Spoofing 66
Camorra 101
Campbell, Liz 31, 92
Camp, L. Jean 182
'cashing out' (identity fraud) 183, 185–7
Cervantes, Miguel de 1
Chicago School of sociology 29
Chilcot Report 20
China 93
CIFAS 191–2, 197
Cohen, Lawrence 87, 90
Companies House 183
Computer Fraud and Abuse Act (US) 49
Computer Misuse Act 1990 (UK) 49
Convention for the Suppression of Terrorism Finances 145
Coolsaet, Rik 161–2
corporate identity crime 183
Corsica National Liberation Front (FLNC) 101
Council Framework Decision 162–3, 170
Council of Europe 4, 15

Council of European Union: counter terrorism financing 146–7, 165; crime-terror nexus 158–9; EU Counter-Terrorism Strategy 135; EU information systems and intelligence sharing 162–3, 168, 170
Counter-Terrorism Implementation Task Force (CTITF) 146
Counter Terrorism Internet Referral Unit (CTIRU) 70
covert channels, terrorist 70–1
crime-terror nexus: criminological definitions 27–9; exclusion/marginalization 31–2; group structure models 43–4, 101; hybrids and overarching etiologies 31–5; joint analyses, ambiguity issues 35–9, 92–4; organization to network 30–1; petty criminality and terrorism cells 143–4, 148–9, 150; power to threaten, online operations 45–6; shareable traits 43, *44*
crime-terror nexus, global dynamics: decentralization and operational flexibility 105–7; Europe, VNSA security challenges 108–9, 110; globalization related benefits 104–5; group structure models 101; resourcing collaborations 101; state fragility and conflict opportunities 107–8; Trans-Saharan hybridized activities 109–11; UN view 100; violent non-state actors (VNSA), impact of 101–4
crime-terror nexus, supranational level: arms trafficking, EU measures 167; cooperation, key to prevention 160–1; counter measures, EU implementation challenges 168–72; criminality and terrorism, linked activities 157, 159–60; criminal radicalization, counter measures 163–4; drug trafficking, EU counter measures 165–6; EU appraisals and findings 158–9; EU information systems, policing/borders 162–3; EU Justice and Home Affairs agency collaboration 161–2, 165, 166–7, 171–2; hazardous substances/explosive limitation 167–8; law enforcement perspective 157; terrorist financing, disruptive/restriction measures 164–6; travel/identity document fraud 162, 166–7
criminological concepts 3–4
criminological definitions 27–9

critical infrastructure sabotage 72–3
Cube Model, anti-crime/terrorism framework: 'case categorization matrix' 122; case pathways 130–2, *131*; counter measure assessment 135–6, *136*; crime/terrorism nexus options 132–5, *133–4*; model development 118–19, **119**; organized cybercrime case 126–7, **127**, *128*; radicalization case **129**, 129–30, *130*; research objectives 117, 136–7; situational crime prevention (SCP) approach 118; stakeholder action/reaction analysis 119–22, *120–1*; terrorism case 123–4, **125**, *125*
cybercrime: critical infrastructure sabotage 72–3; Cube Model, anti-crime/terrorism study 126–7, **127**, *128*; Darknet 67–8, 159; Denial of Service (DoS) 62; depersonalized actions 5–6; Distributed Denial of Service (DDoS) attacks 46–50, 54–5, *54*, 56, 62; diversity of actors 5; identity theft 66–7, 184; online fraud 63–5, 184, 185; power to threaten 45–6; ransomware attacks 45, 61–2; stresser services 46, 47, 48–56, **50, 52**, *53–4*, **54**; terrorist communications 69–71; UK Cyber Security Strategy 193–4

Darknet 67–8, 159
deculturation 32
Department of Health and Social Care (DHSC), UK 45
Dishman, Chris 43
'disposition matrix' 19
Distributed Denial of Service (DDoS) attacks: actions and impacts 46; offender motivations 46–7, 62; prevention approaches 62; stresser services 48–50, 54–5, *54*, 56
drug trafficking: EU counter measures 165–6; organized crime/terrorist links 92, 101, 159; terrorism financing 143, 150; Trans-Saharan activities 109–10
Dupont, Benoit 170
Durkheim, Émile 29

encryption 62
Enterprise Model 43–4
Erdogan, Recep 93
Escobar, Pablo 35
Es Satty, Abdelbaki 91

Index

Estonia: political cyberattack 47
Ethnic–Cultural Model 43
EU Intelligence Analysis Centre INTCEN 171
EURODAC 162, 169
Eurojust 15, 161–2, 168
European Commission (EC): Agenda on Security 19, 158; counter terrorism financing 147–8, 164, 166; hazardous substances/explosives regulation 167–8; intelligence and information systems 169–70, 172
European Counter Terrorism Centre (ECTC) 147–8, 166–7
European Criminal Records Information System (ECRIS) 162
European Parliament 14, 15, 158, 165, 166
European terrorism, since 2004: anti-terrorism challenges 95–6; bullet and bomb attacks 80; combined tactics 91; economic effects 93; improvised explosive devices (IEDs) 83; lone-wolf attacks 79, 82, 83, 90, 94; major incidents and perpetrators 79; vehicular terror-assaults 83, 86, 90–2
European Union (EU): anti-organized crime strategies 15, 156–7; anti-terrorism strategies 19, 135, 156–7; crime-terror nexus, appraisals and findings 157–9; crime-terror nexus, pro-active collaboration 159–68; criminal finances legislation 15, 145, 146–7, 165; drug trafficking legislation 165–6; see also crime–terror nexus, supranational level
Europol: collaboration challenges 169; Counter Terrorism Centre (ECTC) 147–8, 166–7, 169; crime-terror hybrids 37, 43; FIU.net system and financial tracking 146, 164, 165; formation 15; intelligence and information systems 84, 159–60, 161, 162, 171
Euskadi Ta Askartasuna (ETA) 101
EU Strategy for Combating Radicalization and Recruitment to Terrorism 163

Falcone, Giovanni 15, 101
FAST (Families Against Stress & Trauma) 20
Felson, Marcus 87, 90
Financial Action Task Force (FATF) 145, 164

Financial Intelligence Units (FUI) 15, 146, 164
France: Nice truck attack 83, 86, 90; Paris, bullet and bomb attacks 80, 169
Freeman, Michael 144
Frontex 161, 162

Gammell, John Kelsey 48
Germany: Berlin market attack 90–1; Munich mall shooting 90
Gerspacher, Nadia 170
GIA network 145, 150
Grabosky, Peter 33

Hammond, Philip 194
Helser, Susan 182
Hezbollah 110, 142
Hierarchical Model 43
Home Office Identity Fraud Steering Group, UK 182–3, 187, 197

ICSR (International Centre for the Study of Radicalisation and Political Violence) 34, 35
identity crime: CIFAS (fraud prevention) 191–2, 197; credit reference agencies 192–3; definition issues 182–3, 195–6, 198–9; fraudulent gain, services, goods and products 185–7; identity theft, offline/online 183–4; incidence reports and statistics, UK 195–8, *196*, **197**; law enforcement 193, 199; National Fraud Authority, remit and roles 189–91, 195, 198, 199; UK Cyber Security Strategy 193–4; UK public/private sector initiatives 187–8; victims and damage levels 182, 183, 198
identity theft 66–7, 182, 183–4
Improvised Explosive Devices (IEDs) 82–3, 84
information and communication technology (ICT), criminal usage: advanced fee fraud 64–5; auction and trade fraud 63–4; critical infrastructure sabotage 72–3; Darknet 67–8; government/institutional cyberattacks 61–2; identity theft 66–7; propaganda, terrorist groups 69–70; terrorist's covert channels 70–1
Irish National Liberation Army (INLA) 101
Irish Republican Army (IRA) 35, 43, 101

Index   205

ISIS: agitprop propaganda 89; European attacks 79, 80, 83; financial resourcing 110, 147, 148; founding motives 16, 31, 88–9; global terrorism 104; low-tech terrorism 148; radicalization and recruitment pathways 123–4, 128–9, 134–5, 144, 148

Kermische, Adel 123–4, **125**, *125*
Kosovo Liberation Army 101
Kouachi brothers 80
Krieger, Tim 142
Kurdish Workers' Party (PKK) 101

Lahouaiej-Bouhlel, Mohamed 83, 86
Libya 109–10
Lizard Squad 49
London, terrorist attacks 79, 90, 91, 146
Lukes, Steven 44

Maastricht Treaty 15
Macedonia 80
Madrid train bombings 2004 79, 146, 150
Mafia, Italian 28, 101
Mangan, Fiona 109–10
Mararenko, Tamara 43
McIntosh, Mary S. 28
Medellín drug cartel 101
Meierrieks, Daniel 142
Merton, Robert K. 11
MI5, 84
Minsk Metro bomb 2011 79
Morales, Carlos 46
Mudd, Adam 49

Nadir, Ibrahim 61
narco-terrorism 34, 35
National Crime Agency (NCA), UK 34
National Fraud Authority, UK 187, 189–91, 195, 198, 199
National Fraud Intelligence Bureau, UK 189
National Health Service, UK 61
nationalist extremists 79, 80
'Ndrangheta 101
network monitoring (ICT) 68, 69–70
Neumann, Peter 35
Nice, terrorist attack 83, 86, 90
Niemeier, Michael 170
Norway: Utoya island attack 2011 79
Norwegian Defence Research Establishment 150
Not-Petya ransomware attack 45

Oftedal, Emilie 142
online scams and phishing activities 63–7
organized crime: academic literature 1; corruption and manipulation 45; criminological definitions 27–9; decentralized, flexible operations 105–7; elite dissociation and decline 38–9; 'employer' for dispossessed 14; international dynamics 102, 103–4; 'overworld' partnerships 30; private protection and governance 28; structure models 43–4; temporal collaboration 94; wealth accumulation priorities 31
organized crime, TAKEDOWN findings: causes, theoretical approaches 11–12, 21–2; group characteristics 10; main activities 10–11; policing and civilian led prevention 12–13, **13**, 22; reduction, economic/political strategies 14–16, 22; social prevention strategies 13–14
organized crime/terrorism, hybrids and etiologies: analytical comparison critiques 35–9, 92–4; exclusion/marginalization 31–2; neutralization techniques 32; terrorism, criminalized financing 32–3, 34–5; transnational crime alliances 33–4

Palestinian Liberation Organization (PLO) 142
Paris, terrorist attacks 80, 169
Park, Robert 84, 86
Passenger Name Records (PNR) exchange 162, 169–70
people trafficking: organized crime/terrorist links 92; terrorism financing 143; Trans-Saharan activities 109–10
Peterson, M. 10
pharming 66
Picarelli, John 43
political violence: common violence, shared causation 30–1; criminalized financing 32–3; criminological definitions 28–9; ideologically framed motivations 38; neutralization techniques 32; state sponsored 93
Positivist School of criminology 11, 28–9
Powell, William 81
pressure cooker bombs 82–3
'Prevent' programme 20
professional crime 10, 27

propaganda, terrorist tactics 69–70
Provisional Irish Republican Army (PIRA) 95
'Prüm' Decision 162, 165, 170
Public Private Partnership in Financial Intelligence (EFIPPP) 164–5

Radicalisation Awareness Network (RAN) 163–4
ransomware attacks 45, 47, 61–2
Rational Choice theory 88
Redouane, Rachid 91
Reid, Richard 85
Revolutionary Armed Forces of Colombia (FARC) 35, 101
Routine Activities Theory 84, 87–8, 90, 91
Ruehsen, Moyara 144
Ruggiero, Vincenzo 199

Sageman, Marc 16
Salinas de Frías, Ana 35
scambaiting 65
Schengen Information System (SIS) 162, 169
Sen, Amartya 18
Shaw, Mark 109–10
Shelley, Louise 43
SIENA network 161, 169
Simcox, Robin 148
situational crime prevention (SCP) approach 118
Society for Worldwide Interbank Financial Telecommunications (SWIFT) 146
Spain: Alcanar bomb factory 91; Barcelona van attack 2017 91–2; Cambrils attack 92; Madrid train bombings 2004 79, 146, 150
spam detection 65
Stohl, Michael 33
Stolen and Lost Travel Documents, Interpol 167
strain theory 11
stresser services: law enforcement and prevention 49–50, 55; legal purpose 48; malicious and criminal usage 48–9; semi-legal tools 46, 47; StressSquadZ, case study 50–6
StressSquadZ, case study: malicious and criminal usage 53, 54–5, *54*; profits 52, **52**, *53*; service plans, uptake patterns **50**, 50–1, 55; users' activity 53, **54**, 55–6

symbolic interactionism 29

TAKEDOWN project: contributing teams 2–3; objective 2; organized crime, research findings 9–16, **13**; research methodology 8–9
TAKEDOWN project findings: crime reduction, economic/political strategies 14–16; crime reduction, positive integration 12–13, **13**; expert collaboration essential 9–10; organized crime activities 10–11; organized crime drivers 11–12; social prevention strategies 13–14; terrorist activities 16
Taliban 35, 145
terrorism: academic literature 2; agitprop propaganda 81–2, 89; aircraft/airport security measures 85–6, 162; anti-terrorism challenges 95–6; collective identity, mobilizing strategy 37–8; collective identity networks 30, 94; covert communication channels 70–1; criminological definitions 28–9, 31; Cube Model, anti-crime/terrorism study 123–4, **125**, *125*; decentralized, flexible operations 105–7, 148–9, 150; decline through dissociation 38–9; easy victims 90, 95–6; financial loss, criminal economy 92–3; foreign invasion, motivating factor 16, 31, 88; group structure models 43–4; Improvised Explosive Devices (IEDs) 82–3, 84; international dynamics 101–2, 103–4; ISIS radicalization and recruitment 123–4, 128–9, 134–5, 144, 148; Islamic terrorist motivations 88–9; jihadis self-help manual, 'Inspire' e-zine 81–2, 86, 89; lone-wolf attacks, Europe 79, 82, 83, 90, 94; online manipulations 45–6; online propaganda 69–70; public guardians, presence/absence 84, 86–7, 90–2, 95–6; Routine Activities Theory, application of 84, 87–8; tactics defined 78; vehicular terror-assault 82, 83–4, 86–7, 88, 90
Terrorism Convictions Monitor (TCM) 161
terrorism financing: counter terrorism measures, evolution of 144–7, 150–1; criminals, petty crime and recruitment 144–5, 148–9, 150; EU counter measures 164–5; foreign fighters 144; legal and illegal fundraising methods

142–4, 159, 165; low-tech terrorism 148, 149; money transfer methods 144, 165; post-9/11 counter-terrorism measures 145–6; skills and investment strategies 145
terrorism, TAKEDOWN findings: community policing 21; cross-border, pre-emptive interventions 18, 19, 20; cultural and psychological drivers 17–18, 22; military intervention dangers 19–20; prevention effects, expert views **19**; propaganda and recruitment 16; public, soft targets 16; social prevention strategies 18–19, 20–1
Terrorist Finance Tracking Program (TFTP) 146, 164
Turkey 93

UK Payments 195–6, *196*
Ukraine: political cyberattack 47; Volnovakha bus attack 80
United Kingdom (UK): counter-terrorism expansion 84; identity crime, incidence reporting 195–8, *196*, **197**; identity crime, public/private initiatives 187–94; London Bridge attack 2017 90, 91; London transport bombings 2005 79, 146; Manchester Arena attack 2017 83

United Nations (UN) 100, 145
United States (US): Boston Marathon attack 2013 82–3; homeland security 84, 85; post-9/11 counter-terrorism measures 84, 85, 145, 146

Varese, Federico 28
vehicular terror-assault 82, 83–4
Victims of Fraud Service 187–8
Viennese Network Deradicalization and Prevention 20–1
violent non-state actors (VNSA): challenging Europe's security 108–9; decentralization and operational flexibility 105–7; emerging global role 101–2; globalization benefits 104–5; privatized international relations, exploiting 102–4; state fragility and conflict opportunities 107–8; Trans-Saharan hybridized activities 109–11
Visa Information System (VIS) 162, 169

WannaCry ransomware attack 45, 61

Yang, Yongpeng 182
Yemen 81

Zaghba, Youssef 91

Taylor & Francis eBooks

www.taylorfrancis.com

A single destination for eBooks from Taylor & Francis with increased functionality and an improved user experience to meet the needs of our customers.

90,000+ eBooks of award-winning academic content in Humanities, Social Science, Science, Technology, Engineering, and Medical written by a global network of editors and authors.

TAYLOR & FRANCIS EBOOKS OFFERS:

- A streamlined experience for our library customers
- A single point of discovery for all of our eBook content
- Improved search and discovery of content at both book and chapter level

REQUEST A FREE TRIAL
support@taylorfrancis.com

Routledge
Taylor & Francis Group

CRC Press
Taylor & Francis Group